THE FINAL VICTIMS

The Carolina Lowcountry and the Atlantic World

Sponsored by the Lowcountry and Atlantic Studies Program
of the College of Charleston

Money, Trade, and Power
Edited by Jack P. Greene, Rosemary Brana-Shute, and Randy J. Sparks

The Impact of the Haitian Revolution in the Atlantic World
Edited by David P. Geggus

London Booksellers and American Customers
James Raven

Memory and Identity
Edited by Bertrand Van Ruymbeke and Randy J. Sparks

This Remote Part of the World
Bradford J. Wood

The Final Victims
James A. McMillin

THE FINAL VICTIMS

FOREIGN SLAVE TRADE TO NORTH AMERICA, 1783–1810

JAMES A. M^cMILLIN

University of South Carolina Press

© 2004 University of South Carolina

Published in Columbia, South Carolina,
by the University of South Carolina Press

Manufactured in the United States of America

08 07 06 05 04   5 4 3 2 1

Library of Congress Cataloging-in-Publication Data

McMillin, James A., 1950–
  The final victims : foreign slave trade to North America, 1783–1810 /
James A. McMillin.
    p. cm. — (The Carolina lowcountry and the Atlantic world)
  Includes bibliographical references and index.
  ISBN 1-57003-546-6 (cloth : alk. paper)
  1. Slave trade—North America—History. I. Title. II. Series.
  HT1049.M35 2004
  306.3'62'097—dc22   2004002625

For lovely Judy

CONTENTS

ILLUSTRATIONS

ACKNOWLEDGMENTS

Although historical research and writing are inherently solitary and lonely pursuits, they are impossible to do successfully without the help and support of others. With remarkable patience, Peter H. Wood, Robert Durden, and R. Hal Williams have seen me through this project. This work has benefited enormously from their criticisms, suggestions, and encouragement. I also am grateful to Judy Martin, who guided this work through various stages of typing and organization, always with patience and unfailing good humor, and to Jackie Bradley, who provided invaluable assistance with newspapers. I owe a special debt of gratitude to Valerie Hotchkiss and the staff of the Bridwell Library for their unfailing support and encouragement.

The staffs of the following libraries, foundations, and archives assisted with the research for this work: the libraries of Duke University, Harvard University, the University of South Carolina, the University of Georgia, and Tulane University; the New-York Historical Society; the Georgia Department of Archives and History; the Georgia Historical Society; the Historic Charleston Foundation; the Library of Congress; the Massachusetts Historical Society; the National Archives; the North Carolina State Archives; the Rhode Island Historical Society; and the South Carolina Department of Archives and History.

David Eltis and Steven D. Behrendt of the W. E. B. Du Bois Institute of Harvard University kindly shared their records of North American slave voyages with me and patiently answered the most amateurish questions. Stanley L. Engerman provided his natural-growth-rate worksheets from *Time on the Cross*, Edward Countryman suggested the title, and Gwendolyn Midlo Hall generously furnished information on the Louisiana slave trade from her forthcoming book *African Diaspora in the Americas: Continuities of Regions, Ethnicities, and Cultures.* Their expert assistance greatly facilitated my research.

My personal debts to friends and family are many. David Price, R. Hal Williams, and Alex Moore expertly guided me through the publishing maze. I also owe Peter H. Wood much. His generosity, magnanimity, friendship, and the example of his excellent scholarship have meant more to me than I can say. My greatest debt is to my family. My daughters and grandsons have been more than patient. Finally, without the support of my wife, Judy Lee Bryce McMillin, I could not have completed this project. She sacrificed much and never complained. I love and thank you all.

THE FINAL VICTIMS

INTRODUCTION

Near the end of the twentieth century the South Carolina legislature erected a historical marker on Sullivans Island in Charleston harbor to commemorate the arrival of tens of thousands of African captives.[1] The marker was long overdue. The significance of the site—Charleston was "the Ellis Island of black Americans"—had largely been ignored for nearly two centuries.[2]

Despite the good intentions of the legislators, the marker reinforces a popular misconception. By stating that the captives arrived "between 1700 and 1775," the authors imply that the War for American Independence marked the end of the foreign slave trade to Charleston. This was not the case, however. The Revolutionary War only interrupted the trade; soon after British troops withdrew from South Carolina in December 1782, it resumed in earnest. By the time the United States finally outlawed the transatlantic trade in 1808, more than one hundred thousand African slaves had been disembarked in Charleston and other North American ports in the lower South and lower Mississippi Valley.

The misconception is largely a product of scholarship. Historians have studied the colonial trade in great depth. In fact the voluminous scholarship on the important topic covers almost every aspect of historical inquiry. In their studies of the slave trade in the northern colonies, historians have investigated the antislavery movement and the commercial side of the trade, including New England, Pennsylvania, and New York slavers; slave ships; slaving ports; and rum manufacturers.[3]

The southern colonies, where the overwhelming majority of foreign slaves were disembarked in the colonial era, has come under even closer scrutiny. Delaware alone of the southern colonies has not been the subject of at least one slave trade study.[4] Although the Virginia trade lasted longer and delivered more people, South Carolina's trade has been the most closely studied of all the North American colonies, northern and southern. Scholars have researched the volume of the forced immigrants and their origins, the merchants and factors who sold them, the marketing of slaves, the commercial arrangements of the merchants and planters who bought and sold slaves, and the impact that newly arrived Africans had on white and slave societies and South Carolina politics. They have also examined Charleston's role in distributing Africans to other British mainland and West Indies colonies and the volume and profitability of the British slave trade to South Carolina.[5]

The foreign slave trade to the other European colonies in North America, Florida and Louisiana, also have been the subject of several significant studies.[6] And, finally, historians have investigated the British slave trade to colonial North America and North American slavers' participation in the transatlantic slave trade to the Americas.[7]

The post–Revolutionary War foreign slave trade has received far less attention. Most studies that include information on the topic cover the trade before and after the War for American Independence rather than focusing solely on the post–Revolutionary War period. For instance, Jay Coughtry's study of Rhode Island, *The Notorious Triangle*, published in 1981, begins in 1700 and ends in 1807.[8] The articles on the slave trade by Walter Minchinton, "The Seaborne Slave Trade of North Carolina"; Darold D. Wax, "'New Negroes Are Always in Demand,'" on Georgia; Paul LaChance, "The Politics of Fear: French Louisiana and the Slave Trade, 1769-1809"; and Roger Anstey, "The Volume of the North America Slave-Carrying Trade from Africa, 1761–1810" are also overviews.[9] Remarkably, only one scholar has produced a work that has focused solely on the post-Revolutionary trade, and it appeared more than two generations ago. Using information gleaned from her *Documents Illustrative of the History of the Slave Trade to America*, Elizabeth Donnan published "The New England Slave Trade after the Revolution" in 1930. As a result of the lack of scholarly attention, little is known about the volume, economics, politics, nature, and impact of the post–Revolutionary War trade.[10]

A number of factors have contributed to the dearth of scholarship. First, records of the colonial trade have been much more accessible to scholars. From late in the seventeenth century until the 1730s, London-based African and South Sea companies organized the majority of British slaving voyages. Much of the extensive colonial trade from Britain to Africa and to North America was detailed by these chartered companies, and the records were deposited in London offices. Unfortunately for scholars, the African trading privileges were rescinded after 1750, and private British merchants organized all British slave voyages over the next six decades. Although Donnan's *Documents* contained some information on private ventures, most company records have not survived, and scholars have had to turn to other sources—such as newspapers, shipping records, and merchants' accounts, dispersed throughout libraries and archives in Europe and North America—in order to document voyages. Convinced that Donnan had uncovered most, if not all, of the extant records of the post–Revolutionary War slave trade, scholars assumed that further research into the trade was not warranted.[11] After all, because the colonial foreign slave trade to North America covered a longer period than postcolonial trade did, and because participation was more widespread at that time, historians have tended to view the slave trade to North America as a colonial event.

In addition, the dominant historiography of the Constitutional Convention has tended to support this view of the trade. With a few notable exceptions, historians have viewed positively the actions taken by the writers of the Constitution with regard to the slave trade issue at the convention. Needless to say, their argument holds up only if the actions of the delegates resulted in the importation of a relatively insignificant number of foreign slaves. It is significant that estimates regarding the number of slaves imported to North America after the Revolution bolster this standard argument. In 1969 the most widely recognized expert on the Atlantic slave trade, Philip D. Curtin, estimated that only about ninety-two thousand enslaved Africans were imported between 1783 and 1810.[12] Consequently most scholars have credited natural growth, rather than foreign traffic, for the substantial increase in the southern black population while the trade was open. These ideological and quantitative arguments have led most historians, and the general public, to view the foreign slave trade to North America after the Revolutionary War as an insignificant event in American history.[13]

To reassess and revise that prevailing view, four topics need consideration: the number of foreign slaves imported, the origins of the imported captives, the North American merchants who participated in the trade, and the treatment of enslaved workers while they were being transported to North America and then waiting to be sold. Through a careful appraisal of these four areas, three major observations come to light as basic reinterpretations that are central to this study. First, it becomes clear that far more foreign slaves were imported than previously thought. Second, it is apparent that in the lower South the Revolution did little to stop, or even slow, the slave trade. A third observation is that after the war the conditions that captives encountered worsened, rather than improved, as some scholars have suggested. All three of these reappraisals have obvious and far-reaching implications for our understanding of life in the United States during the first generation after the Revolution.

Chapter 1

DEMAND AND SUPPLY

"There seemed to be a rage for negroes."
"A Short Sketch of the Debate," *Charleston Evening Gazette,*
September 28, 1785

When the War for American Independence ended in the early 1780s, many Americans eagerly turned their attention from war to restoration. In a September 1784 letter, Henry Laurens, who had recently made his way down from New York City to Philadelphia, described their activities. "The Merchant, the Farmer, the Mechanic are all busy in their respective vocations," the South Carolina planter wrote, "covering as fast as they can the marks of British cruelty, by new Buildings, Enclosures, and other Improvements, and recovering their former State of happiness and Prosperity."[1] When Laurens finally arrived in South Carolina later that year, he too turned his attention to private interests, and like many other low-country planters he set about restoring his rice and indigo plantations. Reorganizing labor was high on the list of priorities. Convinced that their "happiness" and "prosperity" were linked to intensive commercial agriculture, planters rushed to replace slaves lost in the war. Hoping to profit from the seller's market that ensued, in 1784 a Georgia merchant, quite likely Joseph Clay, wrote to a London firm that "new Negroes from Africa, are, & will be for a very considerable time to come, in great demand with us."[2] For the first post–Revolutionary generation, this claim proved to be accurate. Not only would the call for foreign slaves remain at a historically high level throughout the period, after 1795 it rose rapidly.[3]

The extraordinary demand for black laborers engendered an extraordinary increase in the southern slave population. According to U.S. census records, the southern black population nearly doubled in two decades, rising from 676,637 in 1790 to 909,910 in 1800 and to 1,251,188 in 1810—a net increase of 574,551 in twenty years.[4] The black population rose 34 percent in the 1790s and 38 percent in the first decade of the 1800s, a rate of increase that has not been matched since. The growth in individual states is even more telling. Between 1790 and 1800 the slave population of Georgia more than doubled, increasing from 29,264 to 59,699 workers. Farther south in the Mississippi territory the number of slaves jumped five-fold in the first decade of the 1800s, from 3,489 to 17,088. By 1810 even more slaves could be found in Tennessee, Missouri, Arkansas, Texas, Alabama, and Florida.[5]

For the most part, scholars have credited natural growth, rather than foreign traffic, for the large increase in the southern black population while the trade was open. Relying on the calculations made in the 1850s by H. C. Carey, estimates indicate that between 1790 and 1810 natural increase contributed seven times (505,000) as many people as the foreign slave trade (70,000) to the growth of the southern slave population.[6] No doubt the dramatic events and new ideas and aspirations of the era in which the surge occurred have influenced scholars' perspectives. During what scholar David Brion Davis calls the "age of revolution" many Americans and Western Europeans were becoming more concerned about the oldest and most extreme form of human exploitation and in many cases were trying to end slavery and the slave trade.[7] However, first in the Carolinas and Georgia and than later across much of the Deep South contradictory forces were at work which prevented the promise of the Revolution from being fulfilled. Rather than emancipation being "efficaciously taken up" during the era as Henry Laurens confidently predicted in 1779, the slave trade resumed and slavery expanded.[8]

I.

The foreign slave trade to British North America was among the first casualties of the War for American Independence. In October 1774 the First Continental Congress adopted the Continental Association, which banned all trade with Great Britain. Although many South Carolinians and Georgians were bitterly opposed to parts of the act, when the British snow *Prince Tom* arrived in Savannah in July 1775 with 180 African captives, officials allowed the vessel's captain Benjamin Mason to disembark only 40 slaves destined for a Savannah River planter. "Afraid it may appear improper abroad," officials ordered the vessel to depart with the remaining 140 slaves. The sailing of the *Prince Tom* marked the end of the colonial transatlantic slave trade to British North America and the beginning of a seven-year suspension of the trade to the new nation.[9]

For many the prohibition against slave imports was an answered prayer, especially for the Quakers, or Society of Friends, as they preferred to be addressed. Since midcentury a small but persistent group had been attempting to convince fellow members of the Friends to abandon slaveholding and the slave trade. Certain that slave imports perpetuated and strengthened slavery, they aimed most of their criticisms at slave trafficking. In meetings, newspapers, and tracts Friends condemned the slave trade as "a very wicked and abominable practice contrary to the natural rights and privileges of all mankind, and against the Golden Rule of doing to others as we would be done unto."[10] However, both within and outside the Society of Friends, the Quakers won few converts to their antislavery viewpoint until Revolutionary ideology began to spread in the 1770s. The invocation of universal liberty and equality resonated with black and with many white colonists, and they began moving against slavery and the slave trade.[11]

By the mid-1780s, antislavery supporters had made significant gains. Massachusetts, New Hampshire, and Vermont had abolished slavery; Connecticut, Rhode Island, and Pennsylvania had passed gradual abolition laws; and New York and New Jersey were debating abolition. In the upper South, Quakers, Methodists, and natural-rights proponents had succeeded in bringing the issues to forefront of public consciousness and convinced thousands of slave owners to manumit their slaves. The campaign against the slave trade was even more successful. When the war ended, all of the New England and middle states plus Maryland, Virginia, and Delaware refused to allow slave imports and within a few years they all permanently banned the foreign slave trade. It appeared that American beliefs in liberty and equality, which had triumphed over of the greatest power on earth, were well on their way to vanquishing slavery and the slave trade.[12]

Unfortunately Revolutionary principles, as antislavery supporters would soon learn, were not a panacea, especially in the lower South. This does not mean that Revolutionary ideology and its talk of rights fell on deaf ears in the Carolinas and Georgia. Residents of the region not only mulled over the issue, but there is considerable evidence that many were won over to the antislavery viewpoint.[13] Among the first members of lowcountry society to link the language used by patriots against England and their plight were Charleston blacks. In response to public demonstrations held in Charleston against the Stamp Act in 1765, a group of slaves took to the streets "crying out 'Liberty.'" Henry Laurens dismissed the incident as "a thoughtless imitation" of the white protestors, but other Charlestonians were not so sure.[14] Soon after the incident, rumors spread of an impending slave revolt, and officials called out the militia and imposed extreme controls on the black population.[15] This experience and the ever-present reality that slaves outnumbered whites discouraged public antislavery sentiment in the region for an extended period. The ten year period of calm was broken on the eve of the War for American Independence. In the Darien Resolutions, drafted in early 1775 by a wealthy and influential slave owner, Lachlan McIntosh, a group of Darien, Georgia, freemen declared their "disapprobation and abhorrence of the unnatural practice of Slavery in America."[16] Once fighting began and unrest swept the South, nervous whites became much more cautious. However, once peace was restored in 1782, protests resumed. Condemnations of the recently resumed foreign slave trade were especially vitriolic. Writing in a 1783 Charleston newspaper, "Another Patriot" called attention to the flying of the American flag "in every yard where unfortunate Africans are penned for sale." Veterans of the Revolutionary War, the writer concluded, "must burn with indignation at such an affront to it."[17] Another writer was even more direct: in 1785 he or she described the slave trade as "shocking to human-ity, cruel, wicked, and diabolical."[18]

In public proslavery supporters ignored the attacks. No proslavery responses appeared in South Carolina or Georgia newspapers, and apparently no pressure was brought to bear on newspaper editors to stop publishing the attacks, as they continued until the Haitian Revolution erupted in 1791.[19] Behind closed doors, however, South Carolina, Georgia, and North Carolina political leaders made sure that slavery and the slave trade did not become major issues. When Georgia and South Carolina representatives learned in 1776 that Thomas Jefferson, in an early draft of the Declaration of Independence, had condemned King George III for enslaving innocent Africans, they demanded he strike the entire section, which he promptly did.[20] Less than a month after the Declaration of Indepen-dence was signed, one of South Carolina's delegates to the convention, Thomas Lynch, declared that if it was to be debated "whether their Slaves are their Prop-erty, there is an end of the Convention."[21]

A decade later, at the Constitutional Convention, lower South delegates were not able to head off debate on the slave trade, and it came under serious attack. George Mason of Virginia condemned the trade as "infernal" and "lamented that some our Eastern brethren had from the lust of gain embarked on the nefarious traffic." He concluded with a warning that if slavery was allowed to expand through the slave trade it "would bring the judgment of heaven" on the nation and ultimately "national calamities."[22] Maryland delegate Luther Martin argued that trafficking in slaves was "inconsistent with the principles of the revolution and dishonorable to the American character to have such a feature in the Con-stitution."[23] John Rutledge of South Carolina fired back that "religion and humanity had nothing to do with this question," that it was a matter of "interest" alone. Like many other lowcountry planters he believed that a shortage of labor and an odious climate required a constant supply of slaves. A few days later Rut-ledge brought the debate to an end when he threatened that South Carolina or Georgia "can never receive a plan if it prohibits the slave trade; and if the Con-vention thought" that their states would consent to a prohibition of the trade, "the expectation is in vain."[24] More interested in preserving the union than abolishing the slave trade, a majority of the delegates accommodated the lower South, and slave trafficking remained under the individual state's authority for twenty years.

Despite the fact that the South Carolina legislature had recently banned slave imports for three years, most free residents of the state supported the slave trade clause to the Constitution. They heartily agreed with Rawlin Lowndes when he declared in the South Carolina legislature in 1788 that "Negroes [are] our wealth, our only natural resource."[25] After all, slave-produced rice and indigo had brought great prosperity to the colonial South Carolina lowcountry. Indeed, his-torian Alice Hanson Smith estimates that the private wealth of South Carolina planters and merchants was unsurpassed in British North America. Nowhere else in the region did such a large percentage of the free population live so well.[26] Convinced that this wealth was inseparably linked to slavery, both well-established and newly arrived planters and farmers turned their back on Revolutionary principles and forged ahead with restoration of slavery.

It would not be a simple task. The War for American Independence had wrecked slavery in the lower South. In the "years of general . . . calamity" waves of British soldiers, patriots, Loyalists, Tories, and black maroons swept over large areas of Georgia and South Carolina like a tidal wave disordering plantation life.[27] Some slaves took advantage of the chaos and escaped, while others were evacuated, and still more, abandoned without proper clothing, food, shelter, and medical care, fell victim to starvation, exposure, and disease. The disorder decimated the slave populations of South Carolina and Georgia. In South Carolina the slave population declined by 25,000 people, or 25 percent. In Georgia the decrease was even more precipitous as 10,000, or two-thirds of the prewar population of 15,000 slaves, died, escaped, or left the region on British ships at the end of the war.[28]

As soon as the British vessels disappeared over the horizon, planters began scouring the countryside for labor, but early on most came up empty-handed. In 1782 only a handful of slaves were available for sale in the entire region. The extended interruption of the African trade and losses during the war drove prices up from an average of forty pounds for a "seasoned Negro" in 1776 to two hundred guineas in 1782.[29] Although prices fell after imports resumed in 1783, they remained at a high level, averaging between seventy and one hundred pounds, or 50 percent more than prewar prices, throughout 1783 and 1784. Hoping to profit from the high prices, a group in Charleston formed a company for the purpose of "carrying on the slave trade to the coast of Africa."[30] Many others were attracted as well, and from the fall of 1783 to late 1785 slavers disembarked more than 10,000 enslaved laborers in Charleston alone. Only after most of the planters' capital and credit had been exhausted did prices and shipments begin to decline in early 1785. Although slave ships continued to arrive and sold out quickly, by late 1785 prices had fallen to prewar levels.[31]

As they had during the colonial era, most planters bought slaves on credit; however, they soon discovered that paying back the loans would take much longer after the war than it had before 1775. Exorbitant interest rates, cancellation of England's indigo bounty, a ban on direct trade between the United States and Britain's colonies, and a series of poor rice harvests precluded many slave owners from repaying their prewar debts, much less loans for newly acquired Africans. In an effort to increase the value of slaves, improve the balance of trade, and reduce debts, in 1787 the South Carolina legislature prohibited the importation of slaves for three years.[32] The state government had outlawed imports, but it did not eliminate what one representative described as "a rage for Negroes."[33] Instead, according to historian Winthrop D. Jordan, it was "a matter of men denying themselves what they wanted but could not afford."[34]

Despite the ban slavers continued to land enslaved laborers in North Carolina, Georgia, Spanish Florida, Louisiana, and even South Carolina. Lowcountry planters in South Carolina and Georgia bought some of the captives, but most ended up away from the coast in the upcountry of the lower South and lower Mississippi Valley. Settlers had begun moving into the regions before the war, but when Britain ceded most of the land between the Appalachian Mountains and the Mississippi River to the United States at the end of the war, the migration accelerated. It accelerated again when Thomas Jefferson bought Louisiana in 1803.[35] It is difficult for contemporary Americans to imagine the magnitude of the expansion of the United States that occurred between the end of the war in 1783 and the Louisiana Purchase twenty years later. At the beginning of the era most southerners lived and worked within one hundred miles of the Atlantic Ocean. Two decades later they had pushed the line of settlement more than seven hundred miles inland to the Texas border. In the process the American South added not just hundreds of thousands of acres, but hundreds of thousands of square miles.[36]

The lure of "large bodies of fertile lands . . . yet uncultivated" beckoned the thousands of farmers and planters.[37] Although prices varied, most of the land was extremely cheap, even free. To attract settlers, southern states, territories, and the Spanish crown sold millions of acres for ten dollars per one hundred acres or less. Millions more were awarded to Revolutionary soldiers in headright grants and in enormous speculative grants. In South Carolina alone, more than eight million acres were handed out in speculative grants to 253 individuals between 1785 and 1794.[38] Even after the cotton gin was introduced to the lower Mississippi Valley in 1795, land costs remained at comparatively low levels. At the turn of the century, unimproved land along the Mississippi River in the vicinity of Natchez was readily available for fifty cents per acre, and improved lands under cultivation were selling at from two to ten dollars an acre.[39] Not all southern land was suited for commercial agriculture, for instance, the Appalachian Mountains and the pine barrens, but much of it was productive, especially the Piedmont regions of the Carolinas and Georgia and the fertile valley lands in the lower Mississippi Valley.

To clear their fields, construct buildings and fences, and herd their livestock and cultivate crops, settlers demanded enslaved laborers. Like lowcountry planters, westward-moving settlers were convinced that slaves were a necessity, but, unlike lowcountry planters, western settlers were not ready in 1787 to ban slave imports temporarily. As previously mentioned, Rutledge, Pinckney, and other lowcountry planters claimed that a semitropical climate and labor-intensive crops made slavery necessary, but only in the lowcountry. This argument was based on their assumption that the western lands could develop without slavery. Thus, once they had imported enough Africans to replace the laborers they had lost in the war, lowcountry planters were willing to halt slave imports until they were needed again. Upcountry representatives disagreed and complained that the ban was "a direct Bar to the Increase of the Wealth and population" of their region.[40] This same argument was repeated over and over again by westward-moving Americans. In a 1804 letter to the U.S. secretary of state James Madison, Louisiana's first territorial governor, William C. C. Claiborne, reported that "citizens seem impressed with an opinion that, a great, very great supply of slaves is essential to the prosperity of Louisiana."[41] Slavery and the conviction that it was directly linked to wealth were migrating along with the hundreds of thousands of westward-moving settlers.

To pay for slaves, settlers and well-established planters and farmers produced staples for the commercialized economy. In the lowcountry rice was the major crop, but by the late 1780s sea-island cotton had caught the attention of many planters and was fast becoming popular. Inland planters and farmers also grew cotton but mainly for domestic use. For them tobacco was the cash crop, replacing indigo. When the war ended, westward-moving settlers spread what scholar Joyce E. Chaplin describes as "the well-established commercial cultivation of tobacco," and by the early 1790s tobacco was being cultivated widely in Kentucky, Tennessee, the Carolinas, Georgia, and the lower Mississippi Valley.[42] The new production more than compensated for the decline that was occurring in the Chesapeake as Virginia and Maryland planters switched from tobacco to wheat. Consequently exports of American tobacco increased 36 percent between 1770 and 1790.[43] The growth of inland and lower Mississippi Valley slave populations suggests many planters and farmers used tobacco profits to buy laborers. In the postwar 1780s the backcountry slave population of South Carolina and Georgia increased by nearly nineteen thousand people, or 68 percent. Another twenty-two thousand enslaved laborers migrated into the Kentucky Territory and lower Mississippi Valley.[44]

One case, that of Thomas Foster, mirrored many settlers' experience. In the last year of the War for American Independence, Foster, his widowed mother, and his two older brothers, departed war-torn South Carolina in search of peace and opportunity. By 1783 they had found what they were looking for near the village of Natchez in the lower Mississippi Valley. Foster's mother was able to quickly obtain land through a series of Spanish grants and purchases, and all three of her sons married and started families soon after they arrived in the Natchez area. After his brothers began buying lands of their own, Thomas and his wife Sarah took over responsibility of running his mother's farm. When he purchased an adjoining parcel of 425 acres in 1788, he increased their holdings to nearly a thousand acres. To help clear, improve, and farm the property, he purchased in 1787 an America-born black man, Jesse, brought down from Kentucky, and a year later two newly arrived Africans, Abd al-Rahman Ibrahima and Samba, for $930. For the Africans Thomas paid $150 down in silver, and he gave his bond for the next two tobacco harvests for the balance. Although prices for the crop would decline significantly over the next two years, Jesse, Ibrahima, and

Samba produced enough tobacco to pay off their owner's debt. The following
year their labor funded the purchase of yet another slave.[45]

In five years Foster had significantly increased his holdings in land and people;
however, over the next two decades improvements in agricultural technology,
rich land, plentiful slave labor, and rising cotton prices would allow him and
thousands of other southerners to amass wealth at an even faster pace. In the early
1790s Foster abandoned tobacco for cotton. Although the first few years his slaves
performed the time-consuming task of cleaning the staple by hand, he was able
to profit from cotton cultivation from the very beginning. In 1794 Thomas used
a portion of the profits and the previous harvest, seven hundred dollars and nine
hundred pounds of cotton, to purchase four slaves, twenty-five-year-old Isabella
and her children, Jacob, age ten, Anaky, five, and Limerick, two. The next year,
the first cotton gin began operating in Natchez, and he and many other nearby
farmers and planters entered a period of extended prosperity. During the next fifteen years he would expand his property in land, livestock, and people. His cat-
tle herd grew from 40 head in 1792 to 140 in 1820. He bought his mother's
plantation and other surrounding plots, and by 1812 his plantation sprawled over
1,785 acres. He also purchased a number of valuable lots in Natchez, built an
impressive new home, and constructed a horse-powered cotton gin and a grist
mill. To cultivate cotton and maintain and operate his equipment, he added
more slaves. By 1800 he owned twenty, then by 1810 forty and by 1820 more than
one hundred. Natural increase and inheritance were responsible for some of the
buildup, but most of the slaves were purchased. For all of these additions, Foster
paid cash generated from cotton cultivation.[46]

Certainly not all cotton farmers and planters accumulated wealth as fast as
Foster; nevertheless the staple enriched thousands in the Carolinas, Georgia, and
the lower Mississippi Valley. In many ways it was the ideal crop. Unlike rice,
which required large capital outlays, an extensive, skilled workforce, and extraordinary conditions, cotton cultivation required only a few small tools and access to
a gin and baler. Moreover it thrived in large parts of the South, it could be grown
profitably by one person or a hundred, storage and transportation were inexpensive, and in the 1790s and the first decade of the 1800s prices remained well above
profitable levels. Through hard work, good management, and a run of good luck,
as Thomas Foster had, many southerners were able to acquire more land and
slaves and successfully make the transition from settler to planter.[47]

Cotton, however, was not the only staple that came into its own during the
1790s. At the same time Eli Whitney was developing the cotton gin in Georgia,
Etienne de Boré was perfecting advances in the cultivation and manufacturing
of sugar in Louisiana. For decades planters in southern Louisiana had been
experimenting on a small scale with sugar, but after a series of indigo crop failures and the collapse of sugar production in Santo Domingo, they were ready
to take the plunge. Boré showed them the way. In the mid-1790s Boré built a

modern sugar mill, a drying room, and a warehouse; brought in a skilled sugar maker from Santo Domingo; organized a large slave workforce; and planted sugarcane on a large enough scale to make his investment in land, equipment, and slaves pay. In 1795 he sold his first crop for twelve thousand dollars and cleared five thousand dollars. Word of his success quickly spread and by 1801 seventy-five sugar operations were producing five million pounds of sugar worth four hundred thousand dollars.[48]

Over the next decade many planters were able to replicate Boré's success. In an 1806 letter to President Thomas Jefferson, Gov. William C. C. Claiborne marveled at the wealth sugar planters were amassing. According to Claiborne, "there are several planters, whose field Negroes do not exceed forty who make more than 20,000 Dollars each year."[49] The extraordinary profits did not go unnoticed, and sugar plantations sprang up along the Mississippi River. Consequently by 1811 Louisiana sugar output had nearly doubled. In addition to brown sugar, slaves were producing 3,590 casks of molasses and more than 5,000 gallons of tafia.[50] Convinced that only slaves were suited for heavy work in the hot climate, sugar planters imported thousands of enslaved laborers in the late 1790s and early 1800s. The migration transformed southern Louisiana, especially along the Mississippi River above and below New Orleans. Not well suited for indigo or cotton the region had not supported a large black population before the mid-1790s, but, once the sugar boom commenced, the slave population skyrocketed, and by 1810 sugar parishes contained some of the largest plantations and concentrations of enslaved laborers in the North America. In St. Charles parish, located north of New Orleans, slaves comprised over 70 percent of the total population. More than one visitor to the region noted the similarity of the sugar plantations districts in the West Indies and Louisiana.[51]

From the end of the War for American Independence until 1806 comparatively low slave prices aided the expansion of slavery. When the British army abandoned the lower South in 1782, prices for prime slaves rose to the $400 to $500 range, but after a flood of imports between 1783 and 1785 costs dropped to much more affordable levels, the mid $200s, where they would remain until the mid 1790s. A $250 investment in a slave during this era yielded between 3 and 8 percent. As cotton and sugar culture began expanding in the mid 1790s, demand and prices for slaves increased, but the rate of return on investments in enslaved workers rose as well, especially in the "best lands of the new Southwest, the Mississippi alluvium" and the better Carolinas and Georgia uplands.[52] In the early 1800s prime slaves sold for less than $400 in Natchez, Mississippi, where planters could expect that a field hand could generate from $100 to $200 annually, minus the cost of their food, clothing, and shelter, which was not very great. Natchez planters such as Thomas Foster who used slaves to cultivate cotton achieved rates as high as 10 to 13 percent on their investment. Rice and sugar planters realized even greater returns, in some cases more than two times as much.[53]

As the end of the individual state's authority over foreign slave imports approached, which would come in 1808, the fear that Congress would abolish slave traffic for good sent demand for enslaved laborers through the roof. In response to the possibility of a federal ban, the South Carolina legislature repealed the law prohibiting the importation of slaves in late 1803, and in early 1804 once again slavers began inundating Charleston with African captives. By the time Congress closed the trade four years later, they had disembarked over fifty thousand foreign slaves in the port.[54] Despite the record forced migration, more slaves arrived in North America in that four-year period than in any decade prior to that; African captives brought prices not seen since the years immediately preceding and following the War for American Independence. For instance, in nominal dollars in 1775 Africans brought an average price of $240, in 1783 $360, and in 1807 $390.[55]

Between 1783 and 1810 prevailing ideological, political, and economical forces combined in the South to create a strong demand for slaves. Although many southerners embraced new cultural, intellectual, and technology developments in the Revolutionary era, they could not turn away from the pre-Revolutionary belief that given certain conditions—cheap, fertile land and worldwide demand for agricultural staples—wealth and slavery were intertwined. They knew that in the past and quite possibly in the future a slave–staple crop society would enable many enterprising farmers to enter the planter class, and, of course, it did. The forces translated into good fortune for many well-established farmers and planters and westward-moving settlers and a nightmare for slaves. To meet the demand for enslaved laborers, tens of thousands more Africans were captured and transported to North America, and tens of thousands of American-born slaves were forced to migrate inland.

II.

As slavery expanded across the South, the slave population increased by nearly 575,000, or more than 80 percent, between 1790 and 1810. Scholars maintain that the slave population itself, not emigration from abroad, was responsible for most of the increase. Their argument was buttressed in the late 1960s, when Curtin estimated that only about 70,000 enslaved Africans were imported during the two decades.[56] This would mean that natural growth was responsible for the remaining new African Americans, numbering more than 500,000.[57] Certainly natural increase was the most significant factor in explaining the growth in the period, but the foreign slave trade contributed much more to the growth than previously thought.

Curtin based his estimate on the calculations performed by H. C. Carey in the 1850s. Like most scholars, Carey employed early census records when he made one of the first and most enduring projections. Because it is still repeated by recent authorities, it is important to see just how Carey went about calculating his much-used estimate. Assuming that South Carolina and Georgia were the only states that imported foreign slaves after the American Revolution, Carey based his calculations mainly on the 1790, 1800, and 1810 censuses for these two states. From their combined slave population increase of 69,197 between 1790 and 1800, he subtracted 9,000 to account for the slaves who migrated with their masters from states north of South Carolina and Georgia. He assumed, on average, that each white immigrant family numbered five and brought with them one slave. He subtracted an additional 34,000 to account for natural growth, based on the assumption that the South Carolina and Georgia slave populations grew naturally at a 25 percent decennial rate. He maintained that the difference of 26,197 was the number of foreign slaves imported during the 1790s.

For the next decade, 1800 to 1810, Carey used the same assumptions and formula. He subtracted the estimated number of domestic slave immigrants (25,000) and the estimated natural increase in the slave population (50,000) from 96,000, the difference between the local slave populations in 1800 and 1810. He attributed the resulting figure of 21,000 to the foreign slave trade. However, in a discussion of the nationwide growth of the black population during the decade, Carey correctly concluded that more than 21,000 must have been imported. Consequently he raised the 1800 to 1810 importation volume from 21,000 to 26,000, which conveniently equaled his 1790 to 1800 estimate. To his total for the two decades (52,000), he added 1,400, which he claimed was the number of slaves imported from 1782 to 1790.[58] The additions of these estimates should have added up to 53,400, but a few pages later, when totaling the number of slaves imported into North America from the colonial era through the nineteenth century, with no explanation, Carey lists 70,000 as "imported subsequent to 1790."[59]

Carey's calculations were flawed by questionable assumptions. He assumed that only 1,400 Africans were imported from 1782 to 1790, no foreign slaves were taken to North Carolina, Kentucky, Tennessee, Louisiana, or Mississippi between 1782 and 1810, no Chesapeake slaves were sold and sent West or South without their masters, and no slaves were manumitted. He also used an overly optimistic natural decennial growth rate for the slave population, and he ignored the possibility that newly imported African slaves could have died before census workers could count them. All these mistaken assumptions, when combined, caused Carey to grossly underestimate the volume of the U.S. foreign slave trade, both in his explicit calculations of just over 50,000 and his more familiar general estimate of 70,000. Nevertheless, Carey's 70,000 figure has been, and continues to be, the most widely repeated by historians.[60]

This has not prevented other scholars from estimating the volume of the trade. In 1950, for instance, in his book *The History of Sugar*, Noel Deerr calculated the volume of the slave trade to North America. Deerr based his estimate mainly on New York congressman L. Mitchell's 1804 speech condemning the smuggling of slaves into South Carolina. The congressman quoted an unknown source "who had computed that as many as twenty thousand enslaved negroes had been transported from Guinea" into South Carolina the previous year.[61] With this in mind, Deerr posited that "for the years 1786–1808, an annual average of 15,000 does not seem improbable, giving a total over the period of 420,000."[62] Deerr's estimate was bold. It was more than seven times greater than Carey's, but, not surprisingly, his estimate has largely been ignored, as scholars continued to rely on Carey's calculations.

Historians quoted Carey's 70,000 figure for a number of reasons. First, Carey based his estimate on evidence. Unlike Deerr, for instance, Carey used something concrete, census records, to calculate the volume of the trade. Second, until the late 1960s, scholars had little interest in, and limited tools for, solving quantitative problems, especially one as formidable as estimating the volume of the Atlantic slave trade, in whole or in part.[63] In 1961 Basil Davidson expressed an attitude toward the problem common for a precomputer generation, when he noted in his book on the slave trade that "nobody knows or ever will know; either the necessary records are missing or they were never made."[64] Third, because scholars viewed North American slavery as benign when compared to other slave societies elsewhere in the New World, they credited natural growth for the rapid slave population increases.[65] Finally, through the racial calculus that turned African forced migrants into nonmigrants, many scholars of American immigration almost entirely ignored this inflow from Africa. They too argued, instead, that a high rate of reproduction, not immigration, was the source of black population increases. Harry H. Laughlin expressed this view when he wrote in 1939 that Africans "came to labor, but remained to breed."[66]

Using Carey's estimate, generations of historians argued that slave imports declined precipitously after the Revolution when compared with colonial rates. Even when social science attitudes toward quantitative problems began to change in the late 1960s, historians of the early national period continued to ignore the foreign slave trade of the United States. Following Curtin's lead, scholarly interest in the overall Atlantic slave trade increased, and in this broad context the U.S. slave trade "appeared insignificant" because it accounted for less than 5 percent of the estimated total number of Africans brought to the Americas.[67] When Curtin published his pioneering quantitative overview of the entire trade in 1969, he gave added credibility to Carey's estimate by incorporating it into his authoritative study more than a century after it first appeared.

Curtin's work profoundly revised Atlantic slave trade thinking and scholarship. For most of this century, it was supposed that the Atlantic slave trade was responsible for shipping a minimum of fifteen million persons to the Americas between the fifteenth and nineteenth century. A demographer, R. R. Kuczynski, was responsible for publicizing the figure in the 1930s. Almost everyone, including historians, journalists, and demographers, seemed to use this estimate until Curtin showed that it was based on a nineteenth-century guess. Having demonstrated that the figure could not be supported, he set about calculating a new one based on more concrete evidence. He examined different regions and suggested that the total might be much lower—around ten million, give or take twenty percent.[68]

In the last decade, however, Curtin's overall estimate has been the subject of intense scrutiny.[69] Although he still holds the high ground, his critics have shown that in some areas his estimates are based on uncertain or overly general assumptions. His brief treatment of the U.S. foreign slave trade may represent such a case. Curtin, intent upon showing the overall dimensions of the Atlantic trade in slaves over four centuries, was aware that the entire North American traffic, before and after U.S. independence, represented a very small portion, scarcely 5 percent, of the whole picture, and the majority of arrivals came before the War for American Independence. As a result, he included only a few sentences on the U.S. trade in *The Atlantic Slave Trade*, in which he succinctly concludes that "Carey's further estimate of 70,000 for the period 1791–1807 would complete the period of the legal slave trade at a total in the vicinity of 345,000." When estimating the total volume of the North American slave trade from 1781 to 1810, he did, however, add 22,000 to Carey's 70,000 figure to account for imports from 1781 to 1790 and for foreign slaves imported into the French, Spanish, and English North American regions of Louisiana, Mississippi, and Florida.[70]

Only a handful of historians have questioned Carey's and Curtin's North American post-Revolution estimates. Among the most notable are cliometricians Robert William Fogel and Stanley L. Engerman. Focusing on Carey, they suggested that he had miscalculated the volume of the foreign slave trade. In their controversial 1974 book, *Time on the Cross*, they pointed out that Carey had erred in his original calculations, underestimating the number of foreign slaves imported between 1790 and 1807. According to Fogel and Engerman, Carey overestimated the natural growth rate. They maintained that, instead of 25 percent per decade as Carey had argued, the slave population increased at a much slower natural growth rate of 2 percent per year. Using the 2 percent annual figure, they calculated that 291,126 Africans had been imported between 1780 and 1810.[71] Fogel and Engerman's estimate flew in the face of conventional scholarship, but it appears that they erred on the high side. Their natural growth rate estimate was too low. Certainly, in some regions of the South the annual growth rate equaled 2 percent or was even lower, but overall, as argued in the following chapter, it surpassed their figure. Unfortunately, Fogel and Engerman's discussion of Carey's estimate and their speculation on a much larger volume for the post-Revolutionary foreign slave trade has been largely ignored.[72]

More than a century after Carey published his estimate and almost fourteen years after Curtin upheld it, Allan Kulikoff took the first step toward actually testing Carey's and Curtin's estimates. In a 1983 essay, "Uprooted Peoples: Black Migrants in the Age of the American Revolution, 1790–1820," Kulikoff investigated the massive black migration, domestic and foreign, that occurred in the

South after the War for American Independence. Using U.S. census records and his research on colonial Chesapeake slave natural growth rates, Kulikoff estimated that 113,000 foreign slaves were imported into South Carolina and Georgia, plus Louisiana, Mississippi, and the rest of the Gulf Coast, between 1782 and 1810.[73]

To arrive at his estimate, Kulikoff used similar calculations and made many of the same assumptions as Carey. The difference in their results arose from Kulikoff's allowances for slave manumissions and for forced migrations of domestic and foreign slaves to Tennessee, Mississippi, and Louisiana. Although Kulikoff's calculations were more sophisticated than Carey's, he based his calculations on certain questionable assumptions.

He used a slave population natural growth rate of 2.5 percent for all the southern regions throughout the period. This caused him to overestimate the natural growth rate of the Georgia and South Carolina black populations. He made no allowance for elevated mortality rates for foreign and domestic migrants although he claimed his estimate represents "net migrants." He also assumed that Charleston customs officials enumerated all arrivals of foreign slaves in Charleston between 1804 and 1807. Moreover Kulikoff was wary of straying too far from Curtin's estimate of 92,000. In a discussion of natural growth rates, he posited that lowcountry slaves must have experienced a lower natural growth rate than blacks in other environments, but he drew back from the proposition on the grounds that the lower rate would have raised the total "African survivors to 123,000, an estimate one-third higher" than Curtin's.[74] Despite his reluctance to alter overall estimates, Kulikoff provided insights on natural growth rates and the volume of the domestic slave trade between 1790 and 1820.

The American Revolution was a watershed event. Americans defeated the most powerful army in the world, expanded human liberty, and created a new nation. These changes benefited many Americans including some African Americans. Thousands of slaves won their freedom, and the wellspring of the institution, the transatlantic slave trade, was abolished in 1808. Even those who were not freed were often directly affected. As slavery came under attack and demand and prices for slaves increased, many owners responded by providing improved treatment. As proof of the changes, scholars look to the fast-growing black population. No doubt, in some parts of the nation slave conditions and birth rates improved; however, at first in the lower South and later in the newly acquired regions of the Deep South this was not always the case. As they had during the colonial era, well-established farmers and planters and westward-moving settlers continued to embrace slavery as necessary to their economy, and this conviction led to a robust foreign slave trade.

Chapter 2

THE VOLUME OF THE FOREIGN SLAVE TRADE TO NORTH AMERICA, 1783–1810

"Of these creatures, there are vast numbers and they are continually increasing."

> Edward Hooker to Colonel Noadiah Hooker,
> Farmington, Connecticut, January 7, 1806

In an 1806 letter to his parents back home in Connecticut, Edward Hooker expressed his alarm at numerous "Negroes" he had encountered in Columbia, South Carolina. "They of course are about town (on Sundays) in great numbers," he wrote, "and sometimes pretty noisy. Of these creatures, there are vast numbers in the country, and they are continually increasing." Hooker was quick to point out what he believed was the source of the expansion. "While in Charleston," he noted, "I saw three or four vessels full of them, just brought from Africa, and exposed for sale."[1] Few historians would disagree with Hooker's observation regarding rapid increase, for early national census data suggest that the southern black population was growing at a fast pace—it nearly doubled in two decades, rising from 676,637 in 1790 to 1,251,188 in 1810.[2] Most would, however, disagree with Hooker's impression that the foreign slave trade was responsible for the increase.[3] The most widely recognized expert on the Atlantic slave trade, Philip D. Curtin, estimated that only about 70,000 enslaved Africans were imported between 1790 and 1810.[4] Like many other scholars, he credited natural growth, rather than foreign traffic, for most of the increase.[5] Certainly natural increase was the most significant factor in explaining the growth in the period, but the foreign slave trade contributed much more to the growth than previously thought.

I.

By building on the work of H. C. Carey, Robert W. Fogel, Stanley L. Engerman, Allan Kulikoff and Philip D. Morgan, it is possible to re-estimate the volume of enslaved immigrants entering North America after the Revolution. The starting numbers are those of the slaves and free blacks counted in the federal population censuses between 1790 and 1820, combined with evidence from local observations and Spanish censuses.[6] A number of assumptions are made in the process. First, following other scholars, it is assumed that the numbers provided for black Americans in the first, second, third, and fourth U.S. censuses are reasonably accurate.[7] Second, except for foreign and domestic migrants and South Carolina and Georgia lowcountry populations, a natural growth rate of 2.5 percent per year for southern free blacks and slaves is assumed. This assumption is, of course, highly debatable. A paucity of extant plantation records for this period and the foreign slave variable make estimating the rate of natural growth during the period difficult.[8] However, Kulikoff's research indicated that during the last decades of the colonial era, the Chesapeake black population experienced a 2.5 percent annual natural growth rate, and between 1810 and 1820 a 2.6 percent rate. Obviously conditions varied chronologically and geographically within the broad Chesapeake area over a whole generation, and the displacements of the immediate postwar years are hard to estimate. But if one takes into consideration that a minimum of 60 percent of the country's entire black population resided in the more favorable environments of Virginia, North Carolina, and Maryland from 1790 to 1810, then the 2.5 percent rate seems plausible for most of the southern black population.[9]

Third, for lowcountry slaves on rice plantations, a much lower rate of natural increase is assumed; indeed, no growth at all for the 1780s and .5 percent for the 1790s and the first decade of the 1800s. Rice plantation slaves suffered intensely in the pernicious lowcountry swamp environments of Georgia and South Carolina. Malaria, yellow fever, cholera, dysentery, respiratory diseases, and exposure were just a few of the afflictions attacking the health of slaves in what one member of the Constitutional Convention called "the sickly rice swamps."[10] Harsh work conditions were also the norm; overseers routinely forced pregnant women to work almost their entire pregnancies, and they usually sent the women back to the fields within a week after giving birth. The hostile environment and mistreatment increased mortality rates and reduced birth rates, depressing the overall rate of natural increase.[11]

In the best of times the natural annual growth rate could not have exceeded .5 percent, but in the post–Revolutionary War era it was mostly the worst of times for slaves. For lowcountry planters the War for American Independence had been a financial catastrophe. Trade with England and its other colonies ground to a halt, and invading British soldiers destroyed costly buildings, equipment, and long-term improvements on rice plantations, while liberating or abducting somewhere between twenty-five thousand and thirty thousand slaves.[12] Lowcountry slaves both benefited and suffered from the upheaval. Many workers gained their freedom and managed to relocate, but others died of disease, starvation, and exposure during the war years. For those unfortunate African Americans left behind when British troops departed in 1782, conditions worsened. The end of the war meant that slaves were forced to work that much harder for several years to repair the damage done by British soldiers and years of inattention.[13] It was no small task, as Georgian George Ballie lamented in 1783: "the resettling of plantations that are so intirely gone to ruin, must be attended with nearly as much expence and difficulty, as the first settling of them."[14]

To make matters worse, instead of restoring plantations to their former condition, many rice planters chose to shift to tidal cultivation as a different way of growing rice. Before the war planters had discovered that by harnessing freshwater tidal flows along lowcountry rivers to flood the fields periodically and drown troublesome weeds, rice harvests were made "more certain, and the work of the negroes less Toilsome."[15] The new method eliminated weeks of backbreaking hoeing under a broiling summer sun, but, ironically, tidal cultivation required more arduous work in worse conditions. To control tidal flows, overseers forced workers to construct complex systems of levees, dams, trunks, canals, and ditches in estuary swamps. Slaves moved tons of earth to build the systems, using few tools other than heavy spades, often while standing in water. Not until after the Civil War were the simplest labor-saving devices, like long-handled shovels and wheelbarrows, introduced to lowcountry plantations. Once completed, the tidal systems required extensive maintenance, which was usually performed during the cold winter months.[16] While traveling through the lowcountry in the 1790s, Charles William Janson witnessed the abysmal conditions faced by enslaved workers. A slave "employed in the rice-grounds," he wrote sympathetically, "must toil all day long in soft mud, ditching, and draining . . . often up to his waist in water."[17]

When the Revolution ended, lowcountry rice planters rushed to purchase slaves to repair and renovate their plantations.[18] While traveling through the South Carolina lowcountry in 1783, a Continental Army officer from Pennsylvania, Captain Walter Finney, observed both slaves and planters hard at work. He wrote in his diary that "Labour of all kinds, Mechanical, as well as Agriculture, is parform'd by Negroes, this pollecy being still thought best, evry exirtion is Us'd to incrase ther numbers."[19] There is evidence that lowcountry planters borrowed heavily to purchase black workers. The debt became such a serious problem that in 1787 the South Carolina legislature banned further imports of foreign slaves for a minimum of two years.[20] Not all imported slaves went to the planters, but newspaper advertisements suggest they bought a large percentage of the Africans who passed through Charleston and Savannah slave markets. Runaway ads in South Carolina and Georgia coastal newspapers often described slaves as "new Negroes" speaking African languages or showing "country marks" on their faces as a result of West African ritual scarification. In 1785, for instance, a rice planter advertised for information on four "new Negroes" who had escaped from an Edisto Island plantation in a small boat. A few months later, another planter sought help in locating ten "new Negroes" who had attempted "to return to their own country" in a canoe.[21]

Because the overwhelming majority of imported Africans were adult men, influxes of foreign slaves upset the ratios of adult males to females and adults to children. On two ships about which precise records exist, the *Gambia*, which arrived in Charleston in 1786, and the *Eagle*, which arrived in Savannah in 1797, men outnumbered women two to one, and almost two-thirds of the cargo were adults. Among the children aboard, there were three times as many boys as girls.[22] Inevitably disproportionate ratios decreased birthrates in slave populations. Also imported Africans died at an alarming rate, between 20 and 25 percent within the first ten years after arriving in the lowcountry. The combination of lower birth rates and increased mortality for the region depressed the rate of natural growth. Significantly, in areas such as the parish of Prince William in the lowcountry of South Carolina, where rice was widely cultivated, the slave population *declined* 1 percent in the first decade of the 1800s.[23]

Fourth, for lowcountry cotton plantation slaves, an annual natural growth rate of 1 percent is assumed. Cotton slaves were not forced to work in such extreme conditions as those on rice plantations, but they contracted many of the same diseases that shortened rice slaves' lives. Moreover, although in the 1790s and the first decade of the 1800s the majority of newly arrived Africans were sent inland, census records and plantation inventories evidence that many captives ended up on lowcountry cotton plantations.[24] In an 1810 inventory of Col. John Stapleton's St. Helena Island cotton plantation nearly one-half of the adult workers were newly arrived Africans. On another large cotton plantation in the same parish in 1815, African males headed up eight out of thirteen families. According to South Carolina historians Lawrence S. Rowland, Alexander Moore, and George C. Rogers, Jr. these new Africans, known to lowcountry planters as the "new stock of importations"—arriving between 1795 and 1808—made up nearly one-half the slave population of the sea islands of the Beaufort District in the early antebellum era.[25] Accordingly imports of African captives would have been responsible for all the growth of the slave population of St. Helena Parish that occurred between 1800 and 1810—an increase of 87 percent. No doubt the influx of African workers increased mortality rates and decreased birth rates and, combined with the adverse health environment, reduced the overall reproductive rate.[26]

Fifth, for states and territories that received a large volume of migrants, an annual natural growth rate of 2.2 percent is assumed. Philip D. Morgan, Edward Countryman, and Allan Kulikoff have each argued that forced migration had enormous human consequences. Black migrants left friends, family, and familiar surroundings and regularly experienced extreme hardships. The disproportionate number of male African migrants exacerbated the problem. Combined with physical and psychological stresses, the influx of males increased mortality rates and reduced births in Kentucky, Tennessee, South Carolina, Georgia, Louisiana, and Mississippi.[27]

Sixth, for Louisiana, it is assumed that during the 1780s and 1790s, the black population experienced no natural growth, and, for the first decade of the 1800s, it grew at an annual rate of 1 percent. Philip D. Curtin, Gwendolyn Midlo Hall, and Paul LaChance argue that the black population growth rate in Louisiana was significantly lower than the rate of North American slaves in general. Citing bad health conditions and thousands of African immigrants, they estimate the rate of reproductive change ranged from an increase of much less than 2.2 percent annually to an annual *decrease* of 2 percent.[28]

And finally, seventh, although parts of the Deep South remained foreign possessions for all or part of the period from 1782 to 1807, the slaves imported into these regions are included in the overall estimate of African arrivals in North America. During the entire period Florida and much of the Gulf South were either British, French, or Spanish possessions. Britain relinquished control of Mississippi in 1797, and France sold Louisiana to the United States in 1803.[29]

Using all these assumptions, the following calculations were performed. For the decades 1791 to 1800 and 1801 to 1810, the natural increase of the black population for the southern states and territories was calculated using several different rates of increase as outlined above. From this was then subtracted the projected natural increase from the sum of the decennial growth in the slave population, as calculated from the U.S. censuses that are available during the period of this study. Likewise the total number of slaves manumitted during these decades was subtracted. That total number derives from the determination of the growth rate of the free black population that census records indicate occurred during the period. If natural increase would have accounted for an annual growth of 2.5 percent, growth beyond that was a result of manumissions. This method gives a rough estimate of the manumissions between 1790 and 1810.

For Virginia and Maryland, the calculations suggest that in the 1790s, 40,000 enslaved workers either migrated with their owners to southern and western states and territories or were sent to the regions after being sold. For the remaining southern states and territories, the calculations suggest that these regions experienced an inflow of 100,410 blacks. When the number of domestic exports (40,000) is subtracted from the total number of migrants (100,410), the remainder (60,410) is the estimated number of foreign slaves imported between 1790 and 1800. For the next decade, the calculations suggest that 54,000 enslaved workers from Virginia and Maryland either migrated with their owners to southern and western states and territories or were sent to the regions after being sold. For the remaining southern states and territories, the calculations suggest that these regions experienced an inflow of 164,532 blacks. When the number of domestic exports (54,000) is subtracted from the total number of migrants (164,532), the remainder (110,532) is the estimated number of foreign slaves imported between 1800 and 1810.

Estimating the number of migrants in the 1780s is not nearly as clear-cut. Immediately after the war, officials undertook few, if any, formal statewide census counts in the South, and estimates of the populations vary widely. However, by extrapolating from various reports and observations and applying the same assumptions previously used to estimate the natural growth rates, calculations indicate that planters and traders moved 61,822 enslaved workers to the Carolinas, Georgia, Kentucky, and Louisiana. Of these, 30,000 migrated from the Chesapeake (Virginia and Maryland) and 2,516 from Florida. The remainder were imported from Africa, South America, and the West Indies. When Spain regained control of Florida in 1783, almost all of the British planters residing there chose to leave the colony. Most took their slaves with them to the West Indies, Canada, and England, but some either brought their workers with them to the United States or sent them to Georgia and South Carolina to be sold.[30] When one subtracts the sum of the domestic migrants (32,516) from the total number of migrants (61,822), one arrives at the estimated total of foreign imports for the 1780s (29,306). The sum of the 1780s (29,306), the 1790s (60,410), and the first decade of the 1800s (110,532) puts the estimated number of foreign slaves from Africa, South America, and the West Indies imported into North America from 1783 to 1810, derived from census records, at 200,248. A breakdown of the estimate by decade, state, region, and territory is shown in table 1.

TABLE I — SLAVES IN SOUTHERN STATES, TERRITORIES, AND COLONIES

	1783	1790	1800	1810
Virginia	260,000	292,627	346,968	392,518
Maryland	85,446	103,036	107,707	111,502
North Carolina	83,500	100,572	133,296	168,824
South Carolina	80,000	107,094	146,151	196,365
Georgia	14,750	29,264	59,699	105,218
Kentucky	-0-	*15,847	40,343	80,561
Tennessee	-0-	-0-	13,584	44,535
Florida	1,000**	2,000	4,000	7,500
Mississippi	1,000	2,000	3,489	17,088
Louisiana	12,534	18,700	21,933	34,660
Total	**538,230**	**671,140**	**877,170**	**1,158,711**

SOURCES: J. D. B. De Bow, *Statistical View of the United States, Embracing Its Territory, Population—White, Free Colored, and Slave—Moral and Social Condition, Industry, Property, and Revenue; the Detailed Statistics of Cities, Towns and Counties: Being a Compendium of the Seventh Census, to which Are Added the Results of Every Previous Census, Beginning with 1790, in Comparative Tables, with explanatory and illustrative notes, Based upon the Schedules*

Table 1 (*continued*)

and other Official Sources of Information. By J. D. B. De Bow, Superintendent of the United States Census (Washington: A. O. P. Nicholson, Public Printer, 1854), 63, 82. Evarts B. Greene and Virginia D. Harrington, *American Population before the Federal Census of 1790* (New York: Columbia University Press, 1932), 123–86; Gwendolyn Midlo Hall, *Africans in Colonial Louisiana: The Development of Afro-Creole Cultures in the Eighteenth Century* (Baton Rouge: Louisiana State University Press, 1992), 280–81; Paul F. LaChance, "Politics of Fear: French Louisianans and the Slave Trade, 1786–1809," *Plantation Society* 1 (June 1979): 196–97; David C. Rankin, "The Tannenbaum Thesis Reconsidered: Slavery and Race Relations in Antebellum Louisiana," *Southern Studies* 18 (spring 1979): 21; Patrick Riordan, "Finding Freedom in Florida. Native Peoples, African Americans, and Colonists, 1670–1816," *Florida Quarterly* 75 (summer 1996): 34–40; the U.S. Bureau of the Census, first, second, third, and fourth censuses; Daniel H. Usner, Jr., *Indians, Settlers, and Slaves in a Frontier Exchange Economy* (Chapel Hill: University of North Carolina Press, 1990), 112–16: and Edwin L. Williams, Jr., "Negro Slavery in Florida," *Florida Historical Quarterly* 28 (October 1949): 93–110.

NOTES: *Includes 3,417 slaves residing in Southwestern Territory.

**After British evacuation in 1783.

TABLE 2 — FREE BLACKS IN SOUTHERN STATES, TERRITORIES, AND COLONIES

	1783	1790	1800	1810
Virginia	10,000	12,866	20,507	33,119
Maryland	7,000	8,043	19,987	33,927
North Carolina	4,500	4,975	7,043	10,266
South Carolina	360	1,801	3,185	4,554
Georgia	80	398	1,919	1,801
Kentucky	-0-	114	741	1,713
Tennessee	-0-	-0-	309	1,317
Florida	500	700	800	1,000
Mississippi	-0-	-0-	182	240
Louisiana	2,000	2,400	2,802	7,585
Total	**24,440**	**31,297**	**57,475**	**95,522**

SOURCES: J. D. B. De Bow, *Statistical View of the United States, Embracing Its Territory, Population—White, Free Colored, and Slave—Moral and Social Condition, Industry, Property, and Revenue; the Detailed Statistics of Cities, Towns and Counties: Being a Compendium of the Seventh Census, to which Are Added the Results of Every Previous Census, Beginning with 1790, in Comparative Tables, with explanatory and illustrative notes, Based upon the Schedules and other Official Sources of Information. By J. D. B. De Bow, Superintendent of the United States Census* (Washington: A. O. P. Nicholson, Public Printer, 1854), 63 and 82. Evarts B. Greene and Virginia D. Harrington, *American Population before the Federal Census of 1790* (New York: Columbia University Press, 1932), 123–86; Gwendolyn Midlo Hall, *Africans in Colonial Louisiana: The Development of Afro-Creole Cultures in the Eighteenth Century* (Baton Rouge: Louisiana State University Press, 1992), 280–81; Paul F. LaChance, "Politics of Fear: French Louisianans and the Slave Trade, 1786–1809," *Plantation Society* 1 (June

1979): 196–97; David C. Rankin, "The Tannenbaum Thesis Reconsidered: Slavery and Race Relations in Antebellum Louisiana," *Southern Studies* 18 (spring 1979): 21; Patrick Riordan, "Finding Freedom in Florida: Native Peoples, African Americans, and Colonists, 1670–1816," *Florida Quarterly* 75 (summer 1996): 34–40; Daniel H. Usner, Jr., *Indians, Settlers, and Slaves in a Frontier Exchange Economy* (Chapel Hill: University of North Carolina Press, 1990), 112–16: and Edwin L. Williams, Jr., "Negro Slavery in Florida," *Florida Historical Quarterly* 28 (October 1949): 93–110.

TABLE 3 — SLAVE DISTRIBUTION IN SOUTH CAROLINA AND GEORGIA

	1783	*1790*	*1800*	*1810*
South Carolina				
Lowcountry* rice workers**	22,500	30,000	36,000	34,000
Lowcountry indigo and cotton workers	36,900	48,000	61,170	77,711
Total lowcountry	59,400	78,000	97,170	111,711
Backcountry	20,600	29,094	48,981	85,654
Total South Carolina	**80,000**	**107,094**	**146,151**	**197,365**
Georgia				
Lowcountry rice workers	6,000	10,000	12,000	10,000
Lowcountry indigo and cotton workers	2,000	3,261	4,574	12,780
Total lowcountry	8,000	13,261	16,574	22,780
Backcountry	6,750	16,003	43,125	82,438
Total Georgia	**14,750**	**29,264**	**59,699**	**105,218**

SOURCES: Joyce E. Chaplin, *An Anxious Pursuit: Agricultural Innovation and Modernity in the Lower South, 1712–1911* (Chapel Hill: University of North Carolina Press, 1993), 246–50; J. D. B. De Bow, *Statistical View of the United States, Embracing Its Territory, Population—White, Free Colored, and Slave—Moral and Social Condition, Industry, Property, and Revenue; the Detailed Statistics of Cities, Towns and Counties: Being a Compendium of the Seventh Census, to which Are Added the Results of Every Previous Census, Beginning with 1790, in Comparative Tables, with explanatory and illustrative notes, Based upon the Schedules and other Official Sources of Information. By J. D. B. De Bow, Superintendent of the United States Census* (Washington: A. O. P. Nicholson, Public Printer, 1854), 63 and 82. William Dusinberre, *Them Dark Days: Slavery in the American Rice Swamps.* New York: Oxford University Press, 1996), 460–642; Evarts B. Greene and Virginia D. Harrington, *American Population before the Federal Census of 1790* (New York: Columbia University Press, 1932), 123–86; Gwendolyn Midlo Hall, *Africans in Colonial Louisiana: The Development of Afro-Creole Cultures in the Eighteenth Century* (Baton Rouge: Louisiana State University Press, 1992), 280–81; Paul F. LaChance, "Politics of Fear: French Louisianans and the Slave Trade, 1786–1809," *Plantation Society* 1 (June 1979): 196–97; David C. Rankin, "The Tannenbaum Thesis Reconsidered: Slavery and Race Relations in Antebellum Louisiana," *Southern Studies* 18 (spring 1979): 21; Patrick Riordan, "Finding Freedom in Florida: Native Peoples, African Americans, and Colonists, 1670–1816," *Florida Quarterly* 75 (summer 1996): 34–40; Edmund Ruffin, *Report*

Table 2 (continued)

on the Commencement and Progress of the Agricultural Survey of South-Carolina, for 1843 (Columbia, A. H. Pemberton, 1843), 21–25; Daniel H. Usner, Jr., Indians, Settlers, and Slaves in a Frontier Exchange Economy (Chapel Hill: University of North Carolina Press, 1990), 112–16; Edwin L. Williams, Jr., "Negro Slavery in Florida," Florida Historical Quarterly 28 (October 1949): 93–110; and George K. Holmes, Rice Crop of the United States, 1712–1911 (Washington, D.C.: U.S. Department of Agriculture, Bureau of Statistics, Circular 34, 1912).

NOTES: *The estimate of the number of lowcountry rice workers, was arrived at by dividing South Carolina's average annual rice output by the average of clean rice produced per slave. For rice production, see Dusinberre, Them Dark Days, pp.460–462, Holmes, Rice Crop, and Ruffin, Report, pp. 21–25. For rice worker output, see Chaplin, Anxious Pursuit, pp. 246–250. To estimate lowcountry indigo and cotton workers, the number of rice workers were subtracted from the total number of lowcountry slaves.

**The South Carolina lowcountry includes Beaufort, Colleton, Charleston, and Georgetown districts, and Charleston (also Marion District in 1800 and 1810, and Williamsburg and Horry in 1810). The Georgia lowcountry includes Chatham, Bryan, Liberty, McIntosh, Glynn, and Camden Counties.

TABLE 4 — GROWTH OF SOUTH CAROLINA'S SLAVE POPULATION

	1783–90	1790–1800	1800–1810
Lowcountry Rice Workers*			
Population	22,500–30,000	30,000–36,000	36,000–34,000
Actual increase	7,500	6,000	<2,000>
Hypothetical rate of natural increase	0%	.5%	.5%
Projected natural increase	-0-	1,500	1,800
Net slave in-migration	7,500	4,500	<3,800>
Lowcountry Indigo and Cotton Workers			
Population	36,900–48,000	48,000–61,170	61,170–77,711
Actual increase	11,100	13,170	16,541
Hypothetical rate of natural increase	1%	1%	1%
Projected natural increase	2,583	4,800	6,117
Net slave in-migration	8,438	8,370	10,424
Backcountry Workers			
Population	20,600–29,094	29,094–48,981	48,981–85,654
Actual increase	8,494	19,887	36,673
Hypothetical rate of natural increase	2.2%	2.2%	2.2%
Projected natural increase	3,172	6,401	10,776

	1783–90	1790–1800	1800–1810
Net slave in-migration	5,322	13,486	25,897
Estimated net in-migration for South Carolina (includes allowances for manumitted slaves and migrant free blacks)	22,717	27,290	33,094

Sources: Joyce E. Chaplin, *An Anxious Pursuit: Agricultural Innovation and Modernity in the Lower South, 1712–1911* (Chapel Hill: University of North Carolina Press, 1993), 246–50; J. D. B. De Bow, *Statistical View of the United States, Embracing Its Territory, Population— White, Free Colored, and Slave—Moral and Social Condition, Industry, Property, and Revenue; the Detailed Statistics of Cities, Towns and Counties: Being a Compendium of the Seventh Census, to which Are Added the Results of Every Previous Census, Beginning with 1790, in Comparative Tables, with explanatory and illustrative notes, Based upon the Schedules and other Official Sources of Information. By J. D. B. De Bow, Superintendent of the United States Census* (Washington: A. O. P. Nicholson, Public Printer, 1854), 63 and 82. William Dusinberre, *Them Dark Days: Slavery in the American Rice Swamps.* New York: Oxford University Press, 1996), 460–642; Evarts B. Greene and Virginia D. Harrington, *American Population before the Federal Census of 1790* (New York: Columbia University Press, 1932), 123–86; Gwendolyn Midlo Hall, *Africans in Colonial Louisiana: The Development of Afro-Creole Cultures in the Eighteenth Century* (Baton Rouge: Louisiana State University Press, 1992), 280–81; Paul F. LaChance, "Politics of Fear: French Louisianans and the Slave Trade, 1786–1809," *Plantation Society* 1 (June 1979): 196–97; David C. Rankin, "The Tannenbaum Thesis Reconsidered: Slavery and Race Relations in Antebellum Louisiana," *Southern Studies* 18 (spring 1979): 21; Patrick Riordan, "Finding Freedom in Florida: Native Peoples, African Americans, and Colonists, 1670–1816," *Florida Quarterly* 75 (summer 1996): 34–40; Edmund Ruffin, *Report on the Commencement and Progress of the Agricultural Survey of South-Carolina, for 1843* (Columbia, A. H. Pemberton, 1843), 21–25; Daniel H. Usner, Jr., *Indians, Settlers, and Slaves in a Frontier Exchange Economy* (Chapel Hill: University of North Carolina Press, 1990), 112–16; Edwin L. Williams, Jr., "Negro Slavery in Florida," *Florida Historical Quarterly* 28 (October 1949): 93–110; and George K. Holmes, *Rice Crop of the United States, 1712–1911* (Washington, D.C.: U.S. Department of Agriculture, Bureau of Statistics, Circular 34, 1912).

NOTE: *The estimate of the number of lowcountry rice workers, was arrived at by dividing South Carolina's average annual rice output by the average of clean rice produced per slave. For rice production, see Dusinberre, *Them Dark Days*, 460–62; Holmes, *Rice Crop*; and Ruffin, *Report*, 21–25. For the worker output, see Chaplin, *Anxious Pursuit*, 246–50. To estimate lowcountry indigo and cotton workers, the number of rice workers were subtracted from the total number of lowcountry slaves.

TABLE 5 — GROWTH OF GEORGIA'S SLAVE POPULATION

	1783–90	1790–1800	1800–1810
*Lowcountry Rice Workers**			
Population	6,000–10,000	10,000–12,000	12,000–10,000
Actual increase	4,000	2,000	<2,000>
Hypothetical rate of natural increase	0%	.5%	.5%

Table 5 (continued)	1783–90	1790–1800	1800–1810
Projected natural increase	-0-	500	600
Net slave in-migration	4,000	1,500	<2,600>
Lowcountry Indigo and Cotton Workers			
Population	2,000–3,261	3,261–4,574	4,574–12,780
Actual increase	1,261	1,313	8,206
Hypothetical rate of natural increase	1%	1%	1%
Projected natural increase	140	326	457
Net slave in-migration	1,121	987	7,749
Backcountry Workers			
Population	6,750–16,003	16,003–43,125	43,125–82,438
Actual increase	9,253	27,122	39,313
Hypothetical rate of natural increase	2.2%	2.2%	2.2%
Projected natural increase	1,040	3,521	9,448
Net slave in-migration	8,213	23,601	29,825
Estimated net in-migration for Georgia (includes allowances for manumitted slaves and migrant free blacks)	13,632	27,509	34,974

SOURCES: Joyce E. Chaplin, *An Anxious Pursuit: Agricultural Innovation and Modernity in the Lower South, 1712–1911* (Chapel Hill: University of North Carolina Press, 1993), 246–50; J. D. B. De Bow, *Statistical View of the United States, Embracing Its Territory, Population— White, Free Colored, and Slave—Moral and Social Condition, Industry, Property, and Revenue; the Detailed Statistics of Cities, Towns and Counties: Being a Compendium of the Seventh Census, to which Are Added the Results of Every Previous Census, Beginning with 1790, in Comparative Tables, with explanatory and illustrative notes, Based upon the Schedules and other Official Sources of Information. By J. D. B. De Bow, Superintendent of the United States Census* (Washington: A. O. P. Nicholson, Public Printer, 1854), 63 and 82. William Dusinberre, *Them Dark Days: Slavery in the American Rice Swamps.* New York: Oxford University Press, 1996), 460–642; Evarts B. Greene and Virginia D. Harrington, *American Population before the Federal Census of 1790* (New York: Columbia University Press, 1932), 123–86; Gwendolyn Midlo Hall, *Africans in Colonial Louisiana: The Development of Afro-Creole Cultures in the Eighteenth Century* (Baton Rouge: Louisiana State University Press, 1992), 280–81; Paul F. LaChance, "Politics of Fear: French Louisianans and the Slave Trade, 1786–1809," *Plantation Society* 1 (June 1979): 196–97; David C. Rankin, "The Tannenbaum Thesis Reconsidered: Slavery and Race Relations in Antebellum Louisiana," *Southern Studies* 18 (spring 1979): 21; Patrick Riordan, "Finding Freedom in Florida: Native Peoples, African Americans, and

Colonists, 1670–1816," *Florida Quarterly* 75 (summer 1996): 34–40; Edmund Ruffin, *Report on the Commencement and Progress of the Agricultural Survey of South-Carolina, for 1843* (Columbia, A. H. Pemberton, 1843), 21–25; Daniel H. Usner, Jr., *Indians, Settlers, and Slaves in a Frontier Exchange Economy* (Chapel Hill: University of North Carolina Press, 1990), 112–16; Edwin L. Williams, Jr., "Negro Slavery in Florida," *Florida Historical Quarterly* 28 (October 1949): 93–110; and George K. Holmes, *Rice Crop of the United States, 1712–1911* (Washington, D.C.: U.S. Department of Agriculture, Bureau of Statistics, Circular 34, 1912).

Note: *Estimates of the numbers of lowcountry rice workers, were arrived at by dividing Georgia's average annual rice output by the average of clean rice produced per slave. For rice production, see Dusinberre, *Them Dark Days*, pp. 460–62; Holmes, *Rice Crop*; and Ruffin, *Report*, pp. 21–25. For rice worker output see Chaplin, *Anxious Pursuit*, pp. 246–50. Estimates of lowcountry indigo and cotton workers were arrived at by subtracting the number of rice workers from the total number of lowcountry slaves.

TABLE 6 — CONJECTURAL ESTIMATES OF NET SLAVE MIGRATION TO AND WITHIN NORTH AMERICA

	1783–1790	*1790–1800*	*1800–1810*	*Total*
Virginia	<18,000>	<24,000>	<40,000>	<82,000>
Maryland	<12,000>	<16,000>	<14,000>	<42,000>
Kentucky	15,847	21,612	32,152	69,611
Tennessee	-0-	13,584	28,903	42,487
North Carolina	2,460	5,230	3,660	11,350
South Carolina	22,717	27,290	33,094	83,101
Georgia	13,632	27,509	34,975	76,115
Florida	<2,516>	1,000	4,000	2,484
Mississippi	1,000	1,185	12,849	15,034
Louisiana	6,166	3,000	14,900	24,066
Total	**29,346**	**60,410**	**110,532**	**200,248**

SOURCES: Joyce E. Chaplin, *An Anxious Pursuit: Agricultural Innovation and Modernity in the Lower South, 1712–1911* (Chapel Hill: University of North Carolina Press, 1993), 246–50; J. D. B. De Bow, *Statistical View of the United States, Embracing Its Territory, Population— White, Free Colored, and Slave—Moral and Social Condition, Industry, Property, and Revenue; the Detailed Statistics of Cities, Towns and Counties: Being a Compendium of the Seventh Census, to which Are Added the Results of Every Previous Census, Beginning with 1790, in Comparative Tables, with explanatory and illustrative notes, Based upon the Schedules and other Official Sources of Information. By J. D. B. De Bow, Superintendent of the United States Census* (Washington: A. O. P. Nicholson, Public Printer, 1854), 63 and 82. William Dusinberre, *Them Dark Days: Slavery in the American Rice Swamps.* New York: Oxford University Press, 1996), 460–642; Evarts B. Greene and Virginia D. Harrington, *American Population before the Federal Census of 1790* (New York: Columbia University Press, 1932), 123–86; Gwendolyn Midlo Hall, *Africans in Colonial Louisiana: The Development of Afro-Creole Cultures in the Eighteenth Century* (Baton Rouge: Louisiana State University Press, 1992), 280–81; Paul F. LaChance, "Politics of Fear: French Louisianans and the Slave Trade, 1786–1809," *Plantation Society* 1 (June 1979): 196–97; David C. Rankin, "The Tannenbaum Thesis Reconsidered:

Table 6 (continued)

Slavery and Race Relations in Antebellum Louisiana," *Southern Studies* 18 (spring 1979): 21; Patrick Riordan, "Finding Freedom in Florida: Native Peoples, African Americans, and Colonists, 1670–1816," *Florida Quarterly* 75 (summer 1996): 34–40; Edmund Ruffin, *Report on the Commencement and Progress of the Agricultural Survey of South-Carolina, for 1843* (Columbia, A. H. Pemberton, 1843), 21–25; Daniel H. Usner, Jr., *Indians, Settlers, and Slaves in a Frontier Exchange Economy* (Chapel Hill: University of North Carolina Press, 1990), 112–16; Edwin L. Williams, Jr., "Negro Slavery in Florida," *Florida Historical Quarterly* 28 (October 1949): 93–110; and George K. Holmes, *Rice Crop of the United States, 1712–1911* (Washington, D.C.: U.S. Department of Agriculture, Bureau of Statistics, Circular 34, 1912).

II.

Despite the fact that the estimate here and those made by Carey, Curtin, Fogel, Engerman, and Kulikoff are all based on census records, they vary widely. The new estimate of 200,000 is 2.9 times greater than Carey's, 2.2 times greater than Curtin's, and 1.7 times greater than Kulikoff's. Fogel and Engerman's estimate is 1.5 times greater than the new one. Further evidence as to the precision of the estimates is compiled in appendix B, garnered by new research and that of others into extant records of the post–Revolutionary War North American foreign slave trade. These records are by no means complete, but when available, the data may include vessel arrival dates, the type of vessel and name, the master of the vessel, the origin of the slaves, the consignee, the number of slaves imported, and the source of information. Therefore these records, even though incomplete, provide a useful comparison with quantitative data derived in other ways.

Because not all the information on each arrival is extant, several assumptions have been made to arrive at an estimate of the number of slaves disembarked. Occasionally a general term used in a newspaper advertisement could be matched with a specific number found in a ship manifest or customs report. On the basis of such comparisons, the estimate was that when merchants used the terms *several*, *a few*, *a group*, *a gang*, and *a parcel* in advertisements, they were indicating they had around twenty slaves available to be sold.[31] Other terms dealing with larger groups are even more uncertain. For calculation purposes, it was assumed that when merchants used the term *a number*, they had roughly 30 slaves for sale, on average. When they used the term "a small cargo," it was estimated that they had approximately 35, but for the terms "shipment" or "cargo," in general, about 50, and for the term "shipload," about 100. When totaled, the number of people these terms described amounted to less than 1,800 captives, or less than 2 percent of the known arrivals. Second, for arrivals from Africa where the type of vessel is known, but the number of slaves disembarked is not, information was taken from the volumes merchants assigned to similar vessels. For a sloop, merchant and duties records indicate 80 slaves made up an average cargo; for a schooner, 100; for a brig, 150; for a snow, 180; and for a ship, 235.[32] A third set of assumptions was worked out regarding cargoes arriving from Africa where neither the number of slaves disembarked nor the type of vessel is known. In these instances the assumption was 160 captives for the 1780s and 1790s, and 200 for the first decade of the 1800s. These figures were generated by averaging the number of people who arrived on voyages in which the size of the cargo is known. For vessels that transshipped Africans from the Caribbean to Louisiana, from which the number of slaves disembarked is not known, it was assumed that 80 slaves were delivered. The number of people disembarked was listed on 80 percent of the voyages.[33]

When these assumptions are applied to the data for specific known vessels in appendix B, the imports, which can be documented using this particular approach to the time between 1783 and 1790, total 21,333 foreign slaves. Similarly, the estimate for the time between 1791 and 1800 totals approximately 12,782, and that for the time between 1801 and 1810 totals 72,131. Adding together the calculations for these three decades yields a total of 106,246 for the entire period from 1783 to 1810. (See table 4 for date, place landed, and number of people disembarked.)

TABLE 7 — ARRIVAL OF FOREIGN SLAVES IN NORTH AMERICA, BASED UPON INCOMPLETE NEWSPAPER AND PORT RECORDS FOR THE YEARS 1783–1810

	North Carolina	South Carolina	Georgia	Florida	Louisiana	North America	Total
1783	-0-	1,189	70	-0-	347	-0-	1,606
1784	-0-	4,749	230	-0-	602	-0-	5,581
1785	8	3,904	506	-0-	466	-0-	4,884
1786	145	1,227	380	-0-	957	-0-	2,709
1787	222	1,145	353	-0-	918	381	3,019
1788	84	189	51	-0-	1,041	-0-	1,365
1789	40	-0-	288	-0-	858	-0-	1,186
1790	2	100	302	-0-	419	160	983
Subtotal	501	12,503	2,180	-0-	5,608	541	21,333
1791	-0-	-0-	63	-0-	-0-	-0-	63
1792	-0-	310	1,438	-0-	208	-0-	1,956
1793	-0-	50	779	160	52	-0-	1,041
1794	-0-	-0-	114	-0-	80	-0-	194
1795	-0-	-0-	1,673	-0-	235		1,908
1796	-0-	160	2,918	-0-	-0-	-0-	3,078
1797	-0-	274	1,737	-0-	-0-	-0-	2,011
1798	-0-	67	1,301	-0-	-0-	-0-	1,368
1799	-0-	45	330	-0-	220	-0-	595

Table 7 (continued)

	North Carolina	South Carolina	Georgia	Florida	Louisiana	North America	Total
1800	-0-	100	-0-	50	418	-0-	568
Subtotal	-0-	1,006	10,353	210	1,213	-0-	12,782
1801	-0-	66	160	-0-	123	30	379
1802	-0-	3,100	750	466	250	82	4,648
1803	-0-	400	1,345	200	1,153	0-	3,098
1804	-0-	6,701	786	242	1,162	-0-	8,891
1805	-0-	8,795	-0-	16	279	-0-	9,090
1806	-0-	14,306	235	19	572	-0-	15,132
1807	-0-	21,683	364	-0-	882	-0-	22,929
1808	-0-	887	-0-	-0-	698	150	1,735
1809	-0-	-0-	-0-	-0-	3,460	-0-	3,460
1810	-0-	-0-	-0-	1,281	1,488	-0-	2,769
Subtotal	-0-	55,938	3,640	2,224	10,067	262	72,131
Grand Total	501	69,447	16,173	2,434	16,888	803	106,246

SOURCES: Appendix B.
NOTE: For the number of slaves per vessel, see Appendix B.

The total of 106,000 people, derived from incomplete newspaper and port records of foreign slave arrivals, represents 53 percent of the estimate of 200,000, calculated using census records. The primary reason for this wide discrepancy is the limited scope of surviving arrival records. Extant contemporary observations, slave trade documents, duties and customs records, and newspaper reports and advertisements recording the volume of the post-Revolutionary slave trade to North America document much, but not all, of the foreign slave trade. Many homeport clearances and records of North American slave vessels and imports either were not documented or have been lost or destroyed.

Extant duties and customs records and newspaper reports reveal the extent of the problem. Only two sets of duties and customs records exist today that could be considered anywhere near complete: the Duties on Trade at Charleston, 1784–1789, and a Charleston customs house officer's 1820 report on slave vessel arrivals at Charleston from 1804 to 1807, prepared for U.S. Senator William Smith of South Carolina.[34] The Duties on Trade at Charleston, 1784–1789 appears to be the most reliable. However, it lists arrivals and clearances for only 35 months (May 1784 through March 1787) out of the 47 months in the 1780s when South Carolinians could legally import slaves. Also newspaper advertisements for slave sales and local observations indicate that state officials underreported arrivals. During 1785, for instance, state officials failed to record a minimum of five of the forty-two known slave vessel arrivals, or at least 12 percent of the total.[35] And finally, although it appears that duties officials were responsible for reporting all the state's imports and exports, they listed only a few arrivals and clearances for South Carolina ports other than Charleston. Although more than a hundred vessels entered Beaufort and Georgetown annually in the 1780s, duties officials recorded only five arrivals for the four years the report covered. One of these recorded vessels was the *Brothers*, arriving from Gambia with slaves, but others apparently went unrecorded, indicated by the fact that local officials advanced credit to a merchant for duties on at least 453 more foreign slaves who arrived in Beaufort during these years.[36]

The 1804 to 1807 list of slave vessel arrivals prepared for Senator Smith by customs officials is also incomplete. In 1805 the customs officials failed to record a minimum of thirty vessels, or 52 percent of the total of fifty-eight known arrivals. Edward Hooker's experience cited at the onset illustrates customs officials' inattention. While in Charleston during the last week of 1805, he saw "three or four vessels full of them [slaves], just brought from Africa," but according to the report compiled for Senator Smith, only one vessel carrying slaves docked in December of 1805.[37] As in the earlier list, this report also ignores arrivals at South Carolina's other busiest ports, Georgetown and Beaufort.[38] Records of foreign slave disembarkations at the secondary ports either were not reported or have been lost or destroyed. Smaller shipments of one to thirty slaves were also excluded in the 1804 to 1807 report. In 1805 the arrival of three vessels with small cargoes, the *Little Ned*, *Wenton*, and *Fox*, were not listed in the report.[39] The Duties on Trade at Charleston, 1784–1789 reveals that small cargoes of slaves ranging from one to thirty slaves arrived regularly and constituted as much as 10 percent of the Charleston slave trade.[40] Although the South Carolina legislature prohibited the importation of St. Dominique slaves during the 1800s, it permitted the landing of other black workers from the Caribbean. The report also ignored transshipments of newly arrived Africans from the West Indies, even though newspaper advertisements and cargo manifests clearly demonstrate that merchants received transshipments of Africans from the West Indies.[41]

Customs officials also invariably underreported the number of slaves imported. In the 1800s the *Charleston Courier* irregularly published customs reports listing descriptions, quantities, and origins of items imported during the previous week. During 1806 customs officials underreported the number of foreign slaves imported in thirteen of twenty-four weekly reports. In most cases the reports erred by more than 50 percent. Unfortunately these reports have been used by scholars for more than a century to estimate the volume of the trade.[42]

Besides the Duties on Trade at Charleston and Smith's report, a few random customs manifests from 1783 to 1798 and 1804 to 1807 are extant. They suggest that small numbers of seasoned slaves and African slaves were regularly imported, but because so few manifests have survived, they document only a fraction of the legal North Carolina, South Carolina, Georgia, and Louisiana foreign slave trade.[43]

Newspapers fill some of the gaps left by duties and customs records. They published a report titled "Marine List" or "Shipping Report" and featured advertisements for sales of imported slaves. The daily reports listed arrivals from and clearances for Africa, from time to time, the number and origin of slaves on board vessels arriving from foreign ports, and a cargo's consignee. Below the arrivals and clearances, national and international maritime news was reported. Lifted from other newspapers and interviews with recently arrived passengers and masters, the brief column reported on a wide range of maritime topics, including the Atlantic slave trade. Especially from 1803 to 1808, when the North American foreign slave trade was at its zenith, Providence, Newport, Charleston, Savannah, and New Orleans newspapers reported political developments that affected the slave trade, news from African trading centers, and slaver boardings, seizures, sightings, shipwrecks, crew deaths, revolts, arrivals, and clearances from other ports. Advertisements announced the time and place of slave sales, the origin of the shipment, the quantity of slaves to be sold, the financial terms of sale, the name of the consignee, and a sales pitch as to the gender, age, health, and skills of the slaves.

Newspapers, unfortunately, like duty and customs records, are often an inconsistent and incomplete (and therefore misleading) source. During the period of study, Charleston, Savannah, Newport, and New Orleans newspapers often struggled to survive and then only lasted for a few years, or in some cases, a few months. In the smaller port towns, where slavers also landed cargoes, such as Beaufort, South Carolina, local newspapers did not even appear until decades after the legal slave trade ended.[44] Even when newspapers prospered, many editions are missing, or extant copies are unreadable.

Other factors further limit the inclusiveness of newspaper data. For instance, reports of clearances to Africa from northern ports were reduced from the 1790s onward as federal and state legislation against participation in the slave trade began to induce concealment of the true purpose of slave voyages.[45] Moreover it appears newspapers were largely dependent on the inaccurate daily and weekly reports of customs officials for information on the trade. Therefore, newspapers are an inconsistent source for slave vessel arrivals and clearances during the 1780s and 1790s. In 1785, for instance, the *State Gazette of South Carolina* failed to report thirty-eight out of a total of fifty-four, or 70 percent of known Charleston arrivals.

Slave-sale advertisements further cloud the slave trade picture. They were generally accurate in their listing of the number of slaves a merchant had on hand to sell, but, in doing so, they often misrepresented the original size of a slave cargo upon arrival. Between the time a vessel first appeared in port and a sale was conducted, it was not unusual for a sizable percentage of a slave cargo to disappear in a variety of ways. After ships arrived at the port of disembarkation, slaves who had managed to survive the extreme conditions of the middle passage found themselves physically exhausted, emotionally depleted, and dangerously susceptible to disease. Often the most ill or vulnerable died before they could be sold. Other slaves, called "privileged slaves," were awarded as remuneration to the master and officers of a vessel, who could sell them without paying the usual import duty. Of the remainder the largest number usually went to planters or traders who had placed an order with the merchant handling the sale before a ship departed for Africa.[46]

Deceased, privileged, and presold slaves were not available for sale, of course, and therefore not listed in advertisements. For the periods when duties or custom officials' reports are extant, a comparison between newspaper advertisements and the actual number of slaves disembarked reveals the extent of the problem quite dramatically. In 1785 Duties on Trade at Charleston reported 274 slaves arriving on the *Commerce*, while an ad listed 200 available for sale. In 1807 Customs reported 350 slaves arriving on the *Ann*, while an ad listed 250.[47] Such discrepancies pose a daunting problem, because slave-sale advertisements are often the only extant record of many slave voyages.

Unfortunately no slave-sale advertisements document the arrival of enslaved laborers from the island of St. Dominique (modern day Haiti). Soon after the Haitian Revolution erupted on St. Dominique in 1791, planters began fleeing the island with their slaves. Many of the slaves ended up on the North American mainland where they were sold.[48] Since buyers were wary of purchasing St. Dominique slaves—they considered them rebellious—few, if any, advertisements listing the origin of the enslaved laborers as St. Dominique or describing them as French appeared in newspapers. Customs records are equally scarce. Because North American mainland states and colonies prohibited the importation of West Indies slaves soon after the revolt began, slave owners, merchants, and vessel officers did not report St. Dominique slave arrivals to customs officials.[49]

Nevertheless, other evidence suggests that a substantial number of the enslaved workers ended up on the North American Mainland. In July of 1793, for instance, fifty-three vessels arrived in Baltimore, Maryland, from Cape Francois, St. Dominique. Among the passengers were "500 People of Color and Blacks."[50] About the same time, the commander fo Norfolk, Virginia's militia reported that "two hundred or more Negroes brought from Cape Francois" were in the Norfolk area.[51] No doubt, many of the blacks were free people of color, but a large percentage of the migrants were probably slaves.

Many more of the slaves ended up in the lower South. In the early 1790s newspaper advertisements in Charleston often described runaways as French slaves.[52] Later that decade, in a letter to his wife, Savannah merchant Robert Mackay noted the arrival in Charleston of a St. Dominique planter and his sixty-seven slaves.[53]

The largest contingent, however, passed through New Orleans.[54] Historian Paul LaChance estimates that more than 11,000 St. Dominique refugees, whites, free persons of color, and slaves, landed in the port city between 1790 and 1811. At least 3,226 of the 9,059 refugees that landed in 1809 were slaves.[55] If the ratio of slaves to the total number of refugees, 36 percent, was consistent for the entire period, more than 3,900 St. Dominique slaves were taken to Louisiana.

For Louisiana and Mississippi from 1783 to 1810, few extant records document the arrival of foreign slave ships.[56] According to Gwendolyn Midlo Hall and Paul LaChance, historians of colonial Louisiana, both French and Spanish colonial officials failed to record most slave imports. By comparing a Spanish Custom House list of slaves arriving from the Caribbean in 1786 to slave sales agreements and baptismal registers, Hall estimated that extant records document only 25 percent of the total number of slaves transshipped from the Caribbean to Louisiana during the Spanish period. This count does not include the African captives that arrived directly from Africa. This is especially troublesome because, during the period, census records suggest that merchants and planters imported more than 39,033 foreign enslaved workers into Louisiana and Mississippi.[57]

Documenting smuggling activities also presents a challenge. The census calculations of this work suggest that during the 1790s the volume of the foreign slave trade may have approached 60,000 slaves, which is more than four times the 12,782 persons documented through extant records. Some of the discrepancy can be explained by lost and destroyed records and incompetent customs officials, but bits and pieces of evidence suggest that smuggling was widespread during the 1790s and 1800s.[58] Frequent advertisements for missing Africans appeared in Savannah and Charleston newspapers in the late 1790s and early 1800s, suggesting the substantial presence of newcomers. In 1803, among the many ads that appeared in the *Charleston Courier* for missing slaves, at least twenty-three contain information suggesting that they concerned newly arrived Africans. Slave owners described their missing property as having African markings and as speaking and understanding only African languages.[59]

Smuggling was condoned, especially in and around Charleston and Savannah, after Georgia prohibited further foreign slave imports in 1798. Several months after the Georgia legislature enacted the ban, an advertisement in a Savannah newspaper boldly announced the sale of 330 "New Negroes from Angola."[60] Later that year, South Carolina officials seized the schooner *Phoebe* with its cargo of forty-five Africans.[61] During the last six months of 1799 alone, officials filed six actions for breaking the federal law of 1794. Three years later the Savannah City Council organized a coastal patrol to prevent the landing of 700 to 800 slaves from the Island of Guadalupe.[62] In 1803, three months before the South Carolina legislature lifted the prohibition on importing foreign slaves, W. and E. Crafts advertised goods "for the African trade" in the *Charleston Courier*.[63]

When the schooner *Hannah* was seized near Savannah on August 30, 1803, a local official lamented that "this business of smuggling the Negroes of St. Domingo into this state . . . is becoming truly alarming."[64] A few months later the *Georgia Republican and State Intelligencer* reported two other violations. The Savannah district attorney accused the owners of the brig *Lady Nelson* of illegally importing slaves from Cuba in November 1803, and that same year a local court seized and sold the schooner *Amelia* for violating the prohibition against importing foreign slaves.[65] Even after the South Carolina prohibition was lifted in 1804, smugglers continued to operate in Georgia. State officials filed a complaint against the owners of the brig *Mary* for landing a cargo of slaves on Green Island, Georgia, in January of 1804. The *Mary* was one of the few cases when officials actually mentioned the names of the accused; however, no arrests were made and no convictions were handed down.[66]

Such complaints represent the tip of the iceberg. After perusing the federal census records for his state in 1801, Governor John Drayton of South Carolina estimated that Africans "introduced into this state, both by land and water" accounted for one-half of the 150,000 increase in the slave population from 1790 to 1800.[67] In two 1789 letters penned by Samuel Brown of Boston, Massachusetts, the merchant describes the ins and outs of slave smuggling. According to Brown, two of his vessels, the brig *Don Galvez* and the ship *Pacific* were involved in the illegal trade to South Carolina.[68] Joseph Hawkins wrote a book about his experiences as a supercargo aboard another slave ship involved in smuggling, the *Charleston.* The ship cleared from Charleston in 1794 and later that year took off 500 slaves from the coast of Africa. Although Hawkins failed to mention where exactly the *Charleston* landed its cargo, probably because he did not want to incriminate himself or his colleagues, it is safe to assume that the slaves were unloaded near Charleston. In 1797 the captain and crew of the *Charleston* attempted to deliver another cargo to South Carolina, but because of leaks the ship was diverted to Antigua, where it was condemned and its cargo of slaves was sold.[69]

In a January 7, 1802, letter to his employer (James D'Wolf, the owner of the brig *Nancy*), Charles Clark described how he and other slavers like Hawkins smuggled foreign slaves into Charleston:

> When I wrote you before, I was bound out of the city after my cargo, which had been on the beach to the northward of Charleston. I found them all well, and much better than I expected, for the weather was cold. They had no clothes, and no shelter except for the sandhills and cedar trees, and no person, to take care of them. I arrived in Charleston with them on the 14th of Decr. [1801] without being troubled. I shall not make as much as I expected, for slaves was very high on the African coast, and my time being short, I was obliged to make the best bargain I could. I sailed with 70 cargo, and lost 4 of them; but they are all very good and will bring the highest

price, that is, from $350 up to $500. I don't see that the Trade stops much, for they come in town 2 or 3 hundred some nights. I believe there has been landed since New Years as much as 500 slaves. They land them outside the harbor and march them in at night. 2 or 3 vessels has come in from Africa in ballast. The revenue cutter seized one brig bound from N. Orleans to Charleston. She was cleared from N. O. by calling them passengers. They clear out from there and go into Havana "in distress," and ship from there to the U. States, or sell if the price is high. I think there will be more distressed vessels this winter than ever before. I left on the [African] coast 14 vessels belonging to the U. States, a great part of them for Charleston.[70]

As Clark suggests, smuggling slaves into South Carolina was relatively easy. Smugglers were aided by geography and an ever-increasing demand for slaves, as well as the fact that there were too few authorities to police the Georgia and South Carolina coastlines. During a House of Representatives debate on South Carolina's reopening of the foreign slave trade in 1804, two congressmen described the situation. Rawlins Lowndes of South Carolina attempted to justify lifting the ban by claiming that since the slave trade had been prohibited in Georgia in 1798, South Carolina officials had been "unable to enforce the state ban," because "with navigable rivers running into the heart of it, it was impossible with our means to prevent our Eastern brethren [that is, northern merchants] . . . from introducing them into the country." Lowndes concluded "that the law was completely evaded, and for the last year or two, Africans were introduced into the country in numbers little short, I believe, of what they would have been had the trade been a legal one."[71]

L. Mitchell of New York was more willing to spread the blame. He agreed with Lowndes that northern merchants were engaged in the trade, but he argued that the South Carolina merchants were "countenanced by their fellow citizens at home, who were as ready to buy as they themselves were to collect and to bring to market." In a probable exaggeration for purposes of debate, he estimated that "during the last twelve months, twenty thousand enslaved negroes had been transported from Guinea, and, by smuggling, added to the plantation stock of Georgia and South Carolina."[72]

A pitiful number of law enforcement officers were responsible for policing Georgia's and South Carolina's lengthy coastlines. Only two revenue cutters and crews patrolled over four hundred miles of the coast, dotted with hundreds of islands and breached with innumerable inlets, creeks, and rivers.[73] Moreover no federal or state officials patrolled the southern states' domestic or foreign borders. Slavers took advantage of the lack of law enforcement officers before 1798 and landed foreign slaves legally at or near Savannah and then transported them across the Savannah River into South Carolina, where they were sold in Beaufort, Charleston, or the elsewhere in the state. After Georgia closed its borders to foreign slaves in 1798, transatlantic slavers landed African captives legally in

Spanish East and West Florida, and then merchants, using smaller vessels, smuggled them into Georgia or South Carolina where they were easily sold.[74]

Rising cotton and sugar prices and the fantastic profits they generated kept the smugglers busy, as the demand for labor increased as well. The value of cotton and sugar production skyrocketed from around twenty thousand dollars in 1792 to more than 2.5 million dollars in 1800. Before Georgia closed its borders to further imports of foreign slaves, cotton export value had surpassed the values of tobacco, rice, and indigo in Georgia and the Carolinas.[75] Thus, even though the Georgia legislature disallowed further imports of foreign slaves—mainly because the white population feared that the revolutionary doctrine, so evident in St. Dominique, might be spread by slaves imported from the West Indies —economic forces often overcame moral or political objections to the foreign slave trade. Consequently, until the South Carolina legislature lifted its ban on the importation of foreign slaves in 1804, smugglers could not keep up with the demand.[76]

Smugglers were also active in Louisiana, especially after Congress banned the foreign slave trade in 1808. Soon after the prohibition went into effect the U.S. Navy sent Master-Commander David Porter to New Orleans to stop illegal imports. Like the officers and crews who were responsible for the southeastern coast, the Louisiana force, under the command of Porter, was asked to perform an impossible task. Porter's small squadron of fifteen diminutive craft was expected to patrol a long stretch of the Gulf of Mexico coastline from Dauphine to the Timbalier Islands. The abundance of shallow waterways, which were nearly impossible to patrol with conventional naval vessels, made the task all the more difficult. Over the next year Porter's force was able to apprehend seven vessels carrying foreign slaves and to uncover a conspiracy to illegally import foreign slaves. However, by early 1809 problems with gunboats and crews had severely reduced the squadron's effectiveness, and smugglers essentially came and went as they pleased. They supplied privateer Jean Lafitte's popular slave mart on Barataria Island between Bayou La Fourche and the Mississippi River. At the auctions buyers could purchase African captives landed to the west in Spanish territory and brought in overland or directly off of ships. Evidently local residents approved of Lafitte's operation for his slave auctions were advertised in New Orleans newspapers and were well attended.[77]

III.

To help in overcoming the obstacles presented by lost and destroyed records, undocumented voyages, and misleading extant records, a third means of calculating North American importations of foreign slaves in the post-Revolution generation has been brought into play. This alternative approach involves estimating the slave-carrying capacity of the North American slave ships employed in the transatlantic slave trade. Scholars have used this method (many refer to it as the slave-carrying capacity method) to estimate the volume of the British slave trade. Rather than tabulating records of the disembarkations of African slaves, they assume that they will never be able to document every African slave transported to the Americas; instead, they base their estimate on the total carrying capacity of vessels known to be employed in the slave trade. Scholars prefer this method because much more consistent evidence exists on the number of ships involved in the slave trade than on individual voyages.[78]

To determine slave-carrying capacity, a list of known slave voyages performed by North American vessels between 1783 and 1810 has been compiled (see table 8). These records are by no means complete but may include the name of the ship, captain, tonnage, place of registration, the date of voyage, and source of information. Because not all the information on every vessel is available, a number of assumptions were made to arrive at the slave-carrying capacity. First, for vessels of which the type is known, it was assumed (following the work of Roger Anstey and Stephen Behrendt) that during the 1780s slave "ships" averaged 110 tons and carried 187 people, brigs averaged 61 tons and carried 104 people, snows averaged 76 tons and carried 129 people, schooners averaged 50 tons and carried 85 people, and sloops averaged 45 tons and carried 77 people. For those vessels for which the type and number of slaves disembarked are not known, it was assumed that they averaged 66 tons and carried 112 people.

For the 1790s it was assumed that slave "ships" averaged 170 tons and carried 255 people, brigs averaged 103 tons and carried 155 people, snows averaged 100 tons and carried 150 people, schooners averaged 77 tons and carried 116 people, and sloops averaged 62 tons and carried 84 people. For those vessels for which the type and number of slaves disembarked are not known, it was assumed they averaged 96 tons and carried 144 people. For the first decade of the 1800s, it was assumed that slave "ships" averaged 202 tons and carried 242 people, brigs averaged 117 tons and carried 140 people, snows averaged 216 tons and carried 260 people, schooners averaged 84 tons and carried 100 people, and sloops averaged 65 tons and carried 74 people. For those vessels for which the type and number of slaves disembarked are not known, it was assumed they averaged 130 tons and carried 156 people.[79]

Not all North American slavers delivered their human cargoes to North America; they also disembarked African captives in the Caribbean and South America. However, trade with foreign colonies was often irregular. After the Revolution, England did not reopen trade with its former colony for many years, and between 1788 and 1793 French ports were closed to American slavers. Spain also prohibited foreign ships from landing African captives in its American colonies until 1789, and even then it limited the traffic to Cuba. Moreover, beginning in 1793, European wars curtailed U.S. trade with French, Spanish, and British colonies. Nevertheless, from the mid-1790s until South Carolina lifted its ban on foreign slave imports in late 1803, North American slavers carried on a considerable trade with European colonies in the Caribbean and South America.[80]

   The extent of this trade has, however, not been completely documented. As mentioned previously, especially during the 1790s and in the first three years of the 1800s, American slavers often concealed their activities, and therefore exactly where they disembarked many of their cargoes is not known. In 1796, for instance, extant records suggest that slavers undertook forty-six voyages, but the point of disembarkation is known for only twenty-seven of the forty-six vessels—nineteen landed cargoes in North America and eight in foreign ports. Based on the research of Herbert Klein and Roger Anstey, it is assumed that a majority of the slavers landed their captives in North America, and it is estimated that during the 1780s, 60 percent of the American slave ship cargoes were disembarked in North America; in the 1790s, 50 percent; and in the 1800s, 70 percent.[81] The year, the number of North American vessels involved in the transatlantic trade each year, and each vessel's tonnage and carrying capacity are listed in table 8.

TABLE 8 — ANNUAL NORTH AMERICAN SLAVING VOYAGES AND CARRYING CAPACITY
BASED ON INCOMPLETE NEWSPAPER AND PORT RECORDS FOR THE YEARS 1783–1810

Year	Number of Voyages	Tonnage	Carrying Capacity
1783	3	157	267
1784	8	557	981
1785	18	1,274	2,166
1786	15	995	1,692
1787	13	834	1,418
1788	11	618	1,051
1789	11	752	1,278
1790	11	692	1,176
Subtotal	101	5,879	10,029
1791	21	2,094	3,141
1792	31	3,165	4,748
1793	22	2,245	3,368
1794	23	2,186	3,279
1795	45	4,692	7,038
1796	31	3,295	4,943
1797	15	1,705	2,558
1798	14	1,373	2,060
1799	42	3,181	4,772
1800	23	2,019	3,028
Subtotal	267	25,955	38,935

Table 8 (continued)

Year	Number of Voyages	Tonnage	Carrying Capacity
1801	21	2,666	3,199
1802	32	4,049	4,859
1803	17	2,225	2,670
1804	71	8,293	9,952
1805	116	14,687	17,624
1806	132	17,403	20,883
1807	102	12,642	15,170
1808	5	467	560
1809	-0-	-0-	-0-
1810	1	130	156
Subtotal	497	62,562	75,073
Grand Total	**865**	**94,396**	**124,037**

Sources: See Appendix B.

Table 8 suggests North American slaving ventures increased each decade from the 1780s until the 1810s. The Revolution severely damaged the American mercantile fleet, and, when the war ended in 1783, a lack of capital slowed its recovery. As a result it took American merchants most of the 1780s to reach the late colonial level of participation in the transatlantic slave trade. In 1783 they sent only three slavers to the coast of Africa and, in 1784, eight, but by the middle of the decade their participation had increased significantly. In 1785 the number of voyages rose to eighteen. Although they are not included in the estimate of North American carrying capacity, it should be noted that many vessels transshipped newly arrived Africans from the West Indies to New Orleans. In the first six months of 1786 alone, at least thirty ships delivered Africans bought in Caribbean ports to New Orleans.[82]

During the 1780s North American merchants sponsored 101 voyages to the coast of Africa. However, local observers indicate even more American slavers were involved. In 1789, for instance, a Kingston, Jamaica, newspaper reported that "the Guinea trade to both the Gold and Windward Coasts of Africa, is carried on with vigor from Charleston, South Carolina."[83] In the same year, a British official estimated that as many as forty vessels had been outfitted in New England that year for the African trade.[84] Based on these observations, the documented carrying capacity, 10,000, is raised by 20 percent to 12,000 people. Allowing for known and foreign disembarkations, North American slavers probably landed an additional 3,400 people in the United States in the 1780s.[85]

In the next decade North American involvement in the Atlantic slave trade increased. South Carolina continued to prohibit imports, but North Carolina ports were open until 1794, Georgia ports until 1798, and Louisiana ports until 1796. As previously mentioned, even when the states and colonies prohibited imports, slavers easily evaded authorities and smuggled large numbers of Africans into South Carolina, Georgia, and Louisiana. Moreover, because of the previously mentioned changes in Spanish, French, and British ports in North America, U.S. merchants took advantage of the easier access and sent hundreds of slave vessels to the African coast.[86]

By 1794 U.S. participation in the Atlantic slave trade was so widespread that Congress passed an act designed to prohibit both slave trading from the United States to any other country and the outfitting of slavers for the foreign trade. The statute had little effect, however, except in the middle states, where antislavery groups such as the Quakers made sure the law was upheld. Elsewhere slave traders, especially Rhode Islanders, either avoided or flouted the law. In 1799 a slave ship belonging to James D'Wolf of Bristol, Rhode Island, was libeled and condemned to be sold. On auction day, D'Wolf had the local customs official kidnapped to prevent him from buying the vessel for the government. While the customs official was being rowed across Narragansett Bay, one of D'Wolf's employees bought the ship back for his employer for a fraction of its value. This was not the first nor last time an American slave vessel owner purchased his own condemned ship back at a price far below its value at auction. Because slave traders like D'Wolf continued to violate the law and because many white southerners feared St. Dominique slaves, Congress strengthened the 1794 Act in 1800 by setting more stringent penalties for participation in the foreign slave trade.[87]

Only one group, the slave trade interest, opposed passage of the law. Their advocate, Congressman John Brown of Rhode Island, a wealthy merchant and slave ship owner, maintained that because other countries would quickly fill any void left by the American withdrawal from the slave trade, the act would have little or no effect on the volume of the Atlantic slave trade. This led him to demand before the House of Representatives, "Why should we see Britain getting all the slave trade to themselves? Why should not our country be enriched by that lucrative traffic?" He went on to say that "we might as well enjoy that trade as leave it wholly to others. It was the law of that country [Africa] to export whom they held in slavery, who were as much slaves as those were slaves in this country. . . . The very idea of making a law against this trade, which all our other nations enjoyed, was ill policy." And finally he claimed that the slave trade profited not only slave traders but U.S. manufacturers as well. According to Brown, "all our distilleries and manufacturers were lying idle for want of an extended commerce [in slaves] . . . on those coasts [Africa], New England rum was much preferred to the best Jamaica spirits. . . ." Despite Brown's argument the House and Senate approved the bill overwhelmingly.[88]

In 1801, to avoid the new Federal law and further problems with customs officials, D'Wolf and Brown secured from President Thomas Jefferson the appointment of D'Wolf's brother-in-law and fellow slave trader, Charles Collins, to the position of collector of customs at Bristol, Rhode Island. Needless to say, neither D'Wolf nor any other Bristol slave traders experienced any problems with customs officials while Collins held the position.[89] Other U.S. slavers were just as adept at evading authorities. Slave ship captains adopted a number of strategies to conceal the true purpose of their voyages. According to a report in 1800 by the Pennsylvania Abolition Society, captains "clear out for the West Indies where they dispose of their out cargoes and proceed to Africa for slaves."[90]

Apparently the strategies succeeded. In the 1790s American slavers appeared on the coast of Africa in large numbers. In 1795 alone, at least thirty-two ships cleared Newport, Rhode Island, for Africa.[91] By the middle of the decade, American slavers were flooding the African coast. Zachary Macaulay, governor of Sierra Leone, sadly informed Samuel Hopkins in 1796 that "you will be sorry to learn that during the last year, the number of American slave traders on the coast has increased to an unprecedented degree. Were it not for their pertinacious adherence to that abominable traffic, it would in consequence of the war, have been almost wholly abolished in our neighborhood."[92] Capt. Matthew Benson of Rhode Island, who was on the coast of Africa buying camwood and gum, wrote from Sierra Leone in 1800, to say that, the "American line continues beyond all previous periods. Not a week passes without arrivals. The quantity of rum, tobbacco, and provisions since the tenth of the current [month] is almost incredible."[93] According to officials at the African Institute in London in 1813, the "unprecedented degree" of American slavers had carried [an average of] 15,000 slaves annually from the coast of Africa between 1796 and 1810.[94]

Roger Anstey's and Herbert S. Klein's research confirms that a substantial percentage of the carrying trade of U.S. ships was employed in delivering slaves to North America in the 1790s. Anstey argued that American ships disembarked 180,843 African slaves in Cuba, South America, and the United States from 1791 to 1810. The majority of the people, 108,273, were landed on the North American mainland.[95] Although Anstey bases his estimate in part on the too-large calculations made by Fogel and Engerman, he demonstrates that a substantial number of U.S. vessels were involved in the African slave trade.[96] Klein's research buttresses Anstey's argument. He shows that U.S. vessel arrivals in Cuba ranged from 6 in 1790 to a maximum of 111 in 1797. However, not all of the American vessels Klein documents arrived directly from Africa; many of the ships transshipped people from North America and other Caribbean islands to Cuba. Any ship docking in Cuba was required by Spanish law to deliver a minimum of one slave to the colony. Needless to say, many vessels carried small numbers of slaves to Cuba.[97]

By combining the information from appendix A with the research of Anstey and Klein, one can more accurately estimate the size of the 1790s American slaving fleet. Incomplete records suggest that American merchants sponsored at least 267 slaving voyages to Africa during this decade. From 21 in 1791, the number of voyages increased to 45 in 1795. Three years later they declined to 14 voyages. Conflict with France was responsible for the variations during the latter half of the decade. French seizures of American slavers on the African coast and in the West Indies discouraged American investment in slaving voyages.[98] Despite French interference, the number of American vessels involved in the African trade was probably much greater than table 8 suggests. For instance, Klein documents 111 voyages to Cuba alone in 1797, which is more than 5 times the 21 voyages listed in table 8. Anstey's observations on American participation can help solve the problem. He conjectures American ships delivered 36,000 African captives to North America in the 1790s.[99] If each ship carried an average of 160 slaves, then 225 American vessels disembarked Africans in North America. To compensate for the difference between the number of American slavers that research suggests landed cargoes in North America (100) and Anstey's number (225), the current estimate was raised by 30 percent to 130 voyages. This increases the estimate of the North American carrying capacity to 51,000 people for the 1790s. Allowing for known and foreign disembarkations, it is possible to estimate that North American slavers would have landed an additional 11,000 people in the United States in the 1780s.[100]

In the first decade of the 1800s, American participation continued to increase. Free of French interference, American slavers returned to the African coast in great numbers at the beginning of the new century. The number of known voyages rose from 21 in 1801 to at least 32 in 1802. When South Carolina officials lifted the prohibition on foreign slave imports, the number of voyages skyrocketed from 17 in 1803 to 132 in 1806. By then the American slaving fleet rivaled Britain's, with one official estimating that it was three-fourths as large.[101]

American merchants continued to sponsor voyages after the federal prohibition against imports went into effect on January 1, 1808. In 1808, for instance, at least four vessels cleared Charleston and Savannah for Africa. For the decade, there were 497 documented American voyages to the coast of Africa, although research has not identified all the voyages American slavers sponsored. To compensate for unreported voyages and lost records, the estimate of the carrying capacity was moved upward by 10 percent.[102] This raises the North American carrying capacity to 83,000 people for the first decade of the 1800s. Allowing for known and foreign disembarkations, North American slavers landed an additional 27,000 people in the United States in the first decade of the 1800s.[103] The sum of the adjusted figures for the 1780s (12,000), for the 1790s (51,000) and for the first decade of the 1800s (83,000) puts the estimate of the North American slave carrying capacity at 146,000 people.

IV.

On the basis of the varied approaches to population data given above, it is now possible to generate revised figures for overall North American slave imports for each decade after the War for American Independence. From local observations and federal and Spanish population censuses, it was estimated that during the 1780s merchants and planters imported 30,000 foreign slaves into North America. Documented arrivals and the estimated carrying capacity of American slavers indicate that fewer African and Caribbean slaves arrived during the period. Documented arrivals suggest that a minimum of 21,000 people arrived, and the carrying capacity of American slavers imply more than 24,000, but less than 30,000.

The most problematic regions are the lower Mississippi Valley and Spanish Florida. Spanish censuses indicate that the black population of Louisiana increased 6,200 people during the seven years. If it is assumed that the black population experienced no natural growth (Philip D. Curtin estimated the population experienced a natural *decrease* of 2 percent), then imports would have accounted for all of the increase in population between 1783 and 1790.[104] Taking into consideration the fact that Spanish officials recorded few slave ship arrivals, the Louisiana import total has been raised to 6,200 to compensate for the discrepancy. It is also estimated that Spanish slavers landed 1,000 African captives in Florida and 500 in Mississippi.

For the 1780s the calculations suggest that North American slaving vessels landed 3,400 more captives in the United States than incomplete records of arrivals indicate. It is estimated that 1,500 were disembarked in South Carolina. The additional 1,500 people would increase the estimate of South Carolina imports for the decade to 14,000. Georgia imports are more problematic. The census data calculations suggest merchants and planters imported 13,600 slaves. Since this total exceeds by a factor of six the number 2,200, it is safe to increase the Georgia imports by 3,500 people. The increase raises the Georgia total to 5,700. The adjustments to Louisiana, Florida, Mississippi, South Carolina, and Georgia import figures produce a new estimate of 27,900 for the decade. The 1790s present a much greater challenge. The census calculations have suggested imports increased to 60,410. However, documented arrivals and the carrying capacity of the North American slaving fleet do not support the calculations. Part of the problem lies with reporting. As previously mentioned, except for Georgia, most American states prohibited imports in the 1790s. The South Carolina legislature maintained a ban against imports throughout the 1790s, and North Carolina prohibited the trade after 1794. Slavers disembarked Africans in these states, especially in South Carolina, but surreptitiously. To make matters worse, in Florida, Louisiana, and Mississippi, few records of Spanish and French imports are extant. Even in Georgia, where the imports were legal until 1798, documented arrivals only begin to tell the entire story. Few customs records for the decade are extant, advertisements for slave sales were often limited to one newspaper, and many slave sales to South Carolina planters were not reported.

The carrying capacity of the American slave fleet and census records can help fill in the gaps created by the lack of extant records. The carrying-capacity calculations suggest that during the 1790s American slaving vessels carried 11,000 more African captives to North America than incomplete records of arrivals indicate. Seven thousand probably landed in South Carolina and 4,000 in Georgia. Also an estimated 1,500 St. Dominique slaves were probably introduced into South Carolina and 1,500 in Georgia. Census records indicate that foreign slavers disembarked an additional 2,000 slaves in Florida, 1,500 in Mississippi, and 2,000 in Louisiana. The additional arrivals would increase the total number of South Carolina imports to 9,400, those of Georgia to 16,900, Louisiana to 3,200, Mississippi to 1,500, and Florida to 2,200. For the entire region the additions increase the total to 33,200. This is still considerably fewer people than census calculations suggest landed. One possible explanation for the discrepancy is that in 1800 census takers succeeded in counting a greater percentage of the population than they had in 1790. A more accurate count would have artificially increased the number of migrants. Another and the most probable explanation is that far more foreign slaves were imported, perhaps as many as 15,000 to 20,000 additional people.

In the first decade of the 1800s, the census calculations, documented arrivals, and carrying capacity are much more in agreement. The census calculations suggest that 110,532 African and Caribbean slaves arrived in North America. Documented arrivals total 72,131 people, or 65 percent of the census estimate. As can be seen, however, these figures are still not completely in agreement. A number of factors contribute to the discrepancy. Smuggling was pervasive in large parts of the South during the decade. The foreign slave trade was illegal in Georgia and Mississippi for the entire decade, in South Carolina between 1801 and 1803 and after December 31, 1807, and in Louisiana after 1803. Although Spanish and French officials recorded few slave ship arrivals, census records and local observations indicate foreign slavers were active in Louisiana and Florida. The Spanish crown allowed imports into East and West Florida throughout the decade, and both Spain and France permitted planters and merchants to bring foreign slaves into Louisiana before the United States bought the territory in 1803. Census records suggest that during the first decade of the 1800s foreign vessels delivered 1,800 additional foreign slaves to Florida, and between 1801 and 1804 they disembarked an additional 3,500 enslaved Africans and Caribbean workers in Louisiana and 2,000 in Mississippi.[105]

To further narrow the discrepancy between the total of known arrivals (72,131) and the number census calculations suggest (110,532), the slave-carrying capacity of the American slaving fleet can be used again. These slavers carried about 27,000 more people to the United States than extant records of arrivals suggest. It is assumed the additional people were landed in the following regions: 16,000 in South Carolina, 6,000 in Georgia, 2,000 in Louisiana after 1803, and 3,000 in Mississippi after 1803. Also it is assumed that foreign slave ships (mainly British) landed another undocumented 2,500 captives in South Carolina. The additions raise the total number of South Carolina imports to 74,500, those of Georgia to 9,600, Florida to 4,200, Mississippi to 5,300, and Louisiana to 15,600. The adjustments raise the total number of foreign imports to 109,200 for the first decade of the 1800s. When the estimates of all three decades (27,900 for the 1780s, 33,200 for the 1790s, and 109,200 for the first decade of the 1800s) are combined, they total 170,300 foreign slaves.

TABLE 9 — ESTIMATE OF FOREIGN SLAVE TRADE TO NORTH AMERICA

State, Territory, or Colony Where Disembarked	Number Disembarked			Total Disembarked
	1783–1790	1791–1800	1800–1810	
North Carolina	500	-0-	-0-	500
South Carolina	14,000	9,400	74,500	97,900
Georgia	5,700	16,900	9,600	32,200
Florida	1,000	2,200	4,200	7,400
Mississippi	500	1,500	5,300	7,300
Louisiana	6,200	3,200	15,600	25,000
Total	**27,900**	**33,200**	**109,200**	**170,300**

Sources: Estimates derived from Tables 1–8.

The estimate of 170,000 is much larger than earlier projections by H. C. Carey (70,000), Philip D. Curtin (92,000), and Allan Kulikoff (113,000) and much smaller than the one made by Robert W. Fogel and Stanley Engerman (291,000). This new estimate is more accurate because the calculations are based on more exact black population growth rates. Moreover it has been augmented by using research into North American slave trade records of arrivals and also American slave-carrying capacities. Finally it includes estimates of French and Spanish imports.

Chapter 3

FOREIGN SLAVE ORIGINS

"The Ibo nation lies under a prejudice here and may be excluded."
William Dunbar, February 1, 1807, in Mrs. Dunbar Rowland, ed.,
Life, Letters, and Papers of William Dunbar

In early February 1807, a Natchez cotton planter, William Dunbar, placed an order for enslaved labor with the Charleston commercial firm of Tunno and Price. Much as a present-day businessperson would order a piece of industrial equipment, Dunbar carefully detailed his specifications. He listed the amount he was willing to spend, 3,000 sterling, acceptable credit terms, and expected delivery date. With respect to the "quality of the slaves," the planter indicated his preference for Africans "from the age of 12 to 21; well formed and robust; and the proportion of females about one-fourth to one-third females to that of males, admitting some farther discretionary limitation according to circumstances."[1] He was just as particular about the African origin of his new workers. "The Ibo nation lies under a prejudice here and may be excluded," he wrote, but "there are certain nations from the interior of Africa, the individuals of which I have always found civilized, at least better disposed than those nearer the coast, such as Bornon, Houssa, Zanfara, Zegzeg, Kapina, Tombootoo, all near the river Niger."[2] Like his European colonial predecessors, the Mississippi planter was closely concerned with distinctions among African peoples.[3]

The topic of origins of imported slaves is again receiving attention, but this time from a different group. Ever since the publication of Alex Haley's *Roots* in the 1970s, a growing number of African Americans have begun seeking information on the origin and ethnicity of ancestors, wondering when and where they landed in North America. Unfortunately few specific names of migrants appear in this study. When slave ship captains and supercargoes purchased captives on the coast of Africa, they listed the age, sex, price, and origin of their cargo, but not the names of individuals. The North American merchants and factors who sold newly arrived Africans recorded sales in a similar manner. They listed the age, sex, and price of the slaves and, in some cases, the names of the purchasers. By matching plantation slave inventories with records of slave sales, a few African Americans have been able to trace the origin of their ancestors.

While this study and others cannot provide extensive information on the geographic origins of specific individuals, a more general understanding of the provenance of imported slaves remains an important challenge. The forced migration of millions of Africans had a significant impact on their native continent and on the New World. Their huge numbers and their skills and the knowledge they possessed meant that their removal was a blow to their homeland and a boon to the New World. Especially in North America, African skills and culture played a significant role in shaping regional cultural and economic landscapes.

I.

Scholars of the black diaspora have arrived at a "standard series" of eight coastal regions to aid in the identification of African origin.[4] The northernmost slave-trading region on the western coast of Africa is Senegambia. Bordered roughly on the north by Cape Verde and on the south by the Nunez River, it includes the coastlines of present-day Gambia and Senegal. The second region, Sierra Leone, shares Senegambia's southern border. It extends from the Nunez River in the north to Cape Mount in the south. The third region, the Windward Coast, extends from southeast of Cape Mount to, and including, the Assini River. The region includes much of present-day Ivory Coast and Liberia. The fourth region, the Gold Coast, stretches from west of the Assini River to the Volta River on the east. The fifth region, the Bight of Benin, located east of the Gold Coast, extends from west of the Volta to the Benin River. The sixth region, the Bight of Biafra, centers on the Niger Delta. It runs from the Benin River on the west to Cape Lopez to the south. The seventh region, known as Angola, or West-Central Africa, stretches from Cape Lopez in the north to the Orange River in the south. And finally the eighth region, southeastern Africa, or Mozambique, encompasses the southeastern coast of Africa from the Cape of Good Hope north to Zanzibar, and the island of Madagascar.[5]

From early in the seventeenth century until the War for American Independence began in 1775, Africans were forced to migrate from these regions to New England, the middle colonies, the upper South, the lower South, and the lower Mississippi Valley. However, because the post–Revolutionary War foreign slave trade was confined to the lower South and the lower Mississippi Valley, only the eighteenth-century trade to the Carolinas, Georgia, and Louisiana will be discussed here.[6]

Compared to South Carolina and Louisiana, North Carolina imported few foreign slaves during the colonial era, only around 1,800. Slavers delivered about 300 of these directly from Africa, mainly in the 1750s. Small coasting vessels transported the remaining 1,500 in small groups from one to twenty. Merchants transshipped newly arrived Africans from the West Indies and Charleston to North Carolina, but exactly how many of the 1,500 were Africans is not known.

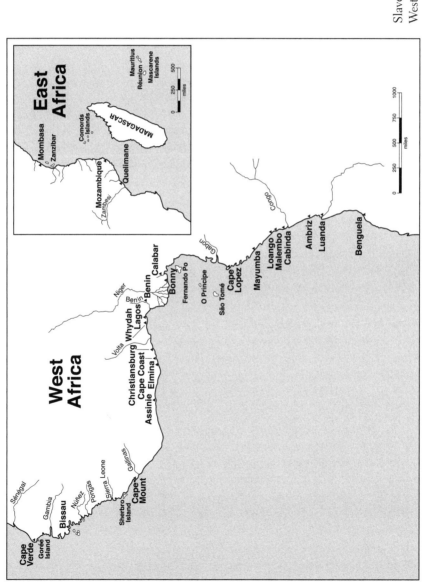

Slave Trading Ports in East and West Africa

Most of the migrants, more than 80 percent, arrived between 1749 and 1775. Coasters delivered the slaves to different ports, including Brunswick, Roanoke, New Bern, Beaufort, Edenton, and Currituck.[7] North Carolina was a minor, although steady, importer during the colonial era.

South Carolina imported more foreign slaves in the eighteenth century than any other mainland colony. Between 1703 and 1775 as many as 90,000 foreign slaves may have arrived in South Carolina. During the first two decades of the eighteenth century, South Carolina planters and traders imported foreign slaves in small lots, mainly from Barbados and Jamaica, but by the 1720s the colony's economy had reached a level that would support direct shipments from Africa. Entire shiploads greatly increased the volume of the trade until 1739, when a slave rebellion brought the slave trade to a screeching halt. Although the slaves that participated in the Stono Rebellion failed to attain their goals, they did succeed in discouraging further imports of Africans into South Carolina for nearly a decade. In the 1750s the transatlantic slave trade was revived, and 17,000 slaves were landed. In the 1760s the volume increased to 23,000 slaves, and, before problems with England halted shipments in 1774, another 22,000 slaves entered the colony in the 1770s. Slavers delivered Africans to a number of locations on the South Carolina coast, including Georgetown and Beaufort, but most landed their cargoes at Charleston. Buyers from South Carolina, North Carolina, Georgia, and Florida traveled to Charleston to purchase newly arrived slaves.[8]

South Carolina planters were well known for their distinct preferences for some African ethnic groups and strong prejudices against others. In a 1756 letter Charleston merchant Henry Laurens made his customers' convictions quite clear: "The slaves from River Gambia," he wrote, "are preferr'd to all others with us save the Gold Coast," while "there must not be a Callabar among them."[9] In another letter he advised that "Gold Coast are best[;] next To Them The Windward Coast are prefer'd to Angolas."[10] The hierarchy was based on characteristics supposedly embodied by regional types. South Carolina slave buyers preferred servile, tall, healthy, male, dark-skinned, young, and blemish-free Africans familiar with rice cultivation. They considered these prime slaves. The coastal regions of Gold Coast and Gambia were the most closely associated with these characteristics. When Gold Coast and Senegambian slaves were not available, or too expensive, planters would buy captives from Sierra Leone, the Windward Coast, and Angola. Those from the Bight of Benin and Bight of Biafra were to be avoided. Viewed as recalcitrant, small, slender, weak, often yellowish in color, and possessing an alarming penchant for suicide, Whydahs, Ibos, Bite, Bonny, and Calabars brought the lowest prices.[11]

The provenances of South Carolina slave shipments reflect the bias of merchants and planters. Philip D. Morgan has documented the arrival of 45,000 African slaves between 1760 and 1774. Of these the origin of 21 percent was listed as Africa, 21 percent Senegambia, 10 percent Sierra Leone, 17 percent Windward

Coast, 12 percent Gold Coast, 3 percent Bight Benin, 1 percent Bight of Biafra, 16 percent West-Central Africa, and 0 percent East Africa.[12] However, it should be noted that exports from Angola made up a much larger percentage of total imports earlier in the century. Between 1735 and 1740, for instance, seven out of every ten slaves imported were Angolans.[13] Nevertheless, Morgan's research is revealing. During the late colonial era South Carolina traders and planters imported slaves mainly from five regions: Senegambia, Sierra Leone, the Windward Coast, the Gold Coast, and Angola. Of these, 27,000 originated in the three regions that South Carolina planters preferred the most, Senegambia, the Windward Coast, and the Gold Coast. Merchants and slave traders included Sierra Leone and, at times, Senegambia and the Gold Coast, as part of the Windward Coast. Therefore shipments from Sierra Leone are included in Windward Coast exports.[14] The two regions at the top of Laurens's hierarchy, Senegambia and the Gold Coast, accounted for 14,300 imports, and the two at the bottom, the Bight of Benin and the Bight of Biafra, for 1,500. The remaining 7,000 came from Angola.[15]

Colonial Georgia planters and traders exhibited the same bias regarding African sources as those in South Carolina. Georgia was the last British southern colony, established in North America in 1732, and the last to enter the slave trade, in 1750. From 1750 to 1765 traders and planters imported some 1,700 foreign slaves, mainly through Charleston. After 1765 the economy of the colony was large enough to absorb direct shipments, and, before the Revolution stopped imports in 1775, another 7,900 foreign slaves entered Georgia. Of these, 5,400 arrived from Africa in 43 ships and 3,400 from the Caribbean in 142 vessels. Most were unloaded in Savannah. During the period, the origin of 26 percent of the total was listed as Africa, 32 percent Senegambia, 21 percent Sierra Leone, 9 percent Windward Coast, 4 percent Gold Coast, 0 percent Bight of Benin, 0 percent Bight of Biafra, 8 percent Angola, and 0 percent Mozambique. Like their South Carolina neighbors, Georgia planters depended on slave labor to cultivate rice and indigo. Accordingly they preferred slaves "from the Coast of Sena Gambia and from as far down as the Gold Coast. Ibos, Conga's, Cape Mounts and Angola Negroes excepted."[16]

During the eighteenth century Louisiana traders and planters imported between 25,000 and 30,000 foreign slaves.[17] Although the origin of only a small percentage of these slaves is known, it appears that most were embarked from three regions. Of the 6,000 slaves who arrived in twenty-three shipments directly from Africa between 1729 and 1743, 29 percent came from the Bight of Benin, 5 percent from West-Central Africa, and 66 percent from Senegambia.[18] Like their South Carolina counterparts, Louisiana traders and planters exhibited distinct preferences. In 1718 the organizers of two voyages to supply Louisiana with Africans instructed captains to purchase slaves who knew how to cultivate rice. The preference for slaves familiar with rice cultivation is reflected in the large numbers of Senegambian imports. No similar records have been located for the Spanish period that began in 1763, but Gwendolyn Midlo Hall has shown in her study of Point Coupee parish that between 1771 and 1802 Africans were present in large numbers, 39 percent, of the slave population. In the parish planters listed Senegambia as the origin of 27 percent of their African slaves, Sierra Leone 2 percent, the Windward Coast 4 percent, the Gold Coast 1 percent, the Bight of Benin 29 percent, the Bight of Biafra 12 percent, West-Central Africa 24 percent, and Mozambique 2 percent.[19]

Louisiana was the only North America colony to import large numbers of Bight of Benin slaves. The presence of large numbers of Senegambian, Benin, and Angolan slaves in Louisiana reflects the preference of French slavers for trade in those regions.[20] Also, like South Carolina traders and planters, Louisiana dealers and slave owners preferred Senegambians, but, unlike South Carolina slave owners, they were quite willing to buy Biafra or Benin slaves when they were available. Their attitudes regarding the desirability of various African groups, and their ties to France, resulted in a slave population with about 80 percent from Senegambia, Benin, and Angola.

When the origins of the slaves shipped to the different colonies are compared, the distinctiveness of each region's African population emerges. Of the three major importing regions, the African populations of Louisiana was the most diverse. Louisiana planters and merchants imported large numbers of slaves from the northernmost and southernmost regions, Senegambia and Angola, and from under the bulge of Africa in the Bight of Benin and the Bight of Biafra. The South Carolina population included few Africans from the Bight of Benin and the Bight of Biafra. Except for Angolans the African population of South Carolina and Georgia was largely made up of slaves from Senegambia, Sierra Leone, and the Windward and Gold Coasts.

When all the North American colonial imports into the lower South and the lower Mississippi Valley are combined, the import pattern that emerges is unique in the Americas. From 1720 to 1770 roughly 30 percent of slaves came from Senegambia, 5 percent from Sierra Leone, 11 percent from the Windward Coast, 10 percent from the Gold Coast, 5 percent from the Bight of Benin, 8 percent from the Bight of Biafra, 30 percent from West-Central Africa, and 1 percent from Mozambique.[21] Although the North American colonies received shipments from all of the conventional eight coastal regions, 60 percent of the colonies' imports originated in Senegambia and West-Central Africa. Only 13 percent came from the Bight of Benin and Bight of Biafra. The remaining 27 percent embarked mainly from Sierra Leone, the Windward Coast, and the Gold Coast. All the French, Spanish, and English colonies in the Americas imported large numbers of Angolans, but none of these had as high a percentage of Senegambian slaves as the North American colonies did. More than anything else, the large number of Senegambian imports sets North America apart from the rest of the Americas during the colonial period.[22]

II.

When the transatlantic trade to Georgia and the Carolinas revived in 1783, merchants picked up right where they had left off. Especially for larger lots, fifty or more slaves, they usually listed the coastal region of origin of newly arrived African slaves in advertisements of slave sales. For sales in Charleston and Savannah, notices appeared proclaiming the superior attributes of African slaves from Gambia, Sierra Leone, the Gold Coast, Angola, and New Calabar.[23] In some cases they noted the loading point within the coastal region. In May of 1784, George Garner announced the sale of a "Cargo of Prime, Healthy, Slaves from the river Gambia, on the Windward Coast of Africa."[24] In rare cases notices also listed the tribe or political state of the newly arrived Africans. In November 1783, for example, R. and Peter Smith advertised the coming sale of two hundred "Very Prime and Healthy Negroes, from the Gold Coast of Africa. They are of the Tantee Country, and esteemed the Best Negroes."[25]

When reporting arrivals, customs agents and newspaper marine reports also employed coastal regions. In June of 1784, Charleston customs agents listed the origin of the cutter *Louisa's* cargo of slaves as simply Gambia. By the early 1800s newspaper "Marine Lists" or "Port News" or "Shipping News" were providing more specific information. They noted the port a ship had "entered from" as well as its cargo. The anchorages where slaves were obtained are mentioned frequently in these reports. Rio Pongus, the river Gambia, Isles de Los, Cape Mount, the Bananas Isles, and the Congo River are just a few of the many that appear. They also used anchorages to inform readers of the progress of slave voyages. For instance, in December of 1807, the "Ship News" reported that "Captain Whitey left in Rio Pongus, ship *Fourth of July,* Brown, for this port, to sail in 2 days; brig *Tartar,* Taylor, and schooner *Kitty,* Maculey, in 10 days."[26]

Unfortunately, the origins of many shipments were not documented. For smaller lots, fifty or less slaves, merchants usually described newly arrived slaves simply as "New Negroes" or "Africans."[27] The coastal origins of many of the larger shipments are also not known. Often cargoes were sold in advance and thus no advertising was done. The only known record for many slave voyages is a newspaper marine list that reports a ship either cleared or arrived from Africa or was bound for a North American port from Africa. Other sources of voyages are also vague. In an August 1786 letter to his New England partner, William Vernon noted the arrival of a slave ship in Charleston from Africa but failed to note the origin of the Africans it landed.[28] Neither the local customs officials nor the newspaper reported the arrival of the ship. This was not unusual during periods when imports were legal, but when they were prohibited, documentation of origin is even more rare. For instance, in January 1802, Charles Clark reported to the owner of the ship he captained that 500 African slaves had been smuggled into Charleston during the first week of the year. Moreover he had left fourteen American slavers on the coast of Africa, most of whom planned to deliver their cargoes to Charleston. Unfortunately he failed to mention the exact source of the smuggled slaves or where on the African coast he had encountered the American ships.[29]

Despite these problems the provenance of 65,600 African arrivals between 1783 and 1810 has been identified. These people represent 68 percent of the 96,200 Africans whom have been documented from written sources as arriving during this era. This is considerably higher than the percentage of known origins on which Philip D. Curtin and Elizabeth Donnan based their estimates for colonial South Carolina and Virginia.[30] The arrival of 9,600 foreign slaves from the Caribbean, South America, Canada, and Europe has been documented. However, except for roughly 750 Guadalupe slaves smuggled into Georgia in 1803 and 3,225 Haitian slaves who arrived in New Orleans in 1809 from Cuba, the majority of the remaining 5,625 slaves had probably originated their journey in Africa. Larger shipments of 50 or more reported as arriving from the Caribbean or South America were usually either transshipments of Africans or were the property of slavers who had stopped for provisions, supplies, or instructions before continuing on to North America. Customs agents and newspapers correctly listed these vessels as arriving from a Caribbean port, but the persons they carried were Africans, not seasoned slaves as the reports seemed to suggest. On March 20, 1804, for instance, the *Charleston Courier* reported that the brig *Sukey and Polly* arrived in Charleston with 175 slaves from Kingston, Jamaica, but four days later an advertisement for the sale of *Sukey and Polly*'s slaves listed the origin of the slaves as Angola.[31] Slave labor was just as much in demand on sugar plantations in the Caribbean and South America as in South Carolina, if not more so; therefore it is doubtful large quantities of slaves would have been removed from other New World plantations to be sold in Charleston.[32] Of the 9,600 documented arrivals from the Caribbean, other than St. Dominique slaves, the overwhelming majority came from Jamaica in lots from 1 to 30 people. An additional 363 slaves arrived from South America, Nova Scotia, and London, and another 300 were advertised or reported as "refuse Negroes" or simply "Negroes."[33]

Although no state laws in North Carolina banned or laid prohibitive import duties on new shipments, historians have not documented any foreign slave arrivals there in 1783 or 1784. In 1785 only 8 slaves arrived from Antigua and Jamaica, but in the next two years imports increased. In 1786 65 slaves arrived from Caribbean ports and 80 from Africa in the brig *Camden*. Despite the passage in 1786 of an act by the General Assembly imposing duties ranging from a minimum of five to a maximum of ten pounds on imported slaves, merchants and traders continued to import slaves. In 1787 the brig *Camden* delivered another 70 Africans to Edenton and the *Jennett* docked with 81 at Roanoke.[34] In 1788 and 1789, no known direct shipments of Africans arrived, but 124 were imported from the West Indies. In 1790 the General Assembly lifted all duties on slave imports, but four years later, in response to the Haitian Revolution, it prohibited further imports. Historians have documented from 1785 to 1790 the arrival of a total of 501 slaves, 231 directly from Africa and 270 from Caribbean ports.[35] Although other slave voyages to North Carolina have not been documented, the region remained a relatively minor importer in the colonial and post-Revolution eras.

The foreign slave trade to South Carolina was much more protracted and extensive. As soon as the war ended in 1783, merchants and planters resumed importing foreign slaves. The trade was brisk until the state legislature temporarily prohibited imports for two years in the spring of 1787. Over the next sixteen years, the legislature maintained the ban and enacted a number of laws that had a direct bearing on the origin of slaves imported into the state. A year after the slave revolt in St. Dominique erupted in 1791, the legislature prohibited slave imports from the West Indies. Soon after Gabriel's rebellion in Virginia in 1800, the assembly also prohibited the domestic slave trade and restricted the free sale of slaves by migrants. When the legislature lifted the prohibition on the slave trade in 1804, it restricted imports to Africans and "no Negro over fifteen years or older . . . from the United States except under a certificate of good character."[36]

Not surprisingly, the overwhelming majority of foreign slaves imported into South Carolina between 1783 and 1810 were Africans. During the period at least 69,400 slaves arrived in the state. The origins of more than 54,000 of the slaves — 53,300 from Africa and 1,300 from the Caribbean and South America — are documented. As previously mentioned, most of the arrivals from Caribbean Islands and South America, more than 95 percent, were in large shipments of 50 or more slaves, which suggests they were Africans rather than seasoned slaves. The late colonial trend of declining seasoned slave imports from the British West Indies continued in the post–Revolutionary War era until the traffic finally dried up completely in the late 1780s. Thus, when the legal trade reopened in 1804, it consisted of only one trade, the direct trade between Africa and Charleston, rather than two, as it had during the colonial era.

The African trade to South Carolina is best understood when analyzed by decade. During the 1780s, the origin of 28 percent of the slaves was listed as Africa, 11 percent Senegambia, 9 percent Sierra Leone, 4 percent Windward Coast, 28 percent Gold Coast, 0 percent Bight of Benin, 3 percent Bight of Biafra, 16 percent West-Central Africa, and 0 percent Mozambique. Large vessels — brigs, frigates, and ships — delivered substantial quantities of slaves in large lots ranging from 200 to 600, but shipments averaged only 90 slaves per vessel. The large shipments came mainly from the Gold Coast and Angola, and smaller from Gambia and the Windward Coast. The main suppliers of slaves to South

Carolina in the 1780s, English slavers, were especially active in three of these regions, the Windward and Gold Coasts and Angola.[37]

The predominance of slaves from Gambia, the Gold Coast, and Angola closely resembles the colonial pattern of African shipments. This should come as no surprise since many colonial planters survived the war and resumed rice cultivation. To replace slaves lost in the war and provide the labor to repair, renovate, and cultivate rice plantations, they bought slaves from the same regions as they had in the past. Merchants attempted to attract planters to their sales by pointing out that slaves from certain regions were familiar with rice cultivation. A notice appeared in the *South Carolina Gazette* in 1785 stating that the 152 slaves from Gambia "are well acquainted with the cultivation of rice and are naturally industrious."[38] Another appeared in July of the same year that advertised "A Choice Cargo of Windward and Gold Coast Negroes, Who have been accustomed to the planting of rice."[39]

Aware that South Carolina planters and farmers raised other crops besides rice, merchants extolled other agricultural skills that Senegambian and Gold Coast slaves supposedly possessed. Notices appeared for Senegambian slaves, claiming that "they are allowed by every Gentlemen that has seen them, to be the finest Slaves that have been imported these 15 years; these Slaves are well acquainted with the cultivation of Indigo, Rice, and Tobacco."[40] A year later another appeared advertising Windward and Gold Coast slaves "accustomed to the planting of both rice and corn."[41] The most sought after of these captives, prime Gambian and Gold Coast slaves, brought the highest prices. In a 1785 letter to the New England owners of the *Gambia*, Charleston merchant Nathaniel Russell boasted that the sale of the vessel's cargo of one hundred Gold Coast slaves, "with proceeds being 6000, are the greatest sales ever made in this State or perhaps anywhere else."[42]

Slavers, especially from England, were able to supply South Carolinians with all the slaves they could buy in the 1780s. Wars in Africa and North America had played havoc with the Atlantic slave trade during the 1770s.[43] When slave shipments to South Carolina resumed in 1783 after a hiatus of nearly a decade, African slaves were available from most of the coastal regions of Africa in large quantities. Africans poured into Charleston, nearly nine thousand in 1784 and 1785, and planters and farmers with the financial resources were able to purchase what they believed they needed.[44]

Although merchants and traders welcomed French and Dutch slavers, the English continued to dominate the trade to South Carolina. A number of merchants who had received and sold cargoes of Africans during the colonial era resumed the practice in the 1780s. David Mitchell, David Oliphant, William Sommersall, Daniel Smith, and Smiths and Co. were just a few of the many who sold slaves both before and after the war. Even Henry Laurens, who claimed he was retired, renewed his ties with English houses and advised them on the South

Carolina slave market.[45] Comfortable with these merchants, the owners of English slavers continued to assign cargoes of slaves to these same firms after the Revolution. Not all South Carolina planters and farmers were happy about buying from English slavers and their agents, but they had few options. Many planters had not paid off colonial debts to these same merchants. Others could not refuse the liberal credit arrangements offered by English traders. Not surprisingly, it was business as usual. Well aware of South Carolina traders' and planters' bias toward Africans, English slavers traded for slaves in regions that slave buyers preferred so that captives would sell quickly and at high prices.[46]

In the 1790s the arrival of only 1,006 slaves in South Carolina has been documented. Many more were imported, but, because the importation of foreign slaves was illegal, most arrivals were not reported. Of the documented African arrivals, 66 percent were listed as arriving from Africa, 17 percent from the Gold Coast, and 17 percent from Sierra Leone. Although few voyages have been documented, extant records indicate that arrivals were large. The *Georgia Gazette* reported that in the fall of 1792 the *Swallow* delivered 300 Gold Coast and West African slaves to Charleston. In the same year one other large vessel, the brig *Favorite*, also arrived in South Carolina with slaves.[47]

In the first decade of the 1800s, a definite shift away from the colonial and late 1700s pattern in African shipments occurred. From 1800 to 1810, 20 percent of arrivals were listed as arriving from Africa, 8 percent from Senegambia, 15 percent from Sierra Leone, 5 percent from the Windward Coast, 13 percent from the Gold Coast, 1 percent from the Bight of Benin, 4 percent from the Bight of Biafra, 35 percent from West-Central Africa, and 1 percent from Mozambique. The percentage of slaves imported from Gambia, the Windward Coast, and the Bight of Benin declined, and the percentage from the Gold Coast, Sierra Leone, the Bight of Biafra, Angola, and Mozambique increased.

The decline in the percentage of Senegambian exports to South Carolina suggests that traders and merchants might have abandoned Laurens's hierarchy of preferences, but in actual numbers, shipments increased from the regions planters preferred most, Senegambia and the Gold Coast. Gold Coast exports increased from 3,100 in the 1780s to 5,800 between 1800 and 1810. A fourth, 2,300, were imported in 1807. In the 1780s South Carolina traders and planters imported 1,300 Gambians. In the first decade of the 1800s, the number of Senegambian imports tripled to 4,500 slaves. More than 40 percent, 1,900, arrived in 1807, the last year imports were legal. But neither of the regions' exports increased nearly as much as those from West-Central Africa. In the 1780s imports from the Congo and Angola totaled 1,900; in the first decade of the 1800s, they jumped more than tenfold to 21,600.

Despite increased West African, Angolan, and Congolese imports, merchants and planters had not abandoned their predilection for Gambian, Windward Coast, and Gold Coast slaves. In 1807 they took delivery of ten "to order" shipments from the African regions. which included three cargoes of Gold Coast slaves. Planters with the financial means contracted with merchants for all or parts of a cargo. This allowed them to specify the quantity, gender, age, and origin of slaves. Of the ten presold cargoes that arrived in 1807, four arrived from Sierra Leone, three from the Gold Coast, two from Gambia, and one from Angola.[48] The three regions at the top of Laurens's hierarchy of preferences, Gambia, the Windward Coast, and the Gold Coast, continued to draw the most buyers. Like Georgians, South Carolinians considered Sierra Leone part of the Windward Coast. According to Laurens, Windward Coast slaves ranked just below Gambian and Gold Coast slaves and above Angolans.[49]

Merchant and planter bias was not the only factor that determined where traders took slaves on the coast of Africa. Gambia was never a major slave market, as exports averaged less than 1,000 persons per year throughout the eighteenth and early nineteenth centuries. North Americans received the lion's share of Gambian exports because slavers knew that South Carolina and Georgia planters would pay inflated prices for slaves from that region. Perhaps because the number of Gambian slaves available for export was so limited, most of the other Caribbean and South American buyers did not bother to compete for shipments from the region.[50] Between 1780 and 1807, Gold Coast exports were also limited. Gold Coast exports averaged more than 5,000 slaves per year during the period, but shipments began to decline just as North American imports were increasing. In 1782 exports fell to 2,300, in 1793, 1,500, and in 1803, 1,700. As supplies dwindled, competition from other slave markets in the West Indies increased prices. Like South Carolinians, Jamaicans viewed Gold Coast slaves favorably. Between 1751 and 1790 they took about 80 percent of the 111,500 persons that British slavers carried away from the Gold Coast. High prices in Jamaica for Gold Coast slaves meant reduced availability and higher prices in South Carolina for exports from the region.[51]

The competition forced British slave captains such as John Adams to abandon the Gold Coast "to seek a better and cheaper market," which he found on the coast of Angola.[52] Traders found purchasing slaves in Angola and the Congo much more to their liking, especially in the late eighteenth century and early 1800s. They took advantage of what Curtin described as the "great Angolan slave rush" after 1800 and delivered 20,000 West-Central slaves to South Carolina alone. Restricted supplies in other regions and the extension of feeder routes into the West-Central interior accounted for the increase in shipments from Angola and the Congo.[53]

Traders also frequented the other major exporting regions, Sierra Leone and the Windward Coast, more often in the early 1800s. As a result exports from the regions increased steadily from 1,000 slaves in the 1780s to 9,700 captives in the first decade of the 1800s. U.S. slavers were responsible for most of the increase. Well aware that slave buyers were willing to pay higher prices for Windward

Coast slaves than for Angolan, Bight of Benin, and Bight of Biafra slaves, they flocked to the region. Sierra Leone was not the most expeditious region from which to acquire slaves, but it was the closest African region to Charleston by sail, and experienced captains of smaller ships could usually fill their holds with slaves by stopping at a number of trading sites there.[54]

For captains and supercargoes of larger ships, mainly British and French, Sierra Leone was not nearly as convenient. Slaves were not available there in the large quantities they required. For faster loading and better prices, they sailed south and east to the Bight of Benin, the Bight of Biafra, the Gold Coast, or West-Central Africa, but voyages to those regions took much more time. To return to Charleston from the Gold Coast, the Bight of Benin, and the Bight of Biafra, vessels were forced to sail down to the equator, away from prevailing westerly winds and currents that hugged the coast. From the equator ships could gain the southeast trades and set course for South Carolina. Winds along the equator were not dependable, however, and ships could be becalmed for weeks at a time. It was not uncommon for ships to take ten weeks to complete the middle passage when departing from under the bulge of Africa.[55] Voyages from Angola were not as time consuming as those from the Gold Coast and the Bight of Biafra, but they took two to three weeks longer than the middle passage from Sierra Leone.[56] Slave traders allowed a year or more for a round-trip to these regions, while voyages to Sierra Leone could be completed in nine months or less.[57] As the number of U.S. slave ships expanded from ten or less in the early 1780s to more than one hundred in the early 1800s, exports to North America from Sierra Leone rose accordingly.

If slaves were not available on the Windward and Gold Coasts, U.S. slavers sailed to West-Central Africa, rather than the Bight of Benin and the Bight of Biafra. Despite the fact that British and French slavers took more than four hundred thousand slaves from the two regions between 1780 and 1807, U.S. vessels rarely traded in either place because of the risks involved. Malaria and yellow fever were just two of the diseases that often killed crew and officers. Dangerous currents and sandbars presented further hazards. Revolts also occurred more frequently in these regions. The Bight of Benin was so perilous that a sailor penned the following popular rhyme: "Beware and take care of the Bight of Benin / Few come out, though many go in."[58] Increased chance of disease and the prospect of revolts required larger crews and more armaments. For American slavers this represented a barrier to trade that they were not willing, or could not afford, to overcome. Operating smaller vessels in general, with little armament and small crews, they traded in regions that they considered to be safer—mainly to the west and north. The extended return trip was another discouraging factor. More days at sea meant greater expenses for supplies and provisions. A longer middle passage also was hazardous to the health of both slaves and crew, and it gave slaves more opportunity to revolt. Once on dry land, planter prejudice against Bight of

Benin and Bight of Biafra slaves cut into profits even more. Slaves from the region usually sold for lower prices and took longer to sell. An extended selling period added more expense for food, clothing, housing, and medical care for slaves. While being held for sale, slaves often contracted disease and died, or they escaped—frequently in surprising numbers.

South Carolinians were willing to overlook their prejudices against Africans from regions such as the Bight of Benin, the Bight of Biafra, and West-Central Africa only when the slaves from regions that they preferred were not available or proved too costly. They found themselves in this position twice during the post–Revolutionary War era. The first occurred between 1783 and 1785. Anxious to replace slaves lost in the war, planters paid extremely high prices, not only for Gambian and Gold Coast slaves, but also for slaves at the bottom of Laurens's hierarchy, those from the Bight of Biafra. In 1784, the first full year of shipments to Charleston after the war ended, a prime cargo of "Ebo males" brought an average of seventy pounds per head.[59] A year later, prices had dropped to between twenty and thirty pounds.[60]

The emergence of cotton as a major southern staple and the approach of a possible prohibition against further slave imports combined to produce a second slave boom in the early 1800s. The pressure for labor to clear land for cotton and cultivate the staple increased demand for Africans in the 1790s and the first decade of the 1800s. Although white southerners did not abandon their preferences for Gold Coast and Gambian slaves, they were more willing to buy Bight of Benin, Bight of Biafra, Mozambique, and Angolan slaves than they had been in the past. Early in the nineteenth century, a Carolina innkeeper advised slave Charles Ball's master that "cotton had not been higher for many years, and as a great many persons, especially young men, were moving off to purchase new land in Georgia, prime hands were in high demand, for the purpose of clearing the land in the new country—that boys and girls, under twenty, would bring almost any price."[61] Ball's master took the innkeeper's advice and sold Ball in Columbia, South Carolina. As he traveled across South Carolina to his new master's low-country plantation, Ball encountered many Africans and noted that "they continued to arrive for several years afterward."[62] Once planters knew that the federal government would halt the trade in 1808, the slave boom heated up even more as traders and planters eagerly snapped up shipments of so-called Bites and Ibos, which they had avoided in the past.

Because the volume of imports to South Carolina in the first decade of the 1800s made up such a large percentage of the overall shipments from 1783 to 1810, the pattern of origins for the last decade closely resembles that of the overall post–Revolutionary War period. From 1783 to 1810, Africa was listed as the origin of 22 percent of the foreign slaves landed, Senegambia, 9 percent, Sierra Leone, 14 percent, the Windward Coast, 5 percent, the Gold Coast, 13 percent, the Bight of Benin, 1 percent, the Bight of Biafra, 4 percent, West-Central Africa,

32 percent, and Southeast Africa, 0 percent. Therefore the conclusions drawn for the first decade of the 1800s for the South Carolina trade also apply to the overall post–Revolutionary War trade. Demand outstripped supplies of the slaves that slave buyers preferred, and as a result Gambian and Bight of Benin imports decreased as a percentage of total imports, Gold Coast imports maintained the same level, and Sierra Leone, Bight of Benin, Mozambique, Bight of Biafra, and Angolan imports increased. The percentage of exports from the coast regions of Senegambia and Angola changed more than the others. Compared to the colonial era, the percentage of post–Revolutionary War Senegambian exports declined almost one-third, while West-Central exports doubled.

The provenance of slave shipments to Georgia between 1783 and 1810 differed significantly from its colonial trade and South Carolina's post–Revolutionary War trade. Soon after the war ended, Georgia merchants and planters resumed importing slaves, but at a much slower pace than the colonial rate. Planters, as mentioned earlier, needed slaves to replace those lost in the war and to repair and renovate their plantations, but they lacked capital and credit. As a result, during the 1780s slaves arrived in small lots from South Carolina and the West Indies. Merchants and planters promoted direct trade with Africa, but most slavers delivered their cargoes to South Carolina or the West Indies.[63] In the 1790s the Georgia economy began to recover, and direct shipments began arriving from Africa more regularly, with volume increasing from 2,200 in the 1780s to 10,400 in the 1790s. After the state legislature prohibited further imports in 1798, slavers smuggled large numbers of slaves into the state. The arrival of more than 3,600 slaves between 1798 and 1810 has been documented.[64]

From 1783 to 1810 Africa was listed as the origin of 34 percent of slaves disembarked in Georgia, Senegambia, 6 percent, Sierra Leone, 27 percent, the Windward Coast, 4 percent, the Gold Coast, 14 percent, the Bight of Benin, 0 percent, the Bight of Biafra, 0 percent, West-Central Africa, 14 percent, and Mozambique, 0 percent. Unlike in the trade to South Carolina, Angolan slaves made up only a small percentage of shipments to Georgia, and Sierra Leone slaves were the predominate imports. When the origins of the colonial shipments are compared to the post–Revolutionary War imports, the percentage of Gambian slaves imported declined by more than three-fourths, and the combined imports from the Gold Coast and Sierra Leone regions increased by more than 50 percent.

The large numbers of slaves imported from Sierra Leone, the Gold Coast, and West-Central Africa reflect the preferences of local planters and farmers. As they had in the late colonial period, they valued slaves from the Windward and Gold Coasts above all others.[65] A colonial slave merchant, Joseph Clay, who survived the war and resumed importing slaves, maintained that in the region "Windward Coast slaves will always obtain a preference."[66] To Georgians, the Windward Coast covered much of the West African coast. As previously mentioned, before the war, Joseph Clay defined the region as stretching from Senegal to the Gold

Coast. Advertisements appearing in Georgia newspapers confirm that after the war traders and slave buyers continued to think the Windward Coast included the conventional regions of the Gold Coast, the Windward Coast, Sierra Leone, and Gambia. In one-inch-high bold type, for instance, an advertisement announced the sale of slaves "Just Arrived from Cape Mount, on the Windward Coast Negroes." Another proclaimed, "Just Arrived from Gorée on the Windward Coast of Africa."[67] Cape Mount is located in conventional Sierra Leone and Gorée in Senegambia. It appears that merchants were aware of the fact that Sierra Leone was a vague term and used more distinctive terms, such as Cape Mount and Gorée, to identify the origin of slaves.

Despite the confusion surrounding the trading centers on the coast of Africa, Sierra Leone exports to Georgia increased in the 1790s. A number of factors contributed to the rise in trade. First, more than 81 percent of documented slave imports arrived in Georgia during the 1790s, mainly between 1794 and 1798. During that period African slaves were available in much greater numbers than in the preceding and following decades. In the 1780s and the first decade of the 1800s, South Carolina and West Indies slave buyers dominated the slave trade in the Northern Hemisphere, but during most of the 1790s they imported fewer slaves, which made more Africans available for export to regions such as Georgia. Second, the largest participants in the transatlantic slave trade, England and France, were at war from 1793 to 1810. This allowed American slavers to gain a much larger share of the slave trade to Cuba, South America, and Georgia. Between 1793 and 1796 Rhode Island slavers dominated the trade to Georgia. One shipper, Cyprian Sterry of Providence, delivered at least thirteen cargoes totaling more than 1,200 people to Savannah.[68] Like other New England slavers who sold cargoes in Savannah, Sterry mainly traded New England rum for slaves, mainly along the Windward Coast in Sierra Leone and the Gold Coast. Third, in the mid-1790s, cotton farmers and planters began realizing sizeable profits on sales of the staple. The cotton boom that ensued not only boosted the economy in Georgia, it also provided the capital necessary to finance the purchase of thousands of slaves.[69]

Georgia buyers imported a significant number of slaves from the West Indies. Nearly 1,900 (or 12 percent) of the 16,200 foreign slaves were brought from the Caribbean. Of these slaves 1,050 arrived in large lots of 50 or more, which suggests that they were transshipments of recently arrived Africans rather than seasoned slaves. But there may have been exceptions to this rule. Georgia planters and merchants preferred Africans, but in some cases they would take seasoned slaves. In 1786 Joseph Clay wrote to a West Indies slave dealer inquiring about the possibility of purchasing 100 seasoned slaves in families "who formerly worked in this state or South Carolina or East Florida (and consequently used to our climate and manner of living)."[70] To work his own rice plantations and to cut timber, Clay wanted "a proportion of such tradesmen, as are among of plantation slaves" and specific proportions of men, women, boys, and girls. These included twelve men and eight women between the ages of thirty and forty; twelve men and eight women between the ages of twenty and thirty; twelve men and eight women between the ages of fourteen and twenty; twenty girls or boys, "none to be under ten;" and twenty girls or boys, "none to be under three."[71] Clay listed the prices he was willing to pay for the slaves by age and sex, and then laid out his remaining conditions. He wrote:

> We have rated them as above on a supposition that negroes in families most probably, consist of nearly, the above proportion of young ones, if there should be more grown people, fewer boys and girls, it will be no objection, but should there be any children under three years of age, we should expect them to be throwed in with out any charge, and we mean all the grown people to be healthy, taskable hands, and free from any known disease! that can or may render them unable to do their duty, if there should be one or two such negroes as last mentioned in a Gang, that probably, it might from family connections or any other reason, be a hardship to separate from the others, we will receive them provided a proper abatement is made in the price.[72]

Clay was attempting to maintain his plantation with not only a skilled workforce but a community of slaves. He wanted slaves to cultivate rice and cut timber and tradesmen to build and maintain the equipment and tools required to operate his plantations. He could have acquired one hundred slaves individually or in small lots, but many may not have been accustomed to the lowcountry climate or rice cultivation. Moreover most would have been recently arrived from Africa or the Chesapeake and consequently subject to disease because of a lack of immunity to lowcountry diseases. In both cases they most likely would have been torn away from their families and therefore prone to depression and likely to run away. It is not known if Clay was able to buy the slaves he sought.

West Indies shipments averaged ten slaves per arrival. The small lots were probably transshipments of Africans, not seasoned slaves. In response to the slave revolt in St. Dominique, the Georgia legislature prohibited further imports of West Indian slaves in 1793. The trade between Georgia and the islands remained fairly active, however, until the state legislature banned all foreign slave imports in 1798.[73] Between 1795 and 1797 eight arrivals from the West Indies have been documented. No doubt these arrivals represented only a fraction of the trade between Georgia and the West Indies.

After Georgia prohibited further imports of foreign slaves in October of 1798, its neighbor to the south, Florida, became a much more important slave-trading region. When Spain regained control of its former colonies, East and West Florida, from England after the War for American Independence, many British residents took their slaves with them to the British West Indies and Canada, while others sent their slaves to be sold in the United States.[74] Between 1783 and 1787 they sent about 1,500 slaves to Georgia, some 1,300 to South Carolina, and around 300 to North Carolina.

By the end of the 1780s, the direction of trade in slaves had been reversed. Spaniards and Anglo-Americans were immigrating to Florida and importing slaves. They settled mainly along the northeast coast around St. Augustine, on St. Mary's Island near the Georgia border, and close by Mobile on the Gulf Coast. They imported more than 7,000 slaves between 1783 and 1810. Many Florida planters and farmers brought slaves into Florida for their own use, but as many as two-thirds may have been imported for resale in the United States. This was particularly true between 1798 and 1804 and after 1808, when foreign slave imports were prohibited in the United States. Florida shared a long unguarded border with the United States, making it relatively easy for smugglers to transport slaves surreptitiously into Georgia, Alabama, and Mississippi.[75]

Of the 7,000 slaves that were probably imported into Florida, only 2,587 can be documented as such. Extant Spanish records are lean, and few illuminate the slave trade to Florida or Louisiana. To make matters worse, records of slave voyages to Florida list the regional origins of only 23 percent of slaves brought from Africa. Although there is not enough data available to draw conclusions about origin, the records do shine a little light on the trade. Almost all the slaves imported were Africans, and most arrived directly from Africa. Of these, 77 percent of the slaves were simply reported as arriving from Africa, 5 percent from Senegambia, 16 percent from Sierra Leone, and 2 percent from Mozambique. More than 90 percent arrived in the first decade of the 1800s in shipments that averaged 103 slaves per arrival. The northeast coast of Florida was the main import zone for East Florida. The ports of disembarkation were not reported, but because Zephaniah Kingsley and Panton, Leslie, and Co. were listed as consignees of the shipments (Kingsley's plantations and trading business were located on the St. Johns River above St. Augustine and Panton, Leslie, and Co. in St. Augustine), it appears that most slaves arrived between St. Augustine and the Georgia border.[76]

Records of Mississippi imports are also scarce. While Mississippi was a Spanish possession from 1783–1798, only a few arrivals of slave shipments are documented. After Mississippi became a United States possession in 1798, only three arrivals are known. Of these all were transshipments from Charleston except one, which came directly from Africa. The African origin of this voyage was not recorded. Obviously more slaves were imported than extant records indicate. According to Spanish censuses Africans began arriving in large numbers as early as 1787. Most were transshipped from Charleston or New Orleans, but some were shipped directly from Africa. The slave ships either sailed up or were pulled up the Mississippi River to Natchez.[77]

Natchez planters preferred "Guiney Negroes" from under the West Africa bulge to slaves from other regions. They believed Windward and Gold Coast slaves were more capable of sustained labor than those from other African regions. They admired Gambian slaves for their intelligence, but they believed that they could not stand up to hard work. Considered "savage and intractable," Ibos from the Bight of Benin were the least in demand.[78] No doubt, the South Carolina and Georgia farmers and planters, who immigrated to Mississippi in large numbers, brought their preferences and biases for Africans with them.[79]

Between 1783 and 1810, Spanish, French, and U.S. flags flew over Louisiana. Spain controlled Louisiana for most of the period, 1783 to 1800, and the French for only a few years, 1800 to 1803, before they sold Louisiana to the United States in 1803. The slave trade was open until 1795, closed from 1795 and 1800, open to Spanish and British ships from late 1800 to 1803, and closed to direct trade after the passage of the Louisiana Ordinance in 1804 by the United States. After 1805 Louisiana traders and planters were restricted to transshipments through Charleston. However, many Louisianians ignored the prohibition against direct imports, as they had when Spain had imposed bans, and smuggled Africans directly into the region.[80]

The illegal shipments and dearth of extant Spanish records make identifying the provenance of slave imports difficult. During this period 16,900 slaves can be documented as arriving. Of these the majority were listed as Africans arriving directly from Africa or Africans transshipped from the West Indies. The other people were mainly from Senegambia, the Gold Coast, Benin, and West-Central Africa. Despite the fact that the origins of most African shipments are undocumented, it is clear that after the Louisiana Ordinance, the Charleston market heavily influenced the provenance of imports to the territory. Although slave ships often circumvented the law, a federal statute forbade imports from "without the limits of the United States."[81] Hence more than 90 percent of documented shipments entered the United States at Charleston, since South Carolina was the only state that allowed foreign imports from 1804 to 1808. Accordingly the shipments from the Bight of Benin and the Bight of Biafra that dominated the colonial Louisiana trade virtually disappeared during the early 1800s. They were replaced by exports from African regions that were popular in the Charleston market: Senegambia, the Gold Coast, and West-Central Africa.

The Caribbean trade was altogether a different matter. Unlike any of the other states or colonies in the post–Revolutionary War era, Louisiana imported large numbers of slaves from the Caribbean Islands. Of the 16,900 slaves documented as arriving in New Orleans, 3,225 were brought from St. Dominique via Cuba in 1809, and 900 from Jamaica, Cuba, and the West Indies between 1803 and 1808. Of the 900 slaves, 580 arrived in groups of 50 or more, which suggests they were newly arrived Africans transshipped from the West Indies. The remaining 320 arrived in small lots of 1 to 20 slaves spread out over the four years of trade. The 3,225 St. Dominique slaves arrived en masse in 1809. No longer welcome in Cuba, the Haitian expatriate slave holders illegally brought their slaves with them to New Orleans. Once on American soil, they convinced the U.S. government their slaves represented no threat, and they were allowed to keep them. Most of the slaves had been born on St. Dominique, and many were mulattoes.[82] The large numbers of Angolan and Haitian imports must have had a significant cultural, social, and economic impact on Louisiana: after they arrived in 1808 the slave population was made up of roughly one-fifth newly arrived Africans and Haitians.[83]

When all documented voyages are combined, a different pattern takes shape. During the first decade of post–Revolutionary War trade, the 1780s, North American traders and merchants exhibited the same preference for Senegambian and Gold Coast slaves that they had during the colonial period. Of the African captives of identifiable origin, slaves from Gambia (19 percent) and the Gold Coast (37 percent) made up 56 percent of total imports. When Gambian and Gold Coast slaves were not available, colonial slave holders would buy those from Sierra Leone (11 percent) and the Windward Coast (6 percent), which together made up 17 percent. Angolans, whom colonists placed near the bottom of their hierarchy, made up 23 percent. The least desired, Bight of Biafra slaves, made up only 4 percent.

As previously mentioned, shipments in the 1790s have not been well documented. The lack of data skews the pattern somewhat. For instance, only 330 captives from West-Central Africa have been documented, and Sierra Leone slaves made up nearly 53 percent of the African captives of identifiable origin.

The busiest decade, the first decade of the 1800s, evidences a continuation of many of the trends established in the previous twenty years. Of the African slaves of identifiable origin, Senegambian captives made up 10 percent of total imports, Sierra Leone, 19 percent, Windward Coast, 6 percent, Gold Coast, 17 percent, Bight of Benin, 1 percent, Bight of Biafra, 4 percent, Angolan, 46 percent, and Mozambique, 1 percent. Imports of Senegambian slaves as a percentage of total imports continued to decline. Sierra Leone slaves made up a much larger percentage than in the 1780s, and the Windward Coast remained on the same level as the 1780s and below the colonial level. The Gold Coast increased in number but as a percentage of total shipments declined significantly. Although one large shipment of 329 arrived in Charleston in 1804 from the Bight of Benin, slaves from the region continued to make up an insignificant percentage of total imports. However, the number of slaves from the other least-desired region, the Bight of Biafra, rose. As the deadline approached, traders and planters were much more willing to buy slaves from any region, even Biafra. The region that supplied the greatest number of slaves was West-Central Africa. Most of the West-Central exports embarked from the Congo. Another 600 arrived from Southeast Africa or Mozambique, and increasing numbers of U.S. slavers delivered large quantities of Sierra Leone, Windward Coast, and Gold Coast slaves.

When compared to pre–Revolutionary War arrival patterns, the imports into the different states and colonies during the postwar era retained their unique characteristics in the 1780s. North Carolina received mainly transshipments of small lots of slaves from Charleston and the West Indies. South Carolina picked up where it had left off before the war and imported mainly Senegambian, Gold Coast, and Angolan slaves on English ships. Georgia received mainly transshipments of Africans from Charleston and the West Indies. Until late in the 1780s Florida and Mississippi received few slaves, while Louisiana's imports continued to arrive mainly from Senegambia, the Bight of Benin, and Angola.

During the 1790s imports began to change. Exports from Sierra Leone and the Windward Coast increased, and exports from Senegambia declined. Wars in Europe reduced British, French, and Portugese participation in the trade, which increased the availability of slaves in Africa. Initially this enabled a growing fleet of U.S. slavers to cater to the preferences of Georgia merchants and planters. However, as cotton production expanded in the 1790s and 1800s and demand for slaves increased, planters and farmers bought Whydahs, Ibos, Bites, and Calabars, whom they had avoided in the past. Their attitudes toward African ethnic groups had not changed, but demand for slaves from the regions South Carolina planters and merchants preferred (Senegambia, Sierra Leone, Windward Coast, and Gold Coast) outstripped supplies.

When the combined postwar origins are compared to the colonial trade, the post–Revolutionary War imports from Senegambia, the Windward Coast, and the Bight of Benin declined, while Sierra Leone, Gold Coast, Bight of Biafra and West-Central shipments increased. Mozambique exports rose slightly. Increases in imports from the region merchants and planters referred to as the Windward Coast and West-Central Africa replaced the decline in the percentage of Senegambian shipments.

Despite the decline in Senegambian imports as a percentage of the overall trade, the ethnic makeup of the African population in North America remained unique within the larger transatlantic slave trade. Compared to those in Jamaica, North American Africans were much more likely to have been exported from the West African regions stretching from the Gold Coast around to Senegambia. Slaves from these regions—Senegambia, Sierra Leone, the Windward Coast, and the Gold Coast—comprised more than one-half of all imports. In Jamaica they made up less than 27 percent. Moreover Africans from Angola and the Congo were much more prevalent in North America. People from the Bight of Benin and the Bight of Biafra, who constituted more than 50 percent of Jamaica imports, were rarely transported to North America after the War for American Independence.[84]

The absence of Bight of Benin and Bight of Biafra postwar imports is significant. The African population of North America was formed by two different streams of trade rather than three, as most scholars have argued. The northern stream comprised mainly Sudanese people from Senegambia, Sierra Leone, the

TABLE 10 — REGIONAL ORIGIN OF AFRICAN SLAVES, 1783–1810

African Coastal Region of Origin	*North American Region of Disembarkation*						
	N. Carolina	*S. Carolina*	*Georgia*	*Florida*	*Mississippi*	*Louisiana*	*Total*
Senegambia	0%	11%	9%	21%	0%	43%	11%
Sierra Leone	0%	18%	42%	73%	0%	11%	21%
Windward Coast	0%	6%	6%	0%	0%	0%	6%
Gold Coast	0%	17%	21%	0%	0%	9%	17%
Bight of Benin	0%	1%	0%	0%	0%	0%	1%
Bight of Biafra	0%	5%	0%	0%	0%	0%	4%
West-Central	0%	41%	22%	0%	0%	0%	38%
Southeast	0%	1%	0%	7%	0%	37%	1%
Total	**0%**	**100%**	**100%**	**101%**	**0%**	**100%**	**99%**
Number of whom origins known	0	53,331	9,407	481	0	753	65,574
Total number of imported Africans	231	68,059	14,414	2,124	150	5,427	96,183

Source: Appendix A.

Windward Coast, and the Gold Coast. The southern stream was made up of Bantu people from the Congo and Angola. The two groups of people speak different languages, and although physical types vary widely within both groups, some distinctions can be made in appearances.[85] Unlike the colonial black populations of Louisiana, the post–Revolutionary War African population contained few people from the Bight of Biafra, who shared cultural elements with both the Bantu and Sudanese people.

Curtin and Morgan are among the few historians who have commented on the regional origin of slaves imported from Africa into North America. Unfortunately Curtin's estimate is for all Africans imported into North America during the colonial and postwar eras. He maintains that imports comprised three streams. A northern stream from Senegambia around to the Gold Coast provided 46 percent of imports, a central stream from the Bight of Benin and the Bight of Biafra contributed 28 percent, and a southern stream from Angola and the Congo sent 25 percent. Combined with colonial studies, new research reveals that fewer slaves arrived from the Bight of Benin and the Bight of Biafra, and more from the northern and southern regions.[86] Morgan limited his research to South Carolina and based his estimate on newspaper reports, customs records, and Donnan's prior research. He concluded that Gold Coast imports dominated the trade in the 1780s and Angolans in the first decade of the 1800s. In both cases this study confirms Morgan's findings, but it also suggests that, for the 1780s and the first decade of the 1800s, Morgan and Curtin underestimated the number of Sierra Leone imports.[87] Like post–Revolutionary War traders and merchants, they counted most of the imports from Sierra Leone as Windward Coast shipments.

A number of factors combined between 1783 and 1810 to shape the slave trade to North America. Geography and economic, political, and social forces, not only in North America, but in Europe and Africa as well, continued to bear on the trade. They determined where slaves were obtained, in what quantities, for how much, who delivered them, where they were imported, who sold them, and who bought them. Although the influence of these factors on the transatlantic slave trade waned in the first decade of the 1800s, South Carolina and Georgia planters and merchants maintained their bias toward African ethnic groups until the trade ended in 1807.

Chapter 4

NORTH AMERICAN SLAVE MERCHANTS

"The Negro business is a great object with us . . . it is to the Trade of this Country, as the Soul to the body."

> Joseph Clay, February 16, 1784, quoted in Elizabeth Donnan, ed.,
> *Documents Illustrative of the History of the Slave Trade to America*

The transatlantic slave trade was an elaborate enterprise. A successful slaving venture required large amounts of capital, special equipment, exceptional trade goods, experienced officers, and knowledge of African and New World markets. Before slave ships sailed, investors advanced substantial sums for specially equipped ships, African trade goods, salaries for officers and crew, insurance, supplies, and provisions. Once on the African coast, captains were faced with a labyrinth of choices. At a hundred or more sales ports, African traders offered male and female captives of varying ages, cultures, ethnicities, agricultural and artisanal skills, physical attributes, religious and political beliefs, and social standing. The preferences of African traders for manufactured goods from Europe, the East Indies, and North America were just as varied. Some preferred fine cloth, others refined iron bars, while still others demanded rum. Across the Atlantic, in the New World, any number of factors affected the outcome of a sale: politics; the season; status of the local crop; the ethnicity; age, gender, and health of the cargo; local currency; and credit conditions. A highly skilled group of European, African, and American entrepreneurs planned, coordinated, oversaw, and carried out the complex and lucrative business.

I.

The transatlantic slave trade to British colonial North America had a long and epochal life. Between 1619 and 1775 British, Dutch, French, and Spanish ships transported between 250,000 and 300,000 African captives and 25,000 seasoned slaves from the West Indies to North America. English slave merchants were the most active participants, transporting nearly 80 percent of the slaves, while French and North American ships brought over the remaining 20 percent.

Specifically New Englanders sponsored most of the American slave ventures. They entered the trade late, but, by the middle of the eighteenth century, the slave trade had become "a staple" of New England commerce.[1]

New Englanders, mainly from Rhode Island, traded their region's most important manufactured product, rum, for slaves on the African coast. Then they transported the captives to the West Indies and southern colonies. In 1770 alone, Rhode Island ships carried 185,000 gallons of rum across the Atlantic Ocean to Africa. More than two-thirds of Rhode Island's ships and sailors participated in the trade, and an extensive service network in Rhode Island, Massachusetts, Connecticut, and New York developed to support them. Shipbuilders, manufacturers, mechanics, and tradesmen built, serviced, and repaired slave ships. In the cities, particularly New York and Boston, a vast number of legal, financial, and clerical workers handled the insurance, taxes, financial transactions, and voluminous paperwork involved in the colonial slave trade.[2]

The trade was even more important to the southern colonies. It provided planters and farmers with inexpensive labor to cultivate the agricultural staples that fueled the economy. In ports such as Charleston, Savannah, and New Orleans, mechanics and tradesmen serviced and repaired slave ships. Planters and merchants hired coasters to deliver slaves up and down the Atlantic coast. Captains bought supplies and provisions for return trips, and slave ships usually sailed with hides or agricultural staples. However, even when fully loaded, a vessel could transport only one-third or less of the remittance in trade goods for slaves sold. Consequently two or more ships were employed to cover the proceeds arising from the sale of one cargo of slaves. City and colonial governments collected substantial import duties on slave shipments. Finally merchants and factors spent considerable sums nursing, housing, feeding, and clothing slaves, entertaining potential buyers, and advertising sales.[3]

For most of the merchants and factors the investment yielded an attractive return. An insatiable demand for slave labor during most of the eighteenth century produced a seller's market, which led to high profits for those who could meet the demand. In 1750 Virginia merchant Francis Jerdone maintained that "there is not the least fear of selling here, for there is in general as many Purchasers as there is slaves imported"; furthermore, "the pay is always better than for any other commodity."[4] Although there were significant risks involved, according to another Virginia merchant, it was "by farr the most profitable trade that we have in this part of the world."[5] Charleston merchant Henry Laurens estimated that between 1755 and 1774 merchants and factors earned from 9 percent to 14 percent on sales of slave consignments. The profit was often more than double the 5 percent profit they earned on other imported goods.[6]

Selling black laborers also gave slave vendors a leg up on their competition. Unwilling to jeopardize their labor supplies, planters maintained sound relationships with slave vendors and in most cases repaid slave merchants before other creditors. In a letter in 1774, a Savannah dry-goods merchant described the advantage slave merchants had over himself and others who did not deal in slaves. He wrote, "We are very apprehensive that the large Quantity of New Negro's sold this Year will absorb the coming Crop and make the Planters at least many of them very backward in discharging of their Store Debts as they will in general support their Credit with the Negro Merchant even if they are obliged to do it at the expense of the Dry Good Merchant."[7] Moreover slave sales and credit payments brought planters into slave merchants' stores, where they bought dry goods. Thus, and most important, as Edward Telfair pointed out, it enabled them "to cary a very considerable part of the Export of this Province."[8]

Close ties with planters and exceptional profits also opened social and political doors for merchants. During most of the colonial era, an elite group of planters and merchants dominated South Carolina and Georgia society and politics. Although a commercial career did not guarantee entry into the group (gentlemen viewed merchants as newcomers until they "acquired a stake in the country"), it did in many cases enable merchants to purchase land and slaves and form close ties with planters.[9] Although merchants and factors were careful to refer to selling slaves as the "African Trade," or "Guinea Trade," participation in the slave trade presented no obstacles to joining the upper class. Lowcountry planters welcomed them into their families, social clubs, and churches and the colonial legislature. In the 1730s prominent members of firms included John Guerard, Richard Hill, Benjamin Savage, and Joseph Wragg; in the 1750s and early 1760s, George Austin, Samuel Brailsford, Henry Laurens, and Thomas Middleton; and, from 1769 to 1774, Miles Brewton, John Hopton, and Roger and Thomas Loughton Smith.[10] The slave trade to Georgia opened only after 1750, but by the 1770s Savannah slave traders Joseph Clay, James Habersham, and John Graham were counted among the elite of Georgia society.[11]

Henry Laurens's rise to prominence was not unlike that of several of his fellow merchants. Born to a prosperous Charleston saddler in 1724, Laurens trained in London for three years before embarking on a career as an importer, factor, and commission merchant in Charleston at the age of twenty-three. Between 1751 and 1761, alone and then with his partners George Austin and George Appleby, he handled nearly sixty cargoes of slaves. Laurens profited greatly from the trade in slaves and other goods he and his partners imported and exported. Although there is some evidence that he invested in slave voyages from time to time, the merchant reinvested most of his profits in rice and indigo plantation, and slaves.

Laurens also married well, and by 1760 he was one of the wealthiest men, not only in South Carolina, but in all of America.[12] Through marriage, wealth, and property in land and slaves, Laurens became a member of the elite group that governed South Carolina. In 1764 Laurens retired from commerce and turned his full attention to planting and politics. He served as a colonial assembly representative, Continental Congress representative, president of the Continental

Congress, and Paris peace negotiator, and he was elected to serve as delegate to the Constitutional Convention. Although Laurens's political career was exceptional, other Charleston slave merchants also became members of the highest social, economic, and political circles during the colonial era.[13]

These men were also among the most active slave vendors. Sooner or later almost all the names of merchants and factors appeared at least once in newspaper advertisements for slave sales. However, a small group of eighteen Charleston individuals and firms imported more than 60 percent of African captives sold in South Carolina.[14] Prominent South Carolinians were partners of these firms, such as Austin, Laurens, and Appleby; Smith and Co.; and Middleton and Brailsford. The operation of Austin, Laurens, and Appleby vended more cargoes, around sixty, than any other firm or individual. Likewise, a small number of prominent Savannah firms also were responsible for handling a majority of slave consignments in Georgia. They included Cowper and Telfair, Joseph Clay, and James Habersham.[15]

The Charleston and Savannah firms and individuals that dominated the trade were not just dealers who sold only slaves. Rather, they were general importing and exporting businessmen who also possessed the resources and skills necessary to profit from slave sales. First and foremost substantial capital was required to finance the sale of Africans. Merchants and factors were responsible for entertaining potential buyers, advertising sales, paying customs duties, and nursing, feeding, housing, and clothing slaves before they were sold. The largest expense, however, was the credit extended to buyers. Planters often did not pay for slaves till the next harvest, which could be up to twelve months. If the harvest failed, then merchants usually had to wait another year for payment. In 1755 Henry Laurens warned a young man considering entering the trade that "we are often in advance more than 10,000."[16]

Second, knowledge of the local market and planters was essential to success. Slavers depended on merchants and factors not only to market their cargoes and care for unsold slaves, but also to keep them abreast of local conditions that often meant the difference between profit and loss. Merchants and factors advised shippers of local preferences for, and prejudices against, African ethnic groups. They also consulted as to when to send cargoes, who were good credit risks, and what sort of slave, crop conditions, and politics to expect. An astute appraisal of the local market and buyers facilitated the quick selling of cargoes at profitable prices with relatively punctual payments.[17]

Marketing skills, however, were of little use during the War for American Independence. Commerce virtually ground to a halt. Invading British troops and roving bands of loyalists destroyed plantation improvements, burned crops, and carried off slaves and livestock. Planters were unable to meet debt payments, and many merchants loyal to the American cause fled. Others lost sons; Laurens's oldest son, John, was killed in a policing action late in the war. When the fighting finally ended in 1783, after eight long years, much of South Carolina and Georgia was in shambles. More than thirty thousand slaves had either died or escaped to British lines, and most plantations were near ruin.[18]

To rebuild their world, merchants and factors began immediately to import slaves. In a 1784 letter Savannah merchant Joseph Clay explained to a London slave merchant why the trade was so important to his business and Georgia. He wrote, "the Negro business is a great object with us, both with a View to our Interest individually, and the general prosperity of this State and its commerce, it is to the Trade of this Country, as the Soul to the body, and without it no House can gain a proper Station, the Planter will as far as in his power sacrifice every thing to attain Negroes, and those who have the disposal of them, will always command their Crops, which is every thing to a Merchant."[19] Six weeks later Clay pleaded again for shipments of slaves, but in his second letter Clay suggested that his suppliers had just as much, if not more, to gain by consigning cargoes to his firm. He wrote, "it is our earnest desire to be interested in Negro Consignments and depend on it tis not more ours than your Interest, that, that should be the Case, tis a foundation for all other business and will always give a preference in the purchasing of produce to the Vendors of them which you know is very essential in expediting and promoting remittances and therefore of the first consequences in point of attention."[20]

The war had not altered the commercial relationship between merchants and planters. The merchants and factors who supplied enslaved laborers maintained a superior advantage over those who did not. Planters kept their relationship with slave traders on a sound financial footing, bought most of their supplies and provisions from them, and consigned their crops to them. Therefore it should come as no surprise that, like colonial merchants and factors, most post–Revolutionary War firms and individual entrepreneurs participated in the trade.

Between 1783 and 1787 nearly one hundred Charleston merchants handled slave sales ranging from one person to cargoes of more than four hundred Africans. Only sixteen firms vended two or more of the cargoes that arrived direct from Africa, which accounted for 60 percent of the imported slaves that passed through Charleston. Most merchants and factors handled small lots of twenty or fewer slaves that were either transshipments of Africans from the West Indies or small lots of Africans they had purchased from other merchants. For instance W. Freeman and Pringle sold two lots of African slaves transshipped from Jamaica in 1785, one of twenty-one and one of twenty. The sloop *Porgy* delivered one of the lots to Freeman and Pringle and several more to other Charleston merchants and factors. Merchants arranged with the captains of vessels like the *Porgy* to purchase newly arrived Africans in the West Indies and transport them to Charleston for resale.[21]

Several colonial merchants were active in the African trade to Charleston and Savannah after the Revolution. William Sommersall, John Edwards, John Lewis

Gervais, and Arthur Middleton and the firms of Ball, Jennings, and Co. and of Smiths, Desaussure, and Darrell survived the war and reentered the trade. Two of these firms, Ball, Jennings, and Co. and Smiths, Desaussure, and Darrell, jointly and alone vended the largest number of Africans, 1,475 in the 1780s.

By 1785, however, most of these older firms and factors had withdrawn from the slave trade for a number of reasons. First, the slave trade in Charleston went from boom to bust in two years. In February of 1783, Savannah merchant Joseph Clay observed that "the vast number [slaves] lost in these two states [Georgia and South Carolina] by the war and the carrying out of them have made them exceeding scarce and in demand from 70 to 100 G's."[22] Aware of the extraordinary prices being paid for slaves, English, Dutch, Danish, French, and American slavers transported as many as 11,000 Africans and West Indies slaves to Georgia and South Carolina between 1783 and 1785. The shipments glutted the market, and by 1785 prices had fallen sharply.[23] Slow collections and bad debts further eroded profits. When the Continental Congress banned trade with England in 1774, it cut off planters from their most lucrative markets for tobacco, rice, and indigo. The end of the war brought little relief. The demand for American indigo evaporated, and rice production recovered slowly. With little to export, most planters could not pay their creditors. To make matters worse, many continued to buy goods on credit from the British merchants who had remained in Charleston during the war. After the British occupying force departed the city in 1782, South Carolinians went on a shopping spree that lasted nearly two years. They bought on credit everything from apples, clothing, building materials, and slaves to carriages, china, playing cards, marble, furniture, beer, wine, and cigars.[24] In 1785, a Charleston newspaper estimated South Carolinians owed 2,000,000 sterling.[25]

The mountain of debt crushed a number of British merchants and factors. In one month alone, August of 1784, "five great American houses" in London "tumbled" and were forced into bankruptcy.[26] Charleston merchants also suffered. Andrew Pleym placed an ad in 1785 in a local newspaper requesting "persons indebted to him since 1783, by bond, note or book account, to settle the same . . . as the heavy expenses of fitting out and loading two Negro vessels renders this request indispensably necessary at this critical juncture . . . unless this last request is complied with, he will put all his debts into the hands of a Lawyer to be sued for."[27] In a 1786 letter to the owners of the slave ship *Betsey*, Nathaniel Russell pled for more time to pay the owners for slaves he had sold for them. Since the vessel's arrival two years before, Russell had not "received one shilling on account of the brig *Betsey*'s cargo of Negroes."[28]

The presence of newly arrived merchants and factors was the second reason prominent Charleston and Savannah merchants and factors withdrew from the trade. When the war ended, competitors poured into Charleston. Northern firms sent clerks to the city to fill what they believed would be a commercial vacuum created by the post–Revolutionary War exodus of British merchants. The overwhelming majority of British traders, however, remained in Charleston.[29] The British commercial presence was further augmented by new arrivals in 1783 and 1784, intent on restoring colonial business ties. Although Charleston harbor was open to all nations of the world, British traders vanquished all challengers and quickly reestablished dominance of South Carolina commerce. The second and more successful British invasion moved an anonymous pamphleteer to describe the 1780s as "the sunshine harvest of British commerce, policy, and influence." The invasion was conducted by "a standing army of merchants, factors, clerks, agents, and emissaries, who out-manoeuver, undersell, and frighten away" the competition.[30]

Despite a vicious and protracted war with England, South Carolina residents quickly resumed trade with their former enemies. Many planters had not repaid prewar debts. Owing an estimated 412,000 sterling to British firms, they had no choice but to trade with their creditors.[31] Others were forced to look elsewhere after many local firms closed either during the war or soon after. Many turned to newly arrived British merchants and factors because they sold goods and African slaves from the regions that planters were familiar with and preferred. French, Dutch, and Swedish traders attempted to vend their manufactured goods in South Carolina, but according to a competitor they sent mainly "needy adventurers" to represent them who imported the "refuse" of their manufactures.[32]

The British traders' greatest advantage, however, was the liberal credit they offered. Merchants of other nations also extended credit, but they screened potential borrowers much more carefully than the British. Pierce Butler escaped financial ruin by borrowing $100,000 from a Dutch firm, but he was able to procure the loan only after he traveled to Holland, negotiated the loan in person, and provided sufficient collateral.[33]

British merchants were much more aggressive. For slave purchases they extended the payment schedule from one to two years and performed little or no screening of applicants for credit. Overall, British credit policies allowed them to dominate South Carolina's commerce, including the slave trade. At the end of 1784, George Abbot Hall, the collector of the port of Charleston, maintained that "until other Nations can give as extensive a credit as the British, they will have the advantage from that credit of a very large proportion of the import trade."[34]

Credit also played a critical role in slave sales. Slave purchases were among the largest, if not the largest, planters made. Lacking sufficient capital, planters often paid as little as one-third of the sales price at the time of purchase, and agreed to remit the balance in twelve to twenty-four months.[35] Slave ship owners, however, demanded payment much sooner. They continued to observe the colonial practice of "bills in the bottom." According to the guarantee arrangement, slave vendors were expected to remit in full the net proceeds of sales of slaves in the ship, or "bottom," that had delivered them. After thirty to forty-five days in port, captains departed carrying cash, staples, or bills that shippers accepted as payment. The bills were drawn against a guarantor, usually the planter's merchant or factor; therefore, if the planters could not or would not pay when accounts came due, it was the slave merchant's or factor's responsibility to cover the loss.[36] According to Henry Laurens, most planters in the colonial era paid punctually, and as a result he wrote off few bad debts. When the trade resumed in 1783, planters continued to purchase slaves on credit, but a series of rice crop failures and depressed indigo prices caused many planters to fall behind on debt payments and, in some cases, to default on loans. Consequently trafficking in humans went from boom to bust in two years, and many merchants were unable to pay their suppliers. The problem became so serious that the legislature prohibited further slave imports in 1787.[37]

The third reason prominent families withdrew from the slave trade was the rift that developed between planters and merchants. During the colonial era successful merchants and factors possessed wealth and the highest social standing; they were no less respected than planters. In fact the distinction between them was difficult to discern, since many of the most prominent plantation families owed their wealth to trade. The rift first appeared after the British army departed in 1782. During the British occupation of Charleston, merchants loyal to the American cause had been forced into exile. When they returned after the war, the South Carolina legislature allowed the British loyalists who had replaced them during the war to remain. It also passed a liberal alien act that attracted new merchants to the state. The act infuriated American merchants and factors, and they took to Charleston streets in the summer of 1783. But fearing a limited number of merchants and factors would restrict imports and increase prices and the demand for locally produced tobacco and rice, legislators ignored the protests and welcomed their former enemies. A local merchant wrote in disgust that "As well might a pigmy be compared to a giant, as the impoverished miserable funds of a American merchant, who lost his fortune in the war, to the immense capitals of British traders."[38]

The American merchants had no other recourse but to protest, for when push came to shove, the lowcountry planters in the legislature looked out for their own interests first. Early on it appeared that the legislators' strategy was working. Prices for imported goods and slaves began to fall, and British merchants accepted rice and tobacco in exchange for imports. Unfortunately planters overextended themselves, and, to make matters worse, Britain withdrew the indigo bounty it had paid during the colonial era and banned direct trade between its colonies and the United States. Even the weather refused to cooperate. Inclement weather damaged rice harvests, and most planters were unable to meet their debt payments. When British merchants began pressing for payment, seemingly overnight the very men that legislators had seen as their salvation were transformed into their worst enemy. Timothy Ford described the situation in 1785. He wrote,

The causes of this additional hatred arose at the conclusion of the war. A number of British merchants found means to remain in the country and foreseeing the great demand there would be for slaves and being the only persons possessed of capital they early imported vast cargoes of Africans. The planters impelled by their necessities to procure slaves eagerly grasped at the first opportunities that offered; and unable to pay down the cash supplied themselves on credit; at whatever rate the British merchants were pleased to fix . . . and advanced upon them 50 to 75 percent.

The merchants influenced by no particular feelings of generosity to their late enemies, or pressed by their credit to make remittances, or as likely as either, expecting to get into their possession the plantations of their debtors for much less than their value, insisted rigidly upon the punctual fulfillment of their contracts. The crisis was important and melancholy for the planters and many of them were torn to pieces by the legal process.[39]

When the American merchants and factors who had also imported Africans and trade goods attempted to collect, they were greeted with the same rancor and resistance that British merchants encountered. Edward Telfair was still attempting to collect for a shipment of slaves in 1793, twenty years after it arrived in 1773. Because they persisted, a wide rift developed not only between planters and British merchants, but also between planters and American merchants. Writing in a Charleston newspaper, IMPARTIAL lamented that "instead of unanimity prevailing . . . [two groups of] inhabitants (for I will divide the inhabitants of this country into two sets, viz. planters and merchants) are endeavoring to get rich at the ruin of the other, how can this or any other country so situated, expect to prosper."[40]

For merchants, the implications of the division were serious. When planters refused or could not pay for slaves and goods purchased on credit, merchants attempted to recover their debts in local courts. After several plantations and their slaves were sold in sheriff's sales to pay creditors in 1784 and 1785, the planter-dominated legislature moved to block further foreclosures. It passed a number of acts in 1785 that prevented merchants from suing debtors. In a Charleston newspaper, EUGENIUS accused recent buyers of slaves of being the main supporters of legal maneuvers to prevent sheriff's sales. The anonymous author maintained that "it would appear that such who had purchased largely at negro sales, and wish to fix the day of payment at as late a period as they possibly can, are those only who reap the advantage of it."[41]

In 1786 the legislature took further action against merchants; it made them liable for duties owed the state treasury. Not only were merchants unable to collect the debts owed to them, they were forced to pay taxes on the goods that debtors still refused to pay for while enjoying their use. "The advantage," John Lloyd lamented, "that men of rank, dignity and wealth take of the present law to avoid paying off their debt is, in the highest degree scandalous."[42]

Before the war, Ford allowed, "the habit of giving and obtaining long and extensive credit implied or begot a great deal of honor and punctuality in dealing," but by the mid-1780s it was engendering conflict and avoidance.[43] Faced with fierce competition, dwindling profits, and declining status, prominent merchants and factors abandoned the trade. Joseph and James Habersham, active colonial Savannah slave importers, dissolved their partnership with Clay, Telfair, and Co.[44] Members of Charleston's and Savannah's most prominent families, the Middletons, Desaussures, Balls, Laurens, and Smiths, withdrew from the slave trade in 1785.[45] Their sons and other well-born young men did not pursue commercial careers. Langdon Cheves chose law over commerce because of "the existing social distinction made between gentlemen (professional men and planters)" and merchants.[46] Most became planters, but many served as judges, councilmen, mayors, assemblymen, and congressmen and senators. William Loughton Smith, the son of a prominent native-born Charleston merchant and slave importer, Thomas Loughton Smith, pursued a career in politics and was elected to the U.S. Congress.

Although there were notable exceptions, for instance, Adam Tunno and Nathaniel Russell, in the nineteenth century, few men of commerce would attain the social or political standing of their predecessors. In the insular commercial, social, and political capital of postwar South Carolina, planters began to distance themselves from merchants and factors. No longer welcome in social clubs where planters, merchants, and factors had once hobnobbed together, the new generation of merchants and factors formed their own.[47] The French traveler Luigi Castiglioni Viaggio observed in 1786 that "the people who attend to commerce are almost all outsiders and rarely mix in gatherings of the gentlemen of Charleston."[48]

Social and credit concerns did not get in the way of the trafficking in slaves. Despite questions raised about slavery and the trade during and after the War for American Independence, most white Georgia and South Carolina residents continued to view the slave trade as vital to their states' economies. Consequently merchants and factors involved in the trade were neither ashamed nor apologetic about selling slaves. On the contrary, some, such as the slave auctioneer Abraham Seixas, were quite proud of their occupation. His poem announcing another sale of slaves appeared in a Charleston newspaper on September 6, 1784:

> Abraham Seixas,
> All so gracious,
> Once again does offer
> His service pure
> For to secure
> Money in the coffer.
> He has for sale

Some Negroes, male
Will suit full well grooms,
He has likewise
Some of their wives
Can make clean, dirty rooms.
For planting, too,
He has a few
To sell, all for cash,
Of various price,
To work rice
Or bring them to the lash.
The young ones true,
If that will do,
May some be had of him
To learn your trade
They may be made,
Or bring them to your trim.
The boatmen great,
Will you elate
They are so brisk and free;
What e'er you say,
They will obey,
If you buy them of me.[49]

Seixas was not the only northern immigrant involved in commerce, but the overwhelming majority of merchants and factors were British. They had become so numerous in the city by 1787 that a Charleston native observed that "in walking our Streets, whether convinced by the Dialect or Names of those who supply our wants . . . we should rather conceive ourselves in the Highlands of Scotland, than in an American State."[50] Other European immigrants sold slaves (for instance, the firm Villepontoux and Co. was probably French), but they were minor traders. Among the most active British vendors between 1783 and 1787 were James and Edward Penman, William Macleod, Adam and William Tunno, and Daniel O'Hara. Alone, and with various partners, the Penmans vended the largest number of Africans, 1,156, while Macleod individually handled the largest cargoes of people: 300 and 260 and 560.[51]

Most of these men had arrived in Charleston during the war years and established themselves as merchants or factors. According to the first *Charlestown Directory*, published in 1782, the Penmans, Macleod, and the Tunnos were operating commercial businesses before the war ended. Only O'Hara appears to have arrived after the war; he began selling slaves in 1785. All the men were in business for a decade or more. In 1802 two decades after the first *Charlestown Directory* appeared, all except the Penmans were listed in the directory as merchants, factors, or planters. James and Edward Penman were listed in the 1790 directory,

Miniature portrait of
Nathaniel Russell
(1738–1820) by Charles
Fraser, 1818. Courtesy of
the Gibbes Museum of
Art/Carolina Art Associa-
tion, Charleston, South
Carolina.

but, because the survey was not published again till 1801, it is difficult to ascer-
tain when they went out of business.[52]

The voids created by retirements and deaths were usually filled by northern or
European immigrants or their sons. Faced with no local representation, many
firms sent family members or talented and trusted clerks to carry on or start up
new businesses. Nathaniel Russell was one of several New Englanders sent to
Charleston during the Revolutionary era. Born in Rhode Island in 1738, Russell
began his mercantile career in 1765, when he and Newport merchant Joseph
Durfee formed a partnership. A few months later Russell moved to Charleston to
represent the firm. Evidently either one of the men or both were unhappy with
their arrangement, and, a few months after arriving in the port, Russell struck out
on his own. Early on the merchant struggled, and by 1769 he was preparing to
return to New England when a prominent Rhode Island house, Nicholas Brown
and Co., contacted him about representing them in Charleston. The offer must
have been attractive for Russell changed his plans and became the firm's agent.[53]

Through the Browns, Russell exported rice, hemp, indigo, tar, pitch, pork, and
Indian corn, and he imported rum, sugar, molasses, oil, candles, and pimento.
Although he did most of his business with the Browns, he also represented other
American and European houses. They sent him household items, small tools,
and slaves. Although slave prices varied widely in the 1780s, selling African
captives appears to have been much more lucrative than the dry and wet goods

business. Slaves usually sold quickly and generated much more revenue than other goods, and until late 1785 purchasers paid promptly. A 1772 invoice shows that after Russell landed, transported, gauged, stored, and sold a hogshead of rum for 67.4.0 he received 3.7.2. Three years earlier the merchant had sold eleven prime slaves from the Grain Coast who netted the merchant more than forty-four times as much as the rum. In 1785 Russell sold a cargo of one hundred Africans for 6,000 sterling. His commission on the sale, which took less than a month, amounted to at least 300 sterling.[54]

Russell's finances and standing in the lowcountry improved dramatically during the 1770s. He purchased four hundred acres on the Santee River, commercial property in the port, and a home on East Bay Street, and he invested £11,088 sterling in South Carolina bonds. Somehow he found the time to serve in the Charleston militia, and in 1780 he was elected to the South Carolina General Assembly. However, for unknown reasons, Russell abandoned Charleston for London soon after the British occupied the city in 1780.[55]

When he returned in 1783, he was able to avoid punitive measures leveled at Tories and resumed his commercial activities, especially selling Africans. Between 1784 and 1805 Russell participated in seven slave sales, which included five shipments that he handled alone. In 1785 the merchant vended two cargoes of 116 and 152 Africans, in 1786 two cargoes of 99 and 92, and in 1805 one shipment of an estimated 200 people. Although he complained in 1785 and 1786 that planters were not paying him promptly, Russell must have profited greatly from the sales for once again he began investing in property, and in 1788, at the age of fifty, he married Sarah Hopton, the thirty-six-year-old daughter of a wealthy and prominent Charleston family.[56]

The marriage increased Russell's wealth and raised his social standing. When they married, Hopton owned one-half interest in a 1,150-acre plantation on the Wando River, commercial properties in Charleston, and twenty-five slaves. More important, Russell gained entry into Charleston's inner circle through Hopton. Before he wed her, Russell had been active locally in politics and commerce, but like most other merchants he was not a member of the so-called lowcountry "aristocracy."[57] This all changed when he married, and from the late 1780s until his death in 1820 he was considered the "prince of Charleston merchants" and a member of the highest standing in society. To reinforce their standing, around 1806 the Russells began construction on one of Charleston's grandest mansions. Built in the most affluent area in Charleston, Meeting Street, the brick house, outbuildings, gardens, and furnishings cost upwards of sixty thousand dollars. Soon after the Russells moved into the mansion in 1808, they announced the engagement of their oldest daughter, Alicia, to a wealthy planter, Arthur Middleton. The series of parties that followed established the home as a center of Charleston privilege. Today the house is considered one of Charleston's architectural treasures and as such is visited by thousands of tourists each year.[58]

Like Henry Laurens before him, Nathaniel Russell amassed tremendous wealth, rose to the highest level of society, and wielded considerable political and commercial power. No doubt both men owed much of their success to hard work, advantageous timing, superior entrepreneurial skills, and gainful marriages. There is also no doubt that they owed as much or more of their success to the slave trade. In Russell's case this is especially true. At critical times in his business career, when he was establishing himself as merchant in Charleston in the late 1760s and early 1770s and again immediately after the War for American Independence, slave sales provided substantial if not vital profits.

The slave trade was also important to Savannah merchants and factors. Like South Carolina, Georgia suffered severe damage during the War for American Independence. An estimated ten thousand slaves fled, were stolen, or died, and British soldiers and loyalists damaged and destroyed many plantations. Although Savannah avoided the debt problems Charleston experienced, it too recovered slowly from the war. Savannah was a much smaller commercial center than Charleston; moreover, when the war began, Georgia lagged behind South Carolina in population, agricultural development and production, and wealth. Consequently, in the decade leading up to the war, British mercantile firms were much less inclined to extend credit to Georgia merchants and planters than their South Carolina counterparts. The policy prevented Georgians from accumulating the nearly insurmountable debt that weighed down the South Carolina economy for more than a decade after the war ended. But, when merchants and planters sought to replace and enlarge their labor force after the war ended, they lacked sufficient capital and credit.[59]

Unable to obtain slave consignments, a Savannah merchant lamented in a 1784 letter that while "slaves are in great demand, many causes have operated to put out of the Planters power in this Country to make immediate payments for slaves."[60] As a result only three slave ships arrived directly from Africa before South Carolina closed its borders to further imports of foreign slaves in the spring of 1787. The closure and the invention of the cotton gin in 1793 significantly increased the slave traffic to Savannah. And between 1787 and 1799 eighty-one ships arrived with African cargoes of fifty or more slaves.[61]

Only one of Georgia's prominent colonial firms, Clay, Telfair, and Co., survived the war and reentered the slave trade. Like most older Charleston firms, Clay, Telfair, and Co. closed its doors in 1785. It was among the forty-two firms and individuals who imported and sold slaves between 1783 and 1798. Eleven firms or individuals handled large cargoes imported directly from Africa, and only four (Crookshank and Speirs, Richard Wayne, Robert Watts, and Caig, Macleod, and Co.) sold two or more cargoes. The four firms and individuals handled 58 percent of the total number of known imports.

A Charleston merchant who had sold slaves in that city in the 1780s, William Macleod, formed a partnership with John Caig, and the firm vended Africans in

Savannah. Robert Watts was by far the most active trader; he vended twenty-nine cargoes totaling 2,498 slaves between 1795 and 1799. Watts's domination of the trade marked the end of an era in the local market. Until the mid-1790s firms and partnerships had handled most slave sales, but after 1795 individuals such as Watts were the most active slave dealers in Savannah and Charleston. Although only Patrick Crookshank and Alexander J. Speirs can be confirmed as British immigrants, it is highly likely that Wayne, Watts, Caig, and Macleod also came over from Britain after the war.[62]

The Georgia legislature prohibited further foreign slave imports in 1798, but South Carolina and Georgia merchants and factors continued to vend cargoes of slaves. Among the many involved were Colcock and Graham of Charleston and Mein and MacKay, Robert Watts, and William Macleod of Savannah.[63] Illegal sales posed a number of risks, but merchants and factors actively pursued the trade. Watts sold Africans openly; in March of 1799 he announced the sale of 330 newly imported Africans in a Savannah newspaper. Others sold imported slaves in a more surreptitious manner.[64] The trade was not trouble-free, however, for some customers refused to pay for contraband. When pressed for payment in 1800, a planter dared a merchant to prosecute. Rhode Island shipper Samuel Vernon, however, considered the threat "a mere bug bear," and he suggested his agent apply more pressure. "If we appear in earnest and resolute to prosecute the affair," he advised, "it will bring them to your own terms."[65]

When South Carolina lifted the prohibition against foreign slave imports effective January 1, 1804, it freed shippers and merchants from any legal impediments. Before the federal government banned further imports in 1808, shippers and merchants pursued the trade with a vengeance. From January 1, 1804, to December 31, 1807, Charleston merchants and factors probably imported more than 75,000 foreign slaves. In only four years, they imported nearly as many slaves as South Carolina merchants and factors had in the seventy-five years leading up to the Revolution.

Needless to say, a large number of individuals and firms were involved. During these four years, 1804 through 1807, 148 firms and individuals vended slaves in Charleston, ranging in lots from "a few" to 478 slaves.[66] As they had in Savannah during the 1790s, individuals, rather than firms, sold most of the cargoes. William Boyd was the most active Charleston slave trader of the early 1800s; between 1804 and 1808 he vended at least twenty-six cargoes totaling more than 7,000 Africans. During the same four-year period, eighty-five firms or individuals vended cargoes of fifty or more captives shipped directly from Africa, and thirty-six of these vended two or more cargoes. Such widespread participation suggests that merchants and factors realized attractive profits from the traffic.[67]

Cotton and sugar booms and fear of a federal ban against further imports fueled the market. Fantastic cotton and sugar profits, and the promise of more to come, provided the capital and credit to buy slaves. Wade Hampton made the most of the boom. Near Columbia, South Carolina, Hampton quickly amassed a fortune at the turn of the century by growing cotton with enslaved workers. He used the income (his first crop brought seventy-five thousand dollars in 1799) to expand his landholdings in South Carolina and Mississippi and purchase Africans to cultivate more cotton. In the early 1800s Hampton borrowed heavily against his cotton plantations and slaves to establish a large sugar operation in Ascension Parish in Louisiana. He, like many other planters, bought Africans in the early 1800s to toil on his plantations. Hampton succeeded in most of his endeavors, and, when he died in 1835, he owned numerous plantations and more than 2,000 slaves.[68]

A book merchant, Ebenezer S. Thomas, witnessed the rush to purchase slaves. He wrote in his diary that "cargoes were bought up with avidity, not only consuming the large funds that had been accumulating, but all that could be procured, and finally exhausting credit, and mortgaging the slaves for payment; many of whom were not redeemed for ten years after. . . . So completely absorbed were the agriculturalists, in many instances, that those who had been in the habit of indulging in every luxury, and paying for it at the moment, took credit for a bundle of quills and a ream of paper."[69] In a speech before the South Carolina House of Representatives, Gov. Charles Pinckney entreated that the trade be prohibited because "the eagerness of the purchasers" was "draining our country of specie, and involving us in pecuniary distress."[70]

Unlike in previous periods, the market suffered no downturns during these four years. Once it reopened in 1804, volume and prices increased each year until Congress prohibited further imports in 1808. In a series of letters to their Barnwell District clients, Charleston merchant David Fleming and his partners chronicled rising slave prices. In September of 1806, Fleming advised Mordecai Cohen that he had not purchased any slaves for him because "Africans being so excessive high at present, $200 to $320, in my opinion it would be the height of extravagance to think of purchasing just now."[71] A month later he informed Cohen that he had purchased three Africans at $300 each for Mordecai Fleming and that he was "expecting to acquire three more . . . my sole motive for purchasing them, was considering them a bargain at that price."[72]

Fleming had, indeed, bought the slaves for a low price. Less than a week later prices had risen to $360 for "likely" men, and they continued to increase despite an influx of shipments. By November of the following year, Africans were bringing $360 to $390. Not coincidentally, Fleming and other merchants kept their clients apprised of the price of cotton. During the period cotton prices fluctuated between eighteen and twenty-two and one-half cents per pound. Although the prices were below the thirty-two cent high reached in 1801, they were profitable (and exceptionally high by the later standards of the 1850s).[73]

The possibility that the federal government would end the foreign slave trade in 1808 added fuel to the fire. Like many South Carolinians, Darling Peoples of the Barnwell District, a state legislature representative, was convinced that "the African trade will be stopped."[74] Sensing that a window of opportunity was rapidly closing, merchants did everything in their power to obtain consignments and increase profits, including sponsoring voyages themselves. Between 1804 and 1808, Charleston merchants sponsored more than sixty voyages to Africa. Gardner and Dean, Christian and D'Wolf, William Boyd, Samuel Grove, and Frederick Tavel were only a few of the many merchants who invested in slave voyages during the period.[75] Those merchants and factors without the means to invest in slaving ventures took on consignments of cargoes that merchants had avoided in the past: women, children, "refuse slaves," and persons from the least-preferred African coastal regions of the Bight of Biafra and the Bight of Benin.[76]

They may have also conspired to fix prices. At the zenith of the Charleston trade, in 1807, an announcement appeared in the *Charleston Courier* stating, "The Merchants who are interested in the African Trade are requested to meet at the Carolina Coffee House This Evening at 7 o'clock."[77] Although it is not known what took place at the meeting, it appears that merchants and factors agreed to hold Africans off the market to prevent prices from declining. Merchant Frances Depau did not begin selling the 247 Congo slaves delivered by the *Governor Claiborne* until February 11, 1808, nearly two months after it arrived on December 18, 1807.[78] William Boyd waited even longer to sell his last cargo. The ship *Cleopatra* arrived in Charleston on December 2, 1807, with 478 Congo slaves on board. Boyd confined the slaves for more than three months before initiating their sale on March 4, 1808. Boyd was still advertising Congo slaves in September. By delaying sales, merchants restricted supply, thus preventing a market glut which would have led to lower prices.[79]

The merchants and factors who vended cargoes in Charleston in 1804 and 1808 were a mixed lot. Fortunately William Loughton Smith, U.S. senator from South Carolina, prevailed on a Charleston customs agent to provide him with a list of the ships that delivered slave cargoes to the port between 1804 and 1808, the place of registry, and the consignees. Although the list is incomplete and often inaccurate, it provides valuable information on the origin of fifty-three slave merchants and factors. The majority, 58 percent, were European immigrants. Great Britain sent the most factors, twenty-five, while France and Ireland sent three each. Among the twenty-two North American merchants and factors, Rhode Island sent eleven, Charleston supplied seven, New Jersey, three, and Massachusetts, one.[80]

Smith used the list to bolster his argument that South Carolina was not responsible for slavery and the slave trade. He asserted that before the War for American Independenc, Britain had foisted the evils on the colony and that after the war Yankee and British merchants resurrected and maintained the trade. Especially between 1804 and 1807, when the largest number of Africans were imported, Charleston merchants and planters had little to do with implementing the expanded trade. In an 1820 speech before the Senate, Smith declared,

> that those [New England] people who most deprecate the evils of slavery and traffic in human flesh, when a profitable market can be found, can sell human flesh with as easy a conscience as they sell other articles. The whole number imported by the merchants and planters of Charleston and its vicinity were only two thousand and six. Nor were the slaves imported by the foreigners, and other American vessels and owners, sold to the Carolinians, only in a small part. They were sold to the people of New Orleans, and a considerable quantity were sent to the West Indies, especially when the market became dull in Carolina.[81]

Smith's claim contained some elements of truth. At least one merchant moved to Charleston solely to vend slaves. Rhode Island merchant James D'Wolf sent his nephew, Henry D'Wolf, to Charleston in 1804 to establish a slave-trading firm. Soon after arriving, D'Wolf formed a partnership with Charleston native Charles Christian to sell slaves imported in D'Wolf ships. In 1806 and 1807, they vended at least eighteen cargoes of African captives. When the Charleston slave trade ended in 1808, Henry D'Wolf returned to Rhode Island.[82] Another Rhode Island commercial house may have also sent representatives to exploit the Charleston trade. John Gardner and John C. Phillips immigrated from Newport, Rhode Island, in 1802 or 1803 to open a commercial house. Between 1804 and 1807, they sold at least twenty-seven cargoes of slaves on a consignment basis.[83]

D'Wolf, Gardner, and Phillips were, however, the exceptions rather than the rule. The overwhelming majority of slave venders had established commercial businesses before the slave trade reopened in 1804.[84] William Boyd, the firm Gibson and Broadfoot, John Price, and John Watson were the most active vendors between 1804 and 1808. Watson may have been an interloper; he sold four cargoes totaling 1,233 slaves in one year, 1806, and promptly disappeared or perhaps died. He was never listed in any of the *Charleston Directories* as a merchant or resident. The other four resided in Charleston before 1804. All of the men were operating commercial establishments as early as 1802, and they remained in Charleston after the slave trade closed. Boyd, Gibson and Broadfoot, and Price were still in business in 1809. Boyd was the most active of Charleston slave traders of the early 1800s; between 1804 and 1808 he vended at least twenty-six cargoes totaling more than 7,000 Africans. He was either a Scottish or Irish immigrant, arriving in South Carolina in the early 1780s and becoming a U.S. citizen in 1800.[85] Rather than being interlopers as Smith had charged, most immigrant merchants and factors had come to Charleston to stay. They actively participated in the slave trade, but like their predecessors they did not specialize in it.

Smith also ignored the many minor slave traders in Charleston. They sold small lots of Africans, rather than entire cargoes. Between 1804 and 1808, Verree

and Blair, M. M. Campbell, David Lopez, and R. Eason were just a few of the
many traders who advertised sales of twenty or fewer imported workers.[86] Lacking
financial resources or connections to sell entire cargoes, they bought Africans
from the merchants who did. Other Charleston merchants and factors bought
slaves for their customers who could not, or would not, journey to the port for
sales. As mentioned earlier, Charleston merchant David Fleming bought several
newly arrived Africans in the fall of 1806 for his clients in the Barnwell District.[87]
Since he did not advertise slave sales, Fleming probably purchased the people
from another merchant. No doubt many backcountry farmers and planters bought
slaves in this manner.

In East and West Florida, merchants and factors involved in the slave trade
were of the same vein; they were either immigrants or immigrants' sons. The
most active firms and merchants were Panton, Leslie and Co., Arrendondo and
Son, Zephaniah Kingsley, and John Fraser. Individually and together they
shipped at least ten groups of captives, totaling 1,260 people, to Florida between
1802 and 1811.[88] The principals of Panton, Leslie and Co., William Panton and
John Leslie, and Fraser were of Scottish descent.[89] Kingsley was born in England,
and the head of Arrendondo and Sons, Fernando de la Maza y Arrendondo, probably was a native of Havana. Fraser and Kingsley were experienced slave traders.
Fraser was born in Scotland in 1769 and before arriving in Florida, had maintained a slave-trading establishment for several years in Sierra Leone on the
African coast. In 1807 he moved to Charleston where he vended slaves mostly
imported by his own ships. To continue his business—the United States banned
foreign slave imports effective January 1, 1808—Fraser relocated to Fernandina
in 1809 and acquired several plantations. A year later he imported two cargos of
Sierra Leone captives into northeast Florida, slaves totaling 266 people. Born in
1765, Kingsley was raised in Charleston, but left South Carolina during the War
for American Independence. By the late 1790s he was actively involved in the
Caribbean slave trade, buying and selling newly arrived Africans. In 1802 he
vended his largest cargo, 250 captives, in Florida. A year later Kingsley settled on
a plantation in East Florida along the St. Johns River and began growing cotton.
Although some of the slaves he and Fraser imported ended up on their plantations, most were probably sold either in Florida or smuggled into Georgia.[90]

In Louisiana, English traveler Thomas Ashe observed in 1806 that "the Scotch
and Irish absorb all the respectable commerce of import and export."[91] Ashe probably counted John McDonogh as one of the more important members of this
group. The son of a Scotch immigrant, McDonogh was born in Baltimore, Maryland, in 1779. After serving an apprenticeship in Baltimore, he moved to
New Orleans in 1800 to represent an east coast firm. Over the next fifteen years
McDonogh participated in the export and import business individually and with
a number of partners. Among many other things, McDonogh imported slaves
and may well have sponsored at least one African voyage. He sold most of the

slaves he imported, but some ended up on his vast landholdings. By 1816 his plantation income had grown to the point that he retired from commerce to concentrate on planting and philanthropy. When McDonogh died in Baltimore in 1850, he bequeathed more than one million dollars to establish schools in Baltimore and New Orleans.[92]

Not all Louisiana slave dealers were of British descent. French merchants and factors John Frances Farmue, Beverly Chew, Alexander Milne, Jr., and M. De Daquin vended cargoes of slaves. Only six of the British and French individuals and firms handled two or more cargoes: Farmue, McDonogh, Milne, De Daquin, Patton and Mossy. At least two, McDonogh and Milne, were active in New Orleans commerce for an extended period. McDonogh was involved in New Orleans trade for fifteen years and Milne for at least four. They, like their South Carolina and Georgia counterparts, mainly imported and exported manufactured goods, supplies, and staples, rather than dealing exclusively in imported slaves.[93]

II.

During the colonial era few southern merchants invested independently in African slave voyages, though many were involved as agents for British or northern interests. Local merchants sponsored three voyages in Virginia in the late 1710s and early 1720s, one in Maryland in 1762, two in Georgia in 1766 and 1768, and two in South Carolina in 1750 and 1751.[94] More merchants probably considered investing in African slaving ventures, but a number of trade disadvantages discouraged participation. British manufacturers produced the dry goods, fine cloth, iron bars, firearms, and gunpowder that slave traders on the African coast preferred, and New Englanders manufactured the most highly prized wet goods, the especially potent "Guinea rum."[95] Southern merchants could have purchased and resold the wet and dry goods, but their costs would have been higher than their New England and British competitors. Moreover British mercantile policy blocked them from purchasing African trade goods at lower prices from foreign manufacturers. And, finally, southern colonists manufactured virtually nothing, and African traders placed little value on their agricultural exports except tobacco, which also had its drawbacks; it took three or more cargoes of tobacco to pay for a single cargo of slaves.

The War for American Independence removed most of the obstacles to American participation in the Atlantic slave trade. Once free of British mercantilist policy, Americans sent ships to foreign ports, where they could trade rice, tobacco, hides, and other products for African trade goods. In England and the French islands in the West Indies and Europe, they bought wet and dry goods. However, southern participation in the African slave trade began slowly. During the war, the American mercantile fleet suffered significant losses, and in the early 1780s most southern merchants lacked the capital to invest in slaving ventures.

Accordingly, in the early 1780s clearances for Africa of only four ships from Charleston and two from Savannah have been documented.[96]

A Charleston merchant, Andrew Pleym, sponsored two other slave voyages to Africa before 1785, but they probably originated in Europe rather than Charleston.[97] A North Carolina merchant who had migrated from England, Josiah Collins, sponsored at least one voyage to Africa. The owner of four ships that traded between the West Indies and North Carolina, Collins fitted out the *Camden* in Boston in late 1784 or early 1785 for a voyage to Africa. The ship returned to Roanoke, North Carolina, in 1786 with eighty African slaves. Collins may have sent the *Camden* back to Africa for more slaves in late 1786.[98] Slave ships may also have cleared Baltimore, Maryland, for Africa. Although there is no evidence to document their sending ships to Africa, Baltimore merchants Samuel and John Smith, William van Wyck, John Hollins, and Stewart and Plunkett actively pursued the slave trade in the West Indies and landed cargoes in Charleston.[99]

Many more voyages were undertaken than have been documented. The main source of information on shipping activity—newspaper marine clearances—reported only a small portion of the Charleston and Savannah vessels that were bound for Africa. For instance, a few months before the South Carolina legislature closed the trade in the spring of 1787, a Charleston paper noted the following observation on local conditions as reported from Jamaica: "Kingston, December 5 . . . the Guinea trade to both the Gold and Windward coasts of Africa, is carried on with vigour from Charleston, South Carolina."[100] As the newspaper suggests, more Charleston vessels were involved than had been reported. Because many vessels bound for Africa cleared for the West Indies or Europe rather than Africa, their ultimate destination was unintentionally concealed. In foreign ports captains could purchase goods for the African trade not available in either Charleston or Savannah. Boston merchant Col. Thomas H. Perkins, who sponsored a number of African voyages, reported from the Caribbean in 1791 that "rum, tobacco, and Coarse Cloths are always to be had here low, such as suit the Guinea Market."[101]

At the same time, Spanish slaving vessels from Louisiana, Florida, and Mississippi were also clearing for the West Indies, but in general they bought slaves in the islands, rather than dry and wet goods. In the late 1780s a number of New Orleans and Natchez merchants sponsored slaving voyages to British Dominica to purchase newly arrived Africans. In 1788, for instance, three New Orleans merchants, Daniel Clark, Thomas Irwin, and Jerome Fuiget, traveled to British Dominica to purchase Africans. Clark, a British immigrant from East Florida, owned and captained his ship, sold slaves, and owned a plantation near New Orleans. He bought 121 Africans off an English slaver in Dominica and later sold them in New Orleans. Irwin, a Philadelphia native, also captained his own ship and sold slaves in Spanish Louisiana and Mississippi. During 1788 Irwin sold roughly one-half of his cargo of fifty-seven Africans in New Orleans and the remainder up the river at Natchez. Another five ships from New Orleans transshipped Africans to New Orleans and Natchez in the first half of the following year.[102]

In May 1789 a British slave trader estimated that in the past few months "no less than Forty Sail of Vessels had been fitted for the Coast of Africa."[103] The merchant may have exaggerated the number of American ships to support his argument that the recently enacted Dolben Act had given Britain's foreign competitors an unfair advantage in the transatlantic slave trade. However, when all the North American slave vessels are counted, including those operating out of the southern states and East and West Florida, his estimate is not far off base. As discussed earlier, vessels operating out of the United States numbered between fifteen and twenty, and those out of Spanish Louisiana numbered between ten and fifteen. Of these twenty-five to thirty-five vessels, as many as twenty may have been registered in South Carolina, Georgia, Maryland, North Carolina, East and West Florida, Louisiana, and Mississippi. By the late 1780s these vessels were transporting a significant number of Africans to North America.[104]

Developments in Europe and North America made it possible for American slavers to make new inroads in the Atlantic slave trade. In 1788 the British parliament had passed the Dolben Act, which established new guidelines for its slave ships, reducing the number of slaves per ton and requiring a surgeon on each voyage to care for slaves. A year later the Spanish crown opened all Spanish New World ports to foreign traders. When war broke out between England and France in 1793, fighting curtailed French, British, and Portugese participation in the Atlantic slave trade. At the same time, an insatiable demand for cotton and sugar and technological advances made cultivation of the staples enormously profitable in southern North America. Cotton and sugar profits increased the demand for enslaved labor in North America and provided the capital for slave purchases and new slaving ventures.[105]

Consequently, in the 1790s southern merchant participation in the trade increased significantly. During the decade documented clearances from Charleston for Africa increased to seventeen. In 1796 alone five ships left Charleston for the African coast. Charleston merchants owned at least ten of the slavers and sponsored more than nineteen voyages to Africa (two Charleston-owned vessels departed for Africa from Savannah). William Macleod owned a number of slave ships and sponsored at least eight voyages to Africa. Another five vessels cleared Savannah for the African coast. At least three of these voyages were sponsored by Savannah merchants.[106]

Local observations indicate that Charleston and Savannah clearances have not been documented. In 1801 an American slave captain reported fourteen American vessels, most of them from Charleston, on one section of the African coast. During 1800, when these ships would have cleared Charleston for the

African coast, extant records document only one clearance. As detailed earlier, the number of American ships participating in the trade exceeded one hundred per year. Fully one-third of those traveling to the coast of Africa were owned or registered in the southern states, while another twenty were transshipping newly arrived Africans to Spanish North America.[107] The size of the ships also increased. During the 1780s American slave vessels averaged less than 100 tons. In the 1790s merchants sent larger vessels, brigs and ships to the coast of Africa. In 1794 the ship *Charleston* cleared from Charleston for the coast of Africa. An enormous ship of 400 tons, it took off 500 slaves from Sierra Leone and delivered them to South Carolina.[108]

The availability of a wider range of manufactured goods at more competitive prices facilitated the growing participation of southern merchants. As the number of English and French slave ships declined in the 1790s, the demand and prices for trade goods bound for Africa that had been produced in Europe and the West Indies fell.[109] American slavers did not completely abandon North American products (for instance, in 1799 the Charleston schooner *Charlotte* transported tobacco and whiskey to the African coast to trade for slaves), but well aware of the fact that European and West Indies products were preferred by many slave suppliers on the African coast, they began carrying foreign-made brandy, rum, gin, tobacco, guns, breast plates, tinsel lace, and glassware to Africa.[110] By the middle of the 1790s they were also sailing with East Indian goods. American shippers transported East Indian goods to New York, Salem, and Baltimore, where they were loaded on coasters bound for Charleston and Savannah. From the southern ports slavers carried the goods back across the Atlantic to the coast of Africa.[111]

In the next decade Charleston merchants experienced their greatest period of slave commerce. Between 1801 and 1810, more than 400 ships arrived in Charleston and disembarked an estimated 75,000 slaves.[112] Ships either owned by Charleston merchants or registered in the port landed 133 slave cargoes in Charleston, the West Indies, and South America. Between 1804 and 1808 Charleston was "one of the great slaving ports of the world."[113] Ebenezer Thomas, whose business declined precipitously after January 1, 1804, witnessed the transformation the city underwent when the prohibition against foreign slave imports was lifted in 1804. According to Thomas, "a great change took place in everything. Vessels were fitted out in numbers for the coast of Africa, and as fast as they returned, their cargoes were bought up with avidity. . . . This state of things continued, until put a stop to by that provision of the Constitution which forbade the trade after the first of January, 1808."[114] Ships registered in Charleston participated in more slaving ventures than all the vessels from Newport and Bristol, Rhode Island.[115] Charleston ships also exceeded the number of vessels that made slave voyages from London and Bristol, England. Only Liverpool vessels outnumbered Charleston slavers during the four-year period.[116]

Among the many Charleston merchants who owned slave vessels or sponsored slaving ventures were the firms Christian and D'Wolf, Mann and Fitz, and Gardner and Dean and the individuals Peter Kennedy, William Boyd, Frederick Tavel, A. Holmes, and Samuel Groves. Baltimore, Maryland, vessels delivered six cargoes to Charleston, and Savannah ships brought two more. The Savannah firm of Maine and Mackay owned a slaver and probably sponsored one of the voyages that landed its cargo in Charleston.[117]

The records of the slave ship *Africa* reveal the economic impact slave voyages had on the port. In September of 1803, William Boyd purchased the *Africa* in Charleston for $9,000. While Boyd owned the ship, it made four voyages to the African coast. The captain, John Connolly, bought dry goods in London for trade on two of the ventures, but for the others Boyd loaded the vessel with wet and dry goods purchased in Charleston. Boyd sent the first two cargoes of African captives to Havana, but he arranged for the third to be sold in Charleston. In October of 1806, the ship *Africa* arrived in Charleston with approximately 300 slaves. William Boyd sold the slaves for an estimated $75,000. For the fourth voyage, which commenced in July 1807 for the river Congo, Boyd purchased rum, crockery, East Indian goods, Manchester cloth, guns, powder, and iron bars for trade on the African coast; rice, brandy, bread, beans, flour, and smoked fish to feed the crew; 280 suits of clothing for slaves and cloth available to make up an additional eighty more, if they were required; and padlocks, chains, powder, and firearms to keep the slaves under control. All of the dry goods and wet goods were imported and most of the provisions and supplies. Only the rice and bread were local products, and even then the flour used to make the bread had probably been brought in. The bill of lading for the cargo totaled $35,329. Boyd paid an additional $379.85 for wharfage, drayage, storage, cooperage and slave hire, and port fees. He hired most of the vessel's twenty-seven crewmen and officers in Charleston. Five of the crew were Americans, the remainder were English, Spanish, Dutch, Prussian, and Italian. In less than one year Boyd had generated over $110,000 in commerce in Charleston. Boyd and other merchants repeated this exercise literally nearly one hundred times over between 1804 and 1807.[118]

During the four years Charleston was the nexus of an elaborate and extensive commercial enterprise, and 75,000-plus Africans were disembarked in Charleston.[119] Planters, farmers, merchants, and factors poured into the city to purchase the Africans. To pay for the slaves, planters and farmers sent more than $18,000,000 in rice, tobacco, and cotton to the port, where it was loaded on several thousand vessels bound for ports in the West Indies, Europe, and the northern United States. Hundreds of additional ships docked in Charleston with more than $3,000,000 in wet and dry trade goods, shackles, chains, clothing, supplies, and provisions for the African trade.[120] Merchants hired more vessels to transship some 5,000 of the slaves to Georgia, Mississippi, and Louisiana.[121] Before they sold or transshipped newly arrived Africans, merchants and factors spent large sums on clothing, housing, feeding, and nursing slaves. They also paid customs duties and wharfage fees, entertained customers, and hired officers and crews. They supported local newspapers by placing advertisements for slave ship crews and officers, runaways, slave sales, slave ships, African trade goods, supplies, and provisions. They employed lawyers to pursue debts and seize ships. Tradesmen and mechanics serviced, repaired, and built slave ships. Crew members and officers bought personal supplies in Charleston and stayed in local inns, where they dined and drank, as did planters in the city for slave sales. Clerks churned out the voluminous paperwork involved in the slave trade. In addition merchants bought and sold slave ships and equipment in Charleston and hired officers and crews to sail them.[122]

Contrary to the beliefs of most traditional scholars, southern merchants played a pivotal role in the post–Revolutionary War transatlantic slave trade to North America. Seeking the superior profits and market advantages slave trading offered, they imported hundreds of cargoes of African captives. When New England and English slavers could not meet the demand for enslaved workers in North America, the West Indies, and South America, many southern merchants, such as Charlestonian William Boyd, bought their own slave ships and sponsored slaving voyages. Between 1783 and 1810 Baltimore, Charleston, and Savannah slavers carried a significant number of Africans to the Americas. Additional vessels owned by Charleston and Louisiana merchants transshipped newly arrived Africans from Charleston and the West Indies to East and West Florida, Mississippi, and Louisiana. However, Charleston merchants were the most active traders by far. They imported the majority of the cargoes of Africans and sponsored the majority of the slaving voyages. Because of their efforts, between 1804 and 1807, Charleston was one of the busiest centers of African commerce in the world. Specifically the city was a major center for slave voyage sponsorship and for the import and sale of enslaved Africans.

Chapter 5

THE NATURE OF THE NORTH AMERICAN SLAVE TRADE BETWEEN 1787 AND 1808

"To get as many slaves as you can"
Quoted in Michael E. Stevens, "To Get As Many Slaves As You Can:
An 1807 Slaving Voyage," *South Carolina Historical Magazine*

The foreign slave trade was one of the last issues addressed by the 1787 Constitutional Convention. Like other slavery-related issues, it quickly gave rise to contentious debate. Delegates from the southernmost states, South Carolina and Georgia, sought to protect the trade, while delegates from Virginia, Maryland, and the North argued for its abolishment. To resolve the impasse, delegates appointed a committee. In less than forty-eight hours the committee returned to the convention floor with a compromise proposal hammered out between lower South and New England delegates. In return for protection of the slave trade for fifteen years, South Carolina and Georgia delegates had agreed to repudiate the provision for the regulation of foreign trade that required a two-thirds vote in Congress. While debating the compromise on August 25, 1787, South Carolina delegate Charles Cotesworth Pinckney demanded that the fifteen-year prohibition proposed by the committee be extended to twenty years. Delegates approved the extension and shortly thereafter the compromise.[1] Before voting for the compromise, Virginia delegate James Madison sadly predicted that "twenty years will produce all the mischief that can be apprehended from the liberty to import slaves."[2] Though a slave owner himself, Madison opposed continuation of the human traffic, which he would later characterize as evil.[3] But unfortunately even he could not foresee the full extent of the destruction the trade would inflict on its victims over the next two decades.

I.

While the Constitutional Convention was in session, only Georgia and North Carolina in the United States and three of Spain's North American colonies, East and West Florida and Louisiana, permitted foreign slave imports. Moreover the slave trade to the United States was slowing. The most active importer, South Carolina, had banned imports for two years in the spring of 1787, and although Georgia and North Carolina merchants and planters continued to bring in enslaved workers, they lacked the capital and credit required to import large numbers of foreign slaves. In Spanish Louisiana the trade had also peaked. Between 1777 and 1788 merchants and planters there imported nearly ten thousand enslaved workers from Africa and the West Indies.[4] In 1786 Esteban Miró, governor of Louisiana, took the first steps toward restricting imports. Concerned about the "detrimental" influence of French and English West Indies black migrants, he ordered merchants to cease imports of West Indies slaves.[5] However, the edict must have failed to bring about the desired result for in 1790, 1791, 1792, and 1795 Miró and other Spanish officials issued additional orders forbidding the import of first French and British slaves and later Africans. Early in the 1790s the combination of local slave insurrections, declining tobacco and indigo prices, the St. Dominique revolt, and European wars slowed shipments of human cargoes.[6]

The dawn of a new century brought the rebirth of African commerce in Louisiana. An ever-increasing population of white Americans in Mississippi and booms in cotton and sugar production increased demand for enslaved workers in the late 1790s and the first decade of the 1800s. In response to the demand, Spain reopened the trade in late 1800 to Spanish and British ships. After France regained Louisiana in 1802, French ships continued the human traffic until the United States took control of the territory in early 1804.[7] Initially Congress banned all imports of foreign slaves. The prohibition included any enslaved workers who had recently arrived in South Carolina; but when Louisiana achieved the second grade of territorial government eighteen months later, Congress lifted the prohibition against transshipments from South Carolina. Charleston merchants wasted no time; by the spring of 1805 they were sending cargoes of Africans to New Orleans.[8]

Most of the enslaved workers sold in New Orleans, Louisiana's main slave market, experienced the middle passage twice. Slave ships traveling from West Africa to the West Indies and North and South America usually completed the three-thousand-mile middle passage in forty to sixty days. Upon their arrival in the New World, crews unloaded the slaves, and merchants sold them to local customers. The workers then traveled a short distance on foot or by boat or wagon to a farm or plantation. In some cases, however, merchants from distant regions such as Louisiana purchased persons for resale to local planters and farmers. For those unfortunate slaves forced to travel on to New Orleans, the nightmare was not over. The trip to Louisiana's main slave market was nearly half again as far as the middle passage and took at least twenty days.

Slaves traveled to New Orleans either on the ship that brought them from Africa or on smaller vessels. Conditions on board smaller vessels were often worse than aboard the transatlantic slave ships. The schooners, sloops, and one-deck vessels that transshipped slaves were built to carry freight, not people. Consequently crews crammed people into "apartments," in between, behind, and over barrels, casks, and crates. In many cases they packed slaves more tightly than oceangoing slave ship crews. The extra time and the abominable conditions on board took their toll on captives.[9] Slaves usually arrived debilitated from the middle passage. Their condition worsened when they were forced to spend weeks longer in compact spaces.[10] Because of the extended time at sea slaves were especially susceptible to "red boils" (scurvy) and many fell victim to the disease and died. John Robinson, Dominica's collector of customs, observed in 1788 that "foreigners only purchase the healthy and merchantable Negroes," for "others would not bear the voyage to the settlements."[11]

Tracing the 1788 journey of the Fulbe prince Ibrahima from Senegambia to Natchez, Mississippi, as Terry Alford has done, reveals the extended length of the tortuous journey. In January 1788, a Heboh army defeated the Fulbe forces led by Ibrahima and captured the prince. They sold him to slave traders, who carried Ibrahima several hundred miles down the Gambia River to Niani-Maru, where they sold him to the captain of an English slaver. From there, along with another 169 captives, Ibrahima traveled three thousand miles to Dominica on the 110-ton brig *Africa*. The voyage took thirty-six days and, according to the captain, was uneventful; only seven slaves died, and all but seven of the survivors were advertised as "prime slaves."[12]

A New Orleans merchant, Thomas Irwin, bought Ibrahima and fifty-six other Gambians on Dominica. After two weeks on the English island, Ibrahima left for New Orleans on May 2 on the 65-ton *Navarro*. The vessel headed west sixteen hundred miles across the Caribbean Sea to the Yucatán Channel. After a few days in port, Irwin set a northwest course for New Orleans, and Ibrahima finally landed in the city about June 2, 1788. The trip from Dominica to New Orleans covered twenty-three hundred miles and took thirty days. The time aboard the *Navarro* was much more pernicious for the captives than the middle passage. During the Atlantic crossing of thirty-six days, seven of the African captives, or 4 percent, died. In the thirty days on board the smaller *Navarro*, fourteen, or nearly 25 percent, perished. For Ibrahima and some of his fellow travelers the nightmare was not quite over. After a month in New Orleans, Irwin transported Ibrahima and twenty-four others upriver on a barge to Natchez. Trips by barge took anywhere between fifteen and twenty-seven days depending on river conditions. When Ibrahima arrived in Natchez in July, he had been traveling for over six months and had covered six thousand miles.[13]

Passage from Charleston to New Orleans, though somewhat shorter in miles than the trip from Dominica Ibrahima experienced, took longer because of prevailing winds and currents. Ships clearing Charleston sailed south for the tip of Florida and then turned toward the west, sailing northwest across the Gulf of

Mexico for the mouth of the Mississippi River. The trip measured thirteen hundred miles and took a minimum of three weeks if everything went well.[14] Since several weeks at sea are always unpredictable, often everything did not go well. Indeed passage from Charleston to New Orleans proved especially hazardous. Between Charleston and the Gulf of Mexico, violent storms, strong currents, reefs, and narrow straits near the Florida Keys could damage or destroy vessels. On at least three occasions slavers traveling between Charleston and New Orleans were wrecked. A violent storm drove the *Lucy* ashore in 1806 and killed many of the slaves on board.[15] The schooner *Sally* went aground on Abaco on March 11, 1807. Its crew and cargo of captives survived, and another ship picked them up and transported them to New Orleans.[16] Another ship, the *Heroine*, with eighty-six slaves on board, also went aground off Whale Key near Abaco in October of 1807. The crew and slaves survived and were taken into Nassau.[17]

Between Charleston and New Orleans, several ships ran out of food and water. In 1806 the brig *Three Sisters* exhausted its supplies and provisions, and thirty Africans died. More would have perished, but forty-one days out of Charleston the brig encountered another ship that came to its aid and provided food and water.[18] Between 1805 and 1808, several ships bypassed the New Orleans slave market and sailed the three hundred miles upriver to Natchez. Sailing against the Mississippi River current was at best difficult and at times impossible. Many oceangoing vessels had to be pulled up the river by slaves. Besides adding another three weeks to the trip, the superhuman effort required to drag vessels against the swift Mississippi current weakened and in some cases may have killed captives.[19] At least the slaves transshipped from South Carolina were allowed to stop off in Charleston to regain their strength before pressing on. Although it was illegal, several ships sailed directly to New Orleans from the African coast without stopping at Charleston. The trips took in excess of sixty days.[20] Whether sailing directly from the coast of Africa or from Charleston, slave ships bound for the Gulf Coast were occasionally slowed further by French and British privateers that stopped and in some cases detained slavers. On July 24, 1806, for instance, a British ship captured the schooner *Lucy* bound for Natchez out of Charleston with fifty slaves and sent it into Nassau.[21]

II.

Foreign boardings and seizures of slave ships occurred often in the 1790s and the first decade of the 1800s. The seizures were related to European conflicts and strife between the United States and France. Beginning in 1792, Europe was engulfed in war for more than two decades. The first war, known as the War of the First Coalition, began in 1792, when the French Legislative Assembly declared war on Austria. Within a few months France was at war with most of Europe. Over the next five years French armies occupied the Low Countries, the Rhineland, Switzerland, Italy, Savoy, and parts of Spain. In 1797 the War of the

First Coalition ended, but France remained at war with Great Britain. A year later Russia, Austria, Portugal, Naples, and the Ottoman Empire formed a new alliance with Great Britain against France, and the War of the Second Coalition began. The war weakened the French government, and in 1799 Napoleon Bonaparte overthrew the Directory and established the Consulate with himself as first consul. While he was reorganizing the French government, Napoleon also took the offensive against France's enemies in the Second Coalition. He defeated the Austrians and fought the British to a draw. In 1802 France and Great Britain signed the Treaty of Amiens, ending the War of the Second Coalition, but in 1803 Great Britain renewed the war against France. In 1805 Austria and Russia joined the war against France, creating the Third Coalition. Although the War of the Third Coalition ended in 1807, Napoleon continued to battle the British. Unable to defeat the British militarily, Napoleon created the Continental System in 1806 to destroy their economy by closing all European ports to British ships and goods. When Napoleon occupied Portugal and the rest of Spain to force Iberian compliance of the Continental System in 1807, war erupted again when Britain sent troops to aid Spanish insurgents' efforts to end French dominance of Spain. The Peninsular War raged well into the next decade.

For the most part the European strife benefited America's African commerce. France and England fought on the sea as well as on land, thereby making the African coast and the routes to the West Indies treacherous for European slavers. Consequently Spanish, French, and British participation in the African slave trade declined. American slavers exploited the opportunity their neutral status afforded them. Except for an outbreak between 1796 and 1800 of undeclared hostilities involving naval skirmishing with France, the United States remained neutral. The status allowed most U.S. slavers to pursue the trade safely, which they did in large numbers. Between 1789 and 1804 the American slaving fleet grew from thirty to more than one hundred vessels. The ships delivered nearly 150,000 slaves in the 1790s and first decade of the 1800s to French, Spanish, and American planters in the West Indies and North and South America.[22]

It was not unusual, however, for American and foreign slavers bound for North America to fall victim to the strife. Problems arose when the European combatants began harassing slave ships in the 1790s. French and British warships and privateers stopped and searched foreign vessels on the coast of Africa and in the West Indies that they suspected of trading with their enemies. In some cases they seized ships and detained them, and when they found sufficient evidence of illegal trade, they condemned vessels and their cargoes of slaves. Americans first experienced problems with European warships and privateers between 1796 and 1800 while the United States and the French were fighting an undeclared naval war. In the first year of the conflict, French privateers seized more than three hundred American merchantmen, mainly in the West Indies. Americans retaliated and captured ninety French vessels in the West Indies. French seizures of slavers discouraged American participation in the Atlantic slave trade until the United States and France negotiated a truce in 1800.[23] Nevertheless French and British warships probably continued to stop and seize American slavers after 1800. The War of the Second Coalition continued until 1802. Americans were delivering African captives to the West Indies and North America; but Americans chose not to report the incidents. Federal law prohibited American participation in the African slave trade to foreign countries, and, since all states banned foreign slave imports between 1798 and 1804, American slave ship owners and captains would have exposed their participation in illegal trade if they had reported seizures.

When the South Carolina legislature lifted its prohibition against foreign slave imports in late 1803, American slavers no longer had to hide their participation in African commerce, and not surprisingly they soon began reporting foreign harassment. In 1804 French privateers seized the schooner *Aurora* in February, the ship *Horizon* near the Cape of Good Hope in June with 543 slaves on board, the *Angola* in the Gambia River with 78 slaves on board in July, and the ship *Mary* in September.[24] The following year seizures increased. French privateers captured the ship *Samuel* in January with 275 slaves and sent it into Point Petre, the *Seaflower* in February, the schooner *Almira* on the Senegambian coast in April, the ship *Two Friends* in early June, the *Montezuma* in August within one day's sail of Charleston, the brig *Jane* in October, and schooner *Yeopum* in December.[25]

The following year the harassment continued, especially near Charleston. By 1806 the port had become a major slaving center. Not only were slavers regularly delivering cargoes of people to the port, but ships with trade goods, supplies, and provisions for Africa were entering Charleston harbor, and slavers were clearing the port for the African coast. The African commerce attracted both French and British privateers hoping to capture prizes, especially slaves. During most of June 1806, for instance, the French privateer *Vengeance* remained off the Charleston bar, watching for slavers. Besides British ships it stopped any vessels entering and leaving the harbor it suspected of transporting slaves to British ports.[26] The *Vengeance* and other French privateers captured the *Fanny* off Charleston in April and the ship *Truxton* in May; and they detained the brig *Port Mary* twice during the summer.[27]

British privateers captured the schooner *Lucy* bound from Charleston to Natchez, and the ship *Washington* in the Congo. They sent the *Lucy* into Nassau, where British officials removed eleven slaves and then allowed it to continue on to Natchez.[28] On at least one occasion both French and British ships seized and detained the same ship. In December 1807, French privateers stopped and detained the brig *Leon* for several days. After being released, the *Leon* resumed its journey, but before it could reach Charleston, a British ship stopped the brig and took it into Nassau. After several days, British officials released the *Leon*, and it went on to Charleston.[29] In 1807 and early 1808, French and British privateers continued to harass slavers bound for North America. In 1807 they seized the ship *Ann* in January, the ship *Juno* and the sloop *Lavinia* in May, the schooner *Eliza* and the schooner *Nancy* in November, and the ship *Amedie* in December.[30] In January of 1808, they detained the ship *Africa* and the ship *Tartar*.[31]

The boardings and seizures had a pernicious effect on the slaves on board. Detainments extended the horrific middle passage and in some cases increased mortality among captives. Already weakened by the middle passage, slaves were much more likely to contract any number of diseases and die when forced to remain on ships for extended periods. Detainments and seizures added anywhere from days to months to time aboard slavers. On October 16, 1806, the ship *Columbia* arrived at the river Platte off Montevideo, Uruguay, from Africa, but it could not enter the harbor because of French privateers. After waiting several weeks for the French to leave, the captain of the ship decided to sail north to Charleston. It took sixty-two days to travel from the Platte to Charleston.[32] In May 1807 privateers sent the schooner *Nancy* into Tortola "with most of [its] slaves suffering much sickness" and detained the schooner for at least fourteen days.[33] Antiguan authorities held the schooner *Eliza* for thirty-five days in November of 1807.[34] British privateers detained the ship *Amedie* on December 20, 1807, near St. Thomas with 103 slaves, holding the ship and its cargo of slaves until mid-February of 1808.[35]

Occasionally a detainment could actually last for years, as when the British warship *Haughty* captured the ship *Africa*, which carried 310 slaves, on January 30, 1808, near Tortola. At least sixteen Africans had died during the middle passage. Between February 13 and March 16, three more perished in Tortola, and by the time British officials awarded the *Africa* and its cargo to the officers and crew of the *Haughty* on November 17, 1810, only 236 "remained." From the time the crew of the *Africa* began loading Congo slaves in October of 1807 until the court released the ship and its cargo of slaves three years later in November of 1810, ninety people had either died or been sold. Local officials may have sold some of the captives to house, feed, clothe, and nurse them, but many of the ninety probably died during the extended detainment in Tortola.[36]

If slavers attempted to avoid capture, foreign warships and privateers often fired on the ships. In June of 1804, the ship *Margaret*, bound for Charleston, engaged two French privateers. The *Margaret* escaped, but cannon fire injured eighteen of its slaves.[37]

The most horrific incident occurred in April 1804 when the ship *Horizon* was seized near the Cape of Good Hope. The captain of the *Horizon*, Alexander M'Clure, and his brother were partners in the Charleston commercial firm of Alexander M'Clure and John M'Clure, and, like most other Charleston merchants and factors, they specialized in importing and exporting, rather than slave voyages. Nevertheless, in 1803, before the South Carolina legislature had lifted the ban on foreign slave imports, the brothers decided to sponsor an illegal slaving voyage to the southeastern coast of Africa.[38]

Alexander M'Clure's destination, Mozambique, was much farther away from Charleston than West or West-Central Africa. From Mozambique to Charleston the middle passage took anywhere from 85 to 134 days.[39] Moreover a successful slaving voyage to Mozambique required special skill and critical timing. To reach Mozambique and return, ships had to sail around the treacherous Cape of Good Hope twice, preferably during the summer months, when the seas were less stormy. Navigating the Mozambique Channel was also tricky. It was best to sail up the southeastern coast of Africa between October and March to take advantage of prevailing southwesterly winds and to return between June and July before northeasterly winds.[40] Sailing against prevailing winds added weeks to the trip; it had taken the *Don Galvez* 62 days to complete the passage from Mozambique to the Cape of Good Hope in 1793.[41] The added distance and hazardous conditions discouraged most merchants from sending slave ships to Mozambique. Those who were willing to take the gamble believed that "though in the long, cold, stormy voyage around the Cape of Good Hope, many more of the slaves died than even in the passage from the coast of Guinea to the West Indies, their cheapness in Mozambique fully compensated for their increased mortality."[42]

It is not known how much experience M'Clure had captaining a slave ship, but it is obvious he had not led a slaving voyage to the southeast coast of Africa. M'Clure left Mozambique too early to take advantage of prevailing northeasterly winds, and he arrived too late to make the summer passage around the Cape of Good Hope. He sailed into St. Simon's Bay in April 1804 with 543 slaves on board, and a French national corvette seized the ship *Horizon*. By then the days were growing shorter and cooler, and by the time the *Horizon* departed a month later in May, the weather had turned cold. Having come from a tropical environment, the captives must have suffered immensely. Although it is not known if M'Clure provided adequate clothing, food, water, heat, or medical care or if exposure, influenza, dysentery, scurvy, or smallpox killed them, during the month that the *Horizon* was detained, nearly 300 slaves died. More may have died during the fifty-one–day passage from the Cape of Good Hope to Charleston. When they arrived in Charleston, the surviving captives had been on board the *Horizon* for at least five months.[43]

M'Clure blamed the deaths on "French inattention," but he must share at least some of the responsibility for the catastrophe. Rather than remain on board to supervise the care of his human cargo during layovers in the southern hemisphere, M'Clure toured the local countryside, collecting exotic birds and pigs and purchasing wine and other goods for resale in Charleston.[44] The *Charleston Courier* described his sojourns:

It gives us considerable pleasure to state that Alexander M'Clure, Esq., who arrived a few days ago from the East-India in the ship *Horizon*, has not been inattentive during his absence, to the interests of this country: for during his stay at the Isle of France, Mozambique, and at the Cape of Good Hope, he, with great pains, collected a variety of seeds of useful plants, which have not heretofore been introduced into this country. The most valuable of these, we believe to be the seed of the Bourbon Cotton, which is in such request among English manufacturers, as to induce them to give nearly double the price for it that is given for the best Cotton raised in this State. We understand that Mr. M'Clure intends to distribute this seed amongst some planters here and in Georgia, with a request that they will use their endeavors to cultivate it, and naturalize it to our climate.

He has also brought with him as curiosities, a number of Birds, either elegant, in their plumage, or celebrated for their notes. And the lovers of exquisite wine may now be gratified with a taste of the far famed Constantia wine, which is produced by one Vineyard only at the Cape of Good Hope: Mr. M'Clure has a considerable quantity of it:—formerly this delicious juice was nearly wholly engrossed by the Dutch Government, who distributed it in presents to the crowned heads and potentates of Europe: what little was for sale, could not be procured in Amsterdam at a less price than a guinea for a pint bottle. When at the Cape, Mr. M'Clure received as a great favor a sow with a pig of the Chinese breed of hogs; this breed is a small species of swine, but the flesh is as tender as chicken, and is esteemed a great delicacy.

We trust Mr. M'Clure's well intended exertions will entitle him to the thanks of the Cotton Planters in the Southern States, and that society will consider him as amongst those who have endeavored to be of service to it.[45]

Neither the article nor any others questioned his care of the slaves on the *Horizon* or the humanity of an enterprise that contributed to so many deaths. The newspaper did, however, run advertisements for the sale of the 243 surviving Mozambique captives, and the *Horizon* itself, along with such exotic imports as cape wine, Constantia wine, batavia arrack, Chinese sugar candy, tamarind, aloes, and columbio root.[46]

III.

When the *Horizon* arrived in 1804, most white Charlestonians were much more concerned about profiting from African commerce than about the pain and suffering inflicted upon its victims. Since late 1803, the Charleston slave trade, no longer prohibited, had flourished, and it continued to expand until 1808. Slave imports rose from seven thousand in 1804 to twenty-two thousand in 1807. In the last two years of the trade, 1806 to 1807, it was especially frantic. The fear of federal intervention fueled the rush. The reopening of the African slave trade to South Carolina had shocked many Americans outside the state, and they began campaigning for its prohibition. President Thomas Jefferson responded positively to their protests, and on December 2, 1806, he delivered a speech calling for Congress to abolish the trade. Congress acted quickly, and on March 2, 1807, he signed a bill abolishing foreign slave imports after December 31, 1807.[47] Once the slave merchants' fears were realized, they expanded their trading activity even more. They sponsored more than ninety slaving voyages in 1806 and 1807. One Charleston firm, Gardner and Phillips, outfitted at least fifteen vessels in 1807 alone for slaving voyages to Africa.[48]

Charleston slavers encountered stiff competition on the African coast. In 1802 Napoleon had reintroduced slavery to the French Empire and revived the French slave trade. British slavers were also present in great numbers. At the same time the United States was moving toward banning the foreign slave trade, the British parliament was considering similar action. The British parliament debated the issue throughout 1806, and finally, on March 25, 1807, a bill received royal assent. The last day British slavers could sail from England was April 30, 1807. With abolition drawing ever nearer, British merchants and planters rushed to transport as many Africans as possible to the New World in 1806 and 1807.[49] Ironically the success of the abolition movement brought a brief but substantial increase in trade during 1806 and 1807, before the cessation of the legalized trade.

Slavers flocked to the coast of Africa. When the ship *Mary* arrived at the Isles de Los in late January of 1807, the ship's captain, Wood, found three English ships, one American brig, and two American ships. Wood went on to Bance Island but encountered even more slavers. "Trade is at a standstill," he lamented, "forty sail of Americans is between Rio Pongos and Cape Mount."[50] Later that year another captain reported that "there is not less than three hundred sail on the coast."[51] The plague of slavers created intense competition for slaves. To fill their holds, captains had to spend more time on the coast. Even then they often returned to Charleston with less than a full hull. In March 1807 a Charleston merchant, Thomas Vincent, outfitted the brig *Venus* for the coast of Africa and ordered the captain he had hired, George Preble, "to embrace the first fair wind and proceed with all possible dispatch for the River Gambia," where Preble was instructed "to get as many slaves as you can."[52] Soon after the *Venus* set sail from Charleston, it encountered problems. Preble fell ill and put into Gorée on the West African coast. While Preble recuperated, Charles Hodgkin, the supercargo, attempted to purchase slaves, but he met with little success. After several weeks Hodgkin decided they should try another port, and they headed for Gambia. Hodgkin failed to buy slaves there also, and the *Venus* continued on down the coast to Sierra Leone, where the supercargo finally was able to trade for eighty-two slaves. He also arranged to transport thirty-one other captives, owned by other merchants, for thirty dollars each. Although Hodgkin had been unable to purchase anywhere near the number of slaves Vincent had hoped, Preble and Hodgkin decided that to beat the December 31 deadline, they should depart for Charleston. They arrived in Charleston on December 14, 1807, with less than one-third of the captives Vincent had hoped for.[53]

In the same region another slaver, the schooner *Kitty*, also failed to take on a full load of captives. While on the coast from January through November 1807, the captain was able to buy only thirty-two slaves.[54] The captain of the brig *Commerce*, R. Long, stopped at numerous trading centers in Senegal in the last six months of 1807, but he was able to purchase less than one-half the total he sought. According to the captain, not only were there few captives available for trade, but slavers had flooded the market with trade goods. Consequently African traders were not interested in his rum, tobacco, dry goods, and powder.[55]

In desperation many captains and supercargoes bought slaves they normally would have avoided. Merchants such as William Boyd of Charleston instructed their representatives to "purchase as many young men and boys, and as few females and small slaves, as possible, . . . but on no account bring any old men or fallen-breasted women."[56] Boyd and others referred to undesirable slaves as "inferior" or "refuse." A Havana firm described the outcome of a sale of an "inferior" cargo of captives. A Charleston merchant owned the cargo and had intended for the slaves to be sold in Charleston, but because of problems with the ship and French privateers, it was sent to Havana. In 1807 the Havana firm Widow, Poey, and Hernandez reported that

> they had carefully examined the thirty-nine new Negroes, consisting of twenty-six males, and thirteen females . . . they were of the opinion that only six were merchantable; that another six or eight might become so, if properly fed and attended to; but that the remainder of them were altogether unsalable, owing to their advanced age, and crippled condition. . . . That at the time the Negroes were sold, it was difficult to procure freight for a vessel bound for Charleston, and only at very extravagant rates, from the dread of being captured by the French privateers; and that considering the deplorable condition of the Negroes, humanity dictated a sale of them at Havana . . . thirty-seven sold, three having died, for $4,685.[57]

It was not unusual for "inferior" slaves to die before they could be sold. Young, old, and weak slaves were much more susceptible to contagious disease. When the ship *Mary* arrived from the coast with 125 people in October 1807, after a sixty-four-day journey, Captain Wood informed the owners of the ship that forty-seven captives had died during the middle passage and "those on board are quite inferior." In the next four days Wood reported "five more have died" and "the slaves are very inferior and much afflicted with sore eyes."[58]

Extended stays on the coast of Africa and shortages of provisions and crewmen contributed to the poor condition of arriving slaves. Most American merchants preferred trading east and north of Cape Palmas in Senegambia, Sierra Leone, and the Windward Coast. Provisions and water were usually readily available, the regions were closer to North America and less hazardous, and the smaller American slaving vessels could usually fill their holds quickly. However, increased competition in 1806 and 1807 eliminated most of the advantages, as the decreased availability of slaves led to longer stays on the coast. The unfortunate captives purchased early on were confined mainly below deck while the search for other slaves continued. The confinement weakened slaves, and they often fell victim to "coast fever."[59] Shortages of provisions further weakened crews and slaves. Numerous captains and supercargoes were unable to purchase food on the coast for the middle passage in 1807. R. Long, master of the brig *Commerce*, searched in vain for bread for a return trip to Charleston that year.[60] According to the captain of the schooner *Kitty*, beginning in August 1807, "such was the scarcity of provisions on the coast, that, till the beginning of November, they were faced with famine."[61] The shortage was widespread above Cape Palmas. Upon returning from Sierra Leone in December 1807, Captain Street reported that "every vessel in Rio Pongus is much in want of rice for their slaves and not a ton to be got there. There was no doubt but the greater part would have to go to the Leeward to procure rice, which is very scarce."[62]

Many captains also encountered problems finding replacements for sick or deceased crewmen. Illness and death were common among officers and crewmen; mortality averaged 20 percent in the eighteenth century.[63] When captains lost crew members before they left the coast, they could usually hire replacements in trading centers. However, between 1806 and 1808, the large number of slavers outstripped the supply of available sailors, and captains often had to sail with less help than usual. The schooner *Kitty* sailed for Africa from Charleston in November 1806 with a captain, two mates, one steward, and seven seamen. It arrived on the coast in January, and by February the second mate and one seaman had died; another passed away in August; the steward ran away; and the captain discharged the first mate for drunkenness. By the end of August, only the captain and five of the crew remained, and the captain had fallen ill in the previous month. When the *Kitty* departed for Charleston in November, only two of the crew were fit for duty. Somehow they managed to sail the schooner into Stono Inlet near Charleston in January 1808.[64] On other vessels crews suffered equal losses. Three of the brig *Commerce*'s crew died in the Gambia River in the fall of 1807, and according to the captain, Long, most of the remaining nine "were ill and entirely unfit for hard duty." Long attempted to hire more, but "No others [were] to be procured," and he set sail for Charleston.[65]

A shortage of crew members must have worsened conditions for slaves during the middle passage, especially on board American slavers, which usually carried fewer crew members than British ships. While on board the American slaver *Charleston* in 1794, Mungo Park observed that to compensate for smaller numbers of crewmen, American officers "confined and secured Negroes" in a more "rigid and severe" manner, which "made those poor creatures to suffer greatly, and a general sickness prevailed upon them."[66] With so many of the crew members of the *Kitty* and the *Commerce* either deceased or sick, the captains of the vessels probably cut back on cleaning, food rations, and exercise periods in the open air. As a result slaves spent more time confined below deck. Weakened by the lack of food and confined in unsanitary conditions, more slaves than normal must have contracted dysentery and other contagious diseases.

Faced with intense competition above Cape Palmas, many merchants chose to send slavers further down the coast to the Bight of Benin, the Bight of Biafra, and West-Central Africa. Slaves were available in these regions in greater abundance at lower prices. However, sailing to and from the regions required much more time. The Atlantic crossing from the regions above Cape Palmas (Senegambia, Sierra Leone, and the Windward Coast) averaged forty-six days. It increased to roughly seventy days from the Gold Coast, the Bight of Benin, and the Bight of Biafra and sixty days from West-Central Africa. It took vessels at least eighty-five days to return from southeastern Africa. Not enough data are available to draw conclusions on the precise rate at which longer middle passages increased mortality. However, because many more slavers traders east and south of Cape Palmas increased during the last four years of the trade, a much higher number and percentage of captives experienced a longer middle passage, a minimum of ten days or 20 percent longer.[67]

In the last few months of the trade, several Charleston merchants gambled and lost on slaving ventures. As late as the end of July 1807, merchants such as William Boyd outfitted ships for the coast. Boyd wanted the captain of his ship the *Africa*, John Connolly, to sail to the African coast, purchase a cargo of slaves, and return in less than five months. Boyd was well aware of the obstacles the captain would encounter, but he was willing to take the chance. In a letter of instruction to Connolly, he explained, "from the very ample investment with which you are provided I flatter myself you will be able to command the trade over any other vessel that may be in the river at the same time; which I beg you will endeavor to every means possible, so as to insure your return by the 1st of January, on which day the act prohibiting the importation of slaves goes into operation, as there is not a moment to be lost." As we have previously seen, Connolly was able to acquire 327 Congo slaves, but purchasing the captives took too long. Realizing that he would not be able to make it to Charleston before the end of the year, Connolly set sail for Cuba, and on January 30, 1808, a British warship seized the *Africa* near Tortola. Connolly could have avoided detainment by departing from Africa sooner or by putting into Nassau and selling his cargo there, but greed intervened. If he had departed West-Central Africa sooner, he could not have purchased as many slaves, but he could have made Charleston before January 1, 1808. If he had sold his cargo in Nassau, it would have brought less than in Cuba. Either decision would have resulted in less profit for Boyd. No doubt Boyd had instructed Connolly to fill his ship on the coast of Africa and, if he could not make the South Carolina deadline, sail to Cuba, where the cargo would have brought less than in Charleston but more than in Nassau. Boyd's gamble failed, and the ship and the remaining slaves were awarded to the captors in November

1810, resulting in the loss of the owner's investment and the deaths of many Africans.[68]

A number of vessels failed to make it off the coast of Africa in 1807. Although the circumstances surrounding the loss of some of the ships is unclear, it appears that as the deadline approached and slaving activity increased, Africans intervened and prevented several ships from leaving the coast. The *Charleston Courier* gave no explanations for the loss of the ship *Lydia* at Rio Pongus in May or the brig *Eliza*, lost in October on the coast. It reported fire destroyed the ship *General Eaton* in June on the coast, and an explosion destroyed the ship *Independence* at Leango Bay. And a captain informed the paper that the brig *Nancy* was left at the Isles de Los in November with ninety-four slaves on board and all the crew dead.[69]

IV.

Many more Africans died in Charleston because of the poor judgement of Boyd and other merchants. Most deaths were linked to extended confinements in poor conditions. When slave ships reached Charleston, captives remained in close confinement on board or in other cramped quarters until they were sold or transshipped or died. To prevent the spread of diseases, especially smallpox, to other migrants and the local population, slavers arriving off Charleston bar were required to proceed first for a ten-day quarantine at James Island, where a "Pest House" had been created in 1798. A doctor inspected the migrants and determined whether or not contagious diseases were present. After ten days, if no disease was found, officials released the slaves, but when they detected smallpox or other diseases, they extended the quarantine for another one to two months. While in quarantine, except for brief periods, crewmen continued to confine captives on board the slave ships. After being released from quarantine, slaves and the slave ships proceeded into Charleston Harbor and then up the Cooper River for a short distance, and docked on the eastern edge of Charleston at Gadsden's Wharf.[70]

Between 1783 and 1808 merchants and factors conducted nearly all foreign, slave sales on Gadsden's Wharf. Before being sold, slaves remained on board the ships that transported them from Africa until the vessels departed, usually in four to six weeks. A few days before the departure, the slaves were moved to buildings on or near the wharf. The slave market was conveniently located near the town's commercial center and close to the ships and buildings that housed unsold captives. Almost all of the commercial houses were located nearby on East Bay or Broad Streets. Close proximity was essential to the merchants, factors, and auctioneers who sold foreign slaves. Slave sales were conducted every day of the week except Sunday. Moreover, since the newly arrived Africans required constant attention and control, sellers had to be nearby to supervise the confining, feeding, housing, clothing, and nursing of the captives.[71]

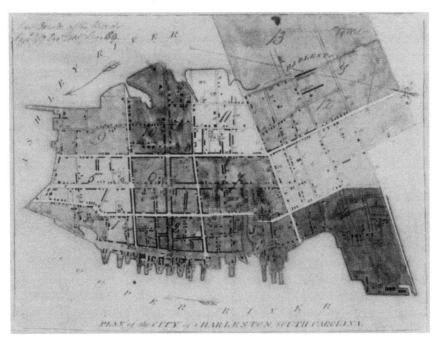

Plan of the City of Charleston, South Carolina, 1805. Courtesy of the South Caroliniana Library, University of South Carolina.

Until 1806 merchants usually sold slaves quickly, in two weeks or less. A number of factors influenced sales: the African origin, prices, skills, gender, age, color, and health of the people, along with local economic conditions, credit, and the quantity of slaves on the market. During 1804, 1805, and the first nine months of 1806, the volume of imports varied, but it rarely exceeded demand, and slaves sold rapidly.[72] The number of slaves held for sale on Gadsden's Wharf ranged from a few to as many as one thousand during the period. The mix of slaves also aided timely sales. Merchants were able to procure substantial numbers of young males from the African regions that planters preferred, Senegambia, Sierra Leone, and the Windward and Gold Coasts. Slow periods occurred during the late fall, winter, and early spring months. Beginning in October of 1806, however, the volume of imports grew steadily until the end of 1807, and the black population held at Gadsden's Wharf increased. As the prohibition against further imports approached in late 1807, imports skyrocketed. During the last two months of 1807 and the first month of 1808, more than 12,000 slaves arrived in Charleston. The mix of captives also changed. The percentage of Angolan, Congo, and "inferior" slaves increased, and the percentage of "prime" Africans from Senegambia, Sierra Leone, and the Windward and Gold Coasts declined. According to one observer, "the market was completely glutted."[73]

As the population of slaves on Gadsden's Wharf grew and the mix changed, the time required to sell cargoes increased. For instance, the sale of the schooner *Edward and Edmond*'s cargo began on November 24, 1807 and was still in progress seven weeks later in the middle of January.[74] The sale of the *Venus'* cargo took even longer. The *Venus* arrived in Charleston on December 14, 1807.[75] Two days later an advertisement appeared in the *Charleston Courier* announcing the sale of "Prime WINDWARD COAST SLAVES."[76] The sale did not go well. A Charleston merchant, Thomas Vincent, sold twenty-five of the captives in December, none in January, seven in February, and sixteen in March. Among the forty-eight slaves sold in Charleston, there were twenty-two men, fifteen women, six boys, and five girls. They averaged about $350 per slave. The remainder of the slaves brought far less. Two slaves died during the middle passage, nine more perished after arriving in Charleston, and Vincent sent nineteen of the captives to Havana to be sold "as they were ill and suffered much from the coldness of this climate."[77]

Conditions on board the slave ships and on Gadsden's Wharf contributed to illness and deaths. Except for the few hours each day, merchants confined captives in cramped, poorly ventilated, and unsanitary ships and buildings. Contagious diseases such as smallpox and measles flourished in the environment.[78] Moreover African populations were particularly vulnerable to European diseases. As Africans were transported from the interior to the coast of Africa, and across the Atlantic Ocean to Charleston, they moved from one diseased environment to another, and their death rates rose.[79] In most cases African captives, accumulated from a large geographic area, first came in contact with European diseases when they were herded together at slave trading centers on the coast of Africa. Exposure to new diseases increased when slaves were loaded on slave ships. Slavers often called on a number of trading centers to fill their holds with captives. In their efforts to purchase slaves, they inadvertently spread diseases that lead to the death of Africans on the coast and during the middle passage.

Upon arriving in Charleston, captives were at their greatest risk. Slaves from all eight trading regions of Africa were confined on ships and in buildings on Gadsden's Wharf. Moreover they were exposed to the diverse crewmen who delivered the slaves to Charleston, to the residents of Charleston, and to the many visitors in the port. The wide range of origins, exposure to Europeans from all across the Atlantic world, the debilitating middle passage, and extended confinement in pernicious quarters contributed to the deaths of hundreds of migrants. A British visitor, John Lambert, toured the wharf in the middle of January, two weeks after prohibition took effect, and recorded his observations. According to Lambert, the din raised by slaves, sailors, sellers, and buyers was akin to the Old Testament Babel.[80]

At the time Lambert visited, the black population of Gadsden's Wharf approached two thousand. Lambert maintained that the market was glutted, but rather than reduce prices, merchants held on to slaves. They realized that because no more imports would be allowed, prices would soon rise. While they waited for the increase, they confined slaves on ships and in buildings on Gadsden's Wharf. Lambert observed that "close confinement, scanty clothing, sharp weather, and improper food created a variety of disorders; which, together with dysentery and some contagious diseases to which the Negroes are subject, considerably increased the mortality. Upwards of 700 died in less than three months and carpenters were daily employed in making shells for the dead bodies."[81] A Charleston merchant told Lambert that "a similar mortality took place a few years ago."[82] During that period dead bodies were thrown into the river to avoid paying for burial or left on vacant lots "to be devoured by the turkey buzzards." So many bodies were thrown into the Cooper River that Charleston residents stopped eating fish for several months.[83]

As we have previously seen, an announcement appeared in the November 28, 1807, *Charleston Courier* stating that "the Merchants who are interested in the African Trade are requested to meet at the Carolina Coffee House This Evening at 7 o'clock."[84] Although it is not known what took place at the meeting, the merchants' actions indicate they may have agreed to hold newly arrived Africans off the market to realize higher prices once the prohibition was in place. Frances Depau did not begin selling 247 Congo slaves delivered by the *Governor Claiboure* on December 18, 1807, when it arrived, until February 11, 1808, more than seven weeks later.[85] William Boyd waited even longer to sell his last cargo. The ship *Cleopatra* arrived in Charleston on December 2, 1807, with 478 Congo slaves on board. Boyd confined the slaves for more than three months before initiating their sale on March 4, 1808. The sale extended for six months through the entire summer and did not end until September.[86]

Merchants did not entirely ignore the needs of slaves confined on Gadsden's Wharf. They provided the basic necessities and medical care, and they buried them when they died. While selling the *Venus*'s cargo, Thomas Vincent paid $361 for clothing and blankets; $17 for rum and brandy; $15 for firewood; $273 for bread, rice, peas, molasses, salt fish, and beef; $35 for a cook named Sam to prepare the food; $94 for vaccinations; $38 for other medical care; and $54 for the burial of the nine slaves who had died.[87] Humanitarianism had little to do with the expenditures, however; merchants such as Vincent were simply maintaining an expensive investment.

Despite efforts by the investors, many Africans expired on Gadsden's Wharf in 1807 and 1808. Charleston doctor David Ramsay reported an outbreak of disease among newly arrived Africans in early 1807. In a letter to a friend, Ramsay wrote:

> the first seven months [of 1807] produced nothing very uncommon, except that dysenteries and dropsies carried off great numbers of the newly imported Africans. It is well known that dysenteries are commonly engendered in camps of foul air. They might, therefore, reasonably be expected in the African slave ships, where such crowds of human beings were almost

constantly shut up without a supply of fresh air, and frequently with a scanty allowance of unwholesome food and bad water. The same causes operated so extensively in producing dropsies, that there was scarcely a cargo of negroes brought into the port, of which there was not a portion laboring under dropsical swellings, most generally of the anasarcous kind.[88]

As previously mentioned, Lambert estimated during the first three months of that span (between October 15, 1807, and January 15, 1808) that seven hundred Africans perished, but the number was probably much higher. While the slaves delivered by the *Venus* were confined, nine out of eighty, or 11 percent, perished. More would probably have died, but because they were ill, Vincent sent nineteen of the slaves to Havana.[89] Not all of the slaves who arrived in Charleston during the period were confined as long as the *Venus* cargo, but a majority spent more than a month there. Also as many as two thousand were on Gadsden's Wharf when Lambert visited, and the majority would remain there for several more weeks. Taking into consideration that imports for the last four months of 1807 approached sixteen thousand Africans, and assuming a 10 percent mortality rate among the severely weakened and disheartened captives who were held on Gadsden's Wharf, as many as sixteen hundred newly arrived Africans may have perished on the Charleston wharf over the four months. When combined with the earlier deaths reported by Ramsay, the total may have approached two thousand.[90] Moreover many more slaves probably died after being sold. Weakened by months of confinement and disease, slaves succumbed either while traveling to plantations or shortly after arriving there.

The slaves' harrowing experience in Charleston conflicts with conventional Atlantic slave trade scholarship. Slave trade demographers, statisticians, and historians have concluded that middle-passage mortality rates declined during the eighteenth century from 14 to near 11 percent by the end of the century. However, when calculating mortality rates, scholars frequently omit what they consider anomalous occurrences, such as wrecks or revolts or epidemics that contribute to an unusually large number of deaths on board slave ships. Moreover they do not include slave deaths that occurred on the coast of Africa, in ports, while slaves were being confined before being sold, or traveling to plantations or shortly after arriving there.[91] By adhering to this practice, they tend to give the impression that the conditions improved as the trade progressed toward abolition. It seems clear, however, that as the prohibition against further foreign imports into North America approached in the first decade of the nineteenth century, rather than improve, conditions worsened and mortality rates increased.

After South Carolina revived African commerce in late 1803, a combination of factors contributed to the further deterioration of bad circumstances. Shipments to Louisiana extended the middle passage by at least twenty days and exposed captives to the hazardous journey between Charleston and New Orleans or Natchez. Slavers racing against the calendar wrecked and ran out of provisions during the passage, killing a number of migrants. French and British seizures and detainments added to the misery. Between 1804 and 1808, by seizing slavers bound for North America, these privateers extended the middle passage of at least twenty-six different groups of migrants. In one case three hundred captives died; in another detainment lasted three years. North American merchants must also bear responsibility for the deaths of Africans. In their rush, as one merchant put it, "to get as many slaves as you can," they imported ill, old, and weak individuals who often perished, and they exposed sailors and slaves to famine and disease.[92] Moreover, to increase profits, they confined people in cramped, unsanitary, and poorly ventilated quarters. In that environment contagious diseases flourished and killed hundreds of defenseless victims. Although the high mortality may have been typical for only North America as opposed to South America and the West Indies in the late 1790s and in the first decade of the 1800s, it does offer convincing evidence that the Atlantic slave trade to North America continued to be "a cruel and wasteful operation—most damaging to the slaves themselves."[93]

CONCLUSION

This reassessment has portrayed the post–Revolutionary War foreign slave trade to North America in a different light than previous accounts did. Factors that combined to create a strong demand for enslaved laborers in the first post–Revolutionary War generation include the conviction that slavery and wealth were intertwined, the loss of slaves during the war, technological advances, rising staple prices, comparatively low land and slave prices, and the race to beat the foreign slave deadline of December 31, 1807.

Questionable quantitative arguments have contributed to the acceptance of inaccurate estimates of the post–Revolutionary War foreign slave trade to North America. Philip D. Curtin's numerical analysis of the Atlantic slave trade, *The Atlantic Slave Trade: A Census*, buttressed this scholarship. In this influential study he argued that natural growth, rather than imports, was responsible for the considerable increase of the southern black population between 1783 and 1810. Accordingly he estimated that only ninety-two thousand Africans arrived during the period. Curtin, however, based his estimate on the erroneous calculations of nineteenth-century scholar H. C. Carey. Relying more on conjecture than fact, Carey underestimated the volume by a wide margin.[1]

To arrive at a more accurate estimate, three different approaches were used. First was the use of the same quantitative methods that previous scholars had used, but with a different assumption of natural growth rates for the black low-country populations of Georgia and South Carolina as well as for black immigrant populations. This approach generated a new immigrant estimate of 200,000 newcomers arriving in North America via the foreign slave trade between 1783 and 1810 (see table 5). Second was the use of research into customs records, newspaper reports and advertisements, contemporary observations, and merchants' accounts to extract information on the documentable number of foreign slaves landed in North America for the period of this study. Information on arrival sources and data is in appendix B. Calculations show that credible data existed concerning at least 106,000 of the captives who arrived in this era (see table 8). Third was research into the same sources to extract information on North American slave-carrying capacity for the period of this study. Information on slaving voyage sources and data is in appendix B. Calculations indicated that the total carrying capacity of North American slavers in this generation totaled 146,000 people. This are fewer persons than Roger Anstey's estimate for the period

(220,000), but more than Curtin's (120,000).[2] All three of these methods are incomplete in different ways, but when integrated, they provide a considerably more trustworthy and larger estimate than scholars have been using in the past. It is now estimated that between 1783 and 1810 North American merchants and planters imported 170,000 foreign slaves (see table 9).

Data from appendix B has been used to analyze the origins of the foreign slaves disembarked in North America. In the past most historians have relied on Elizabeth Donnan's *Documents Illustrative of the History of the Slave Trade to America*, published in 1935, to identify the origins of captives. The new research presented here filled many of the gaps in *Documents* and other studies. Data from appendix B indicates that after the War for American Independence, planters continued to exhibit their prejudice against Africans from the Bight of Benin and the Bight of Biafra. It also suggests that they would purchase West-Central captives when Senegambian, Sierra Leone, and the Windward and Gold Coasts slaves were not available or were too dear. Between 1783 and 1810, of the Africans of identifiable origin, Sudanese people from Senegambia, Sierra Leone, and the Windward and Gold Coasts made up 55 percent of the total number of people landed, and Bantu people from the Congo and Angola made up 38 percent. It should be noted that shipments from Angola and Congo predominated in the market during the last two years of the legal trading period.

Research into customs records, newspaper reports and advertisements, contemporary observations, and merchants' accounts helps create a picture of the American merchants who sponsored slaving voyages and the merchants from various countries who sold foreign slaves in North America. Information on merchant sources and data is in appendices A and B. The sources and data demonstrate that as soon as the Revolutionary War ended, South Carolina and Georgia merchants and factors enthusiastically reentered the slave trade. However, they soon discovered that selling slaves no longer guaranteed the attractive profits or trading advantages that they had enjoyed during the colonial era, and they abandoned African commerce to a new generation of merchants and factors. Other changes ensued. Individuals rather than firms and partnerships vended the majority of African cargoes, and, during the last four years of the legal trade, Charleston merchants were intimately bound up in the transatlantic slave trade.

During the 1790s and the first decade of the 1800s, increased competition for slaves, longer voyages, French and British interference, and a precipitous rise in Charleston imports worsened the conditions captives were forced to endure. In Charleston alone, as many as two thousand newly arrived slaves may have died while being confined in cramped, unsanitary, and poorly ventilated slave ships and warehouses. These findings suggest that mortality rates for Africans transported to North America remained at high levels or may even have increased rather than declined during the final decades of the trade, as most scholars have argued.

Three major observations emerge from these investigations. First, far more for-eign slaves were imported than previously thought. This appraisal has important demographic, economic, political, social, and cultural implications. Conserva-tive estimates of the number of Africans landed in North America during the colonial and post-Revolution eras total 430,000.[3] When the new larger estimate of volume from 1783 to 1810 is factored into the overall total, it appears that North American imports exceeded 500,000 persons during the period. This appraisal also bears on the overall volume of the transatlantic trade. Curtin esti-mated that from 1451 to 1870, 10,000,000 African captives were imported into the Americas.[4] The difference (78,000) between the estimate presented here (170,000) and Curtin's (92,000) of imports into North America from 1783 to 1810 totals less than 1 percent of Curtin's overall estimate. However, when one considers the fact that numerous "insignificant" regions such as North America imported Africans, and several minor carriers such as the United States trans-ported captives, it becomes obvious that more inquiries regarding minor im-porters and carriers could raise the overall figure above Curtin's 10,000,000 projection.

The new estimate for the period also indicates that Africans were by far the largest ethnic group of immigrants that arrived in North America from 1783 to 1810. They probably made up nearly 45 percent of the 380,000 immigrants who arrived during the period.[5] Despite the fact that these Africans did not constitute as high a proportion in the lower South's total population as they had in the colo-nial era, they had a significant impact on the South and the nation. By import-ing Africans, white southerners increased their representation in the U.S. House of Representatives and their electoral college votes. Importing enslaved Africans also aided the southern economy. The reopening of the slave trade after the Revo-lution allowed low country planters to re-entrench and sustain slavery in their region. Planters and farmers were also able to extend it to the backcountry regions of Georgia and South Carolina and the lower Mississippi Valley. More-over the inexpensive labor that the foreign slave trade provided helped fuel the cotton and sugar booms. Without foreign slave imports farmers and planters would have had to rely solely on domestic imports during the 1790s and 1800s. A limited supply of labor would have increased slave prices quite possibly to such high levels that most farmers and planters could not have afforded to purchase slaves.[6]

Whether they ended up on rice, tobacco, sugar, or cotton plantations, Africans constituted a sizeable percentage of the slave population. Philip D. Morgan has estimated that Africans composed 27 percent of South Carolina's adult popula-tion in 1790 and 20 percent in 1810.[7] Allan Kulikoff has shown that nearly three-quarters of all slaves, domestic and foreign, sold in Natchez, Mississippi, from 1786 to 1788 were Africans.[8] In both regions significant black migrations were underway. It is possible that from 1783 to 1810 nearly 100,000 slaves from the

Caribbean, Africa, and the Chesapeake arrived in these two regions alone.[9] This reappraisal suggests that in the lower South and lower Mississippi Valley, the long period of evolution of slavery and black society did not end in 1790 as some have argued.[10] Indeed any understanding of African American societies and cultures in the nineteenth-century South should begin with an appreciation of the fact that Africans continued to arrive in large numbers until 1810. Undoubtedly their presence in black communities had an impact on the lives of slaves.

The second observation is that the Revolution did little to stop, or even slow, the foreign slave trade to the lower South. Thus the writers of the Constitution are cast in a different light. For the most part interpretations of their actions have reflected a Whig view of history, meaning that it assumed a positive progress in which today was always better than yesterday. The Constitutional Convention slave trade compromise and the momentous foreign traffic in slaves that it allowed undermines the Whig view. Instead of circumscribing the slave trade or slavery, for that matter, as some historians have argued, delegates to the Constitutional Convention protected both institutions. Many delegates were embarrassed by their actions, especially granting the slave trade a twenty-year immunity from federal restriction in exchange for southern votes to eliminate any restrictions on navigation acts. Knowing that they had failed to uphold the precedents of the Revolution, particularly the 1774 slave trade resolution, and the Declaration of Independence, they offered conflicting and often dubious interpretations of the compromise. Convention delegate James Wilson of Pennsylvania interpreted the slave trade clause as "laying the foundation for banishing slavery out of this country; and though the period is more distant than I could wish, yet it will produce the same kind of gradual change which was pursued in Pennsylvania."[11] In the South, where the truth served them better, delegates scoffed at these illusions and accurately reported to their state conventions that the Constitution protected slavery and the slave trade and that the Constitution in no way ruled that the slave trade must cease in 1808.[12]

By agreeing not to interfere with the slave trade, the delegates also prevented the federal government from regulating slavers. Unlike the British government, which moved in 1788 to reduce mortality on slave ships by imposing limits on the number of slaves carried and requiring surgeons on each voyage, the federal government could do nothing because the Constitution barred it from interfering. Consequently, in the 1790s and the first decade of the 1800s, American slavers carried more people per ton than British slavers and, with few exceptions, refused to carry surgeons to care for the human cargoes they transported.[13]

If it did anything with regard to slavery, the Constitution freed merchants of restrictions that had limited their participation in the transatlantic trade before and during the War for American Independence. Once British colonial mercantile and Confederation Congress commercial barriers were removed, merchants enthusiastically exploited their commercial liberty. They bought slaves from non-British slavers, purchased African trade goods from non-British suppliers, and sold captives to non-British customers in South America and the West Indies. Not surprisingly their participation in African commerce grew rapidly, and by the mid-1790s North American slavers had eclipsed their competitors in North America and Cuba. The rise in African commerce had a profound effect on Charleston. Between 1804 and 1808 Charleston was a major center for importing slaves and outfitting slave voyages. Indeed, during the last two years of the legal trade, 1806 and 1807, only in Liverpool, England, did merchants sponsor more slaving voyages.[14]

The extensive participation of Charleston's middle class merchants in the transatlantic slave trade suggests that they were just as vigorous and enterprising as their northern counterparts. Especially during the first decade of the 1800s, Charleston exhibited all the signs of entrepreneurial development that had appeared in the origins of American economic development in several northern cities. Fortunately the merchants' participation in the slave trade ended by 1810, but unfortunately their capitalistic spirit was snuffed out at the same time, and enterprise and versatility languished. Perhaps, if they had not been constrained by a slave society, the merchants could have channeled their entrepreneurial spirit into other branches of commerce and fulfilled the promise of Revolution.[15] Although numerous factors contributed to its decline, after decades of colonial and post–Revolutionary War growth and prosperity, Charleston shipping and commerce slumped soon after the slave trade ended in 1808. It remained in the doldrums throughout most of the antebellum era.[16]

A third observation is that after the war conditions that slaves encountered worsened rather than improved, as some scholars have suggested. That much of the suffering must be attributed to the greed of Charleston merchants is especially disturbing. Somehow, most white southerners and historians have managed to disassociate the United States from the transatlantic slave trade. According to this view, Americans had nothing to do with enslaving Africans, forcibly removing them from their homes and families, and inflicting the suffering and deaths of the middle passage. However, as this study shows, the slave trade was not something peripheral to the city. Charleston-owned slavers transported Africans to South Carolina, the Caribbean, and South America. Moreover they confined Africans for extended period in pernicious conditions in Charleston, which led to several thousand deaths.

These three concluding observations, prompted by the reappraisal undertaken here, open up a series of related issues that deserve to be explored with renewed vigor. Only by pursuing such questions actively and openly is it possible to begin to understand more clearly life in America during the first generation after the War for American Independence.

Appendix A

SLAVE MERCHANTS AND COMPANIES OF SAVANNAH, NEW ORLEANS, CHARLESTON, AND THE FLORIDA TERRITORY

Merchant or Consignee	Years in Trade	Sales	Slaves Vended
Savannah			
Mordecai Sheftall	1783	1	20
Richard Leake	1784	2	13
Joseph Clay	1784	1	35
Crookshank and Speirs	1784	4	157
Joshua Halton	1785	1	20
Newell and Bolton	1785	1	35
Clay, Telfair, and Co.	1785	1	30
John and William Wallace	1787	2	215
Owners and Thomas; and John and William Wallace	1787	1	20
Robert Montfort	1787	1	8
John Penman	1787	1	20
Patrick Cookshank and C.	1787	1	20
Montfort and Pinder	1787	1	20
Watts and Cole	1787	1	3
Andrew McCredie and Co.	1788	1	11
George Hopkins	1788	1	20
Speirs, Macleod, and Co.	1788–91	5	65
John Olderman (master)	1789	1	68
Richard (Robert?) Wayne	1789, 1792, 1795, and 1798	5	463

Merchant or Consignee	Years in Trade	Sales	Slaves Vended
Bannard Wathington (master)	1789	1	8
Michael Byrne, William Anderson, and Richard Wayne	1790	1	12
John Holman	1790	1	200
Johnston and Robertson	1790	1	4
John Mitchell	1790	1	2
Samuel Wright	1790	1	6
Stephen Hammond	1791	1	25
George Houstoun	1792	1	20
E. Steele (master)	1792	1	4
John Gardner	1792	1	1
Jeremiah Condy	1792	1	360
William Vander Locht	1792	1	18
James Wallace	1793 and 1798	3	41
William Stephen and Joseph Miller	1793	1	80
John Cunningham and Co.	1793	1	70
Robert Watts	1795–99	22	2,697
Anthony Macleod	1795–96	2	114
John Gibbons	1795	2	40
Papengross	1795	1	95
John Caig and Co.	1795	1	500
Robert Gamble	1795	1	1
Belcher and Dickinson	1795	2	80
Gardner and Dickinson	1795–96	3	79
Kennedy and Parker	1796–98	3	244
Caig, Macleod, and Co.	1796–97	4	903
Robert Watts and William Sears	1796	1	87
Ewing and McCalls	1796	1	255
Charles O'Hara and Samuel Austin	1797	1	100
Robert Watts and Robert Miffit	1797	1	95
Edward Swarbreck	1797–98	1	138
James Wallace and William Godfrey (master)	1798	1	19

Merchant or Consignee	Years in Trade	Sales	Slaves Vended
Alexander Watt	1798	1	330
Mein and Mackay	1803	1	200
Hills and Monnox	1803	2	24
Joseph Arnold	1803–4	3	64
Fairchild and Pope	1803	1	20
I. M. Monnox	1804	1	10
John I. Gray	1804	1	25
N. Macleod	1807	1	25
Thomas Lawrence	1807	1	54

New Orleans

McKenzie	1784	1	150
Charles La Chapell	1785 and 1787	2	350
Daniel Clark	1786–88 and 1803	5	651
Francis Mayronne	1788	1	150
Pedro Branley and Zenon Bulls	1790	1	200
William Butler	1794	1	80
Jean Raymond and Co.	1795	1	235
Santiago (James) Fletcher	1799	1	200
Berquin Duvallon	1799	1	20
Jean-Francois Merienlt	1803	1	80
John Frances Farmuel	1803	3	463
Patten and Evans	1804	1	5
William Evans	1804	1	1
John McDonough	1804	3	306
Chew	1804	1	108
Paul Lanusse	1804	1	34
Remy, Pucet, Milet, Ranert, Rowe, Marceline, and Hung	1804	1	120
Dubourg	1804	1	40
Alexander Milne	1804	1	11
P. S. Dubourg and M. De Daguin	1804	1	41

Merchant or Consignee	Years in Trade	Sales	Slaves Vended
Kenner and Henderson	1806–7	3	127
John Ramsey and Co.	1806	1	40
Alexander Milne, Jr.	1806	1	9
Henry Molier and Co.	1806	2	30
Patton and Mossy	1806–7	7	366
Chew and Relf	1807	2	322
T. B. Mitchell	1807	1	50
Phillipe Loubert	1807	1	50

Charleston

David Bourdeaux	1783–85	5	530
J. Versey (Vessey) and Co.	1783–84	4	175
William Sommersall	1783 and 1785	3	299
James and Edward Penman	1783–85	5	538
John Jacobs	1783–84	2	60
R. and Peter Smith	1783	1	200
Hort and Warley	1783	1	30
A. Wilkinson and Co.	1784	2	150
Villepontoux and Co.	1784	1	13
Lewis McPherson	1784	1	20
John Elworthy and Robert Norris	1784	1	440
Smiths, Desaussure, and Darrell	1784	3	102
George Garner	1784	1	90
John Mitchell	1784	1	50
Huger and Fair	1784	1	20
Clay, Telfair, and Co.	1784	1	300
L. Mitchell	1784	1	15
Adam Tunno	1784 and 1786	2	96
Whitter Saltus, Joseph Nessey, and Richard E. Hinson	1784	1	5
Thomas Stewart	1784	1	12
Ralph di Pass	1784	1	15

Merchant or Consignee	Years in Trade	Sales	Slaves Vended
Colcock and Gibbons	1784–85	2	26
Cudworth and Waller	1784	1	25
Bryan (master)	1784	1	2
Smiths, Desaussure, and Darrell; and Ball, Jennings, and Co.	1784	4	1,156
John and Thomas Manson	1784	1	280
Fisher, Hughs, and Edwards	1784	3	546
Alexander Ross and Nathaniel Russell	1784	1	10
John Edwards	1784	1	23
Courtauld and Ogier	1784	2	96
Edward Penman	1784–87	10	155
John Walter	1784	1	5
Miller	1784	1	4
William Duncombe	1784	1	2
William Macleod and Co.	1784–85, 1799, and 1804	4	984
Scarborough and Cooke	1784	1	13
John Blake and Josiah Smith	1784	1	7
John Todd	1784	1	2
Grant	1784	1	12
Grant and Simmons	1784	1	4
Edwin Neusville and Thomas Bonsall	1784	1	59
William Pitt	1784	1	2
Winthrop, Todd, and Winthrop	1785	1	117
Winthrop and Co.	1785	1	130
J. Teasdale	1785	1	29
Scarborough	1785	2	58
M. Timmel	1785	1	19
Penman, Freeman, and Co.	1785	1	21

Merchant or Consignee	Years in Trade	Sales	Slaves Vended
Daniel Jennings, Winthrop, and Co.; and Smith and Co.	1785	1	15
Smiths, Desaussure, Darrell, and Co,; and Jennings and Winthrop	1785	1	214
Freeman and Pringle	1785	1	20
Russell and Co.	1785	1	1
Robert Hazelhurst and Co.	1785	1	152
Nathaniel Russell	1784–86 and 1805–6	7	832
John Walters Gibbs	1785	1	20
Robert Norris	1785	1	206
Andrew Pleyn and Lorentz Waaban (master)	1785	1	188
Andrew Pleyn	1785	4	228
Ben Gardin	1785	1	164
Scarborough and Cooke; and Theodore Galliard	1785	1	340
Lawrence Campbell	1785	3	61
James Anderson and R. and W. Lindsey	1785	1	157
W. Freeman	1785	1	15
William Lee	1785	1	9
R. Vaughn (master)	1785	1	18
Fisher and Edwards	1785	2	715
Daniel O'Hara	1785–87	6	126
Nathaniel Cudworth and Co.	1785	1	30
Theodore Gaillard	1785	1	6
John Penman	1785	1	20
McCully Righton and T. T. Tucker	1785	1	4
Hall and Edward Penman	1785	1	6
Jacob Milligan	1786	1	20
Conyers and Holmes	1786	1	32
Daniel Hall and Co.	1786	1	10

Merchant or Consignee	Years in Trade	Sales	Slaves Vended
H. Grant	1786	1	8
Bowman	1786	1	88
F. McKenzio	1786	1	5
Crafts and Co.	1786	1	1
A. Sasportas	1786	1	10
Smith	1786	1	2
F. E. Moore	1786	1	15
W. Thompson, A. Ewing, and A. Urisholm	1786	1	8
Thomas Stewart	1786	2	5
B. Modie and Edward Penman	1786	1	31
Brailsford and Co.; Adam Tunno and Putman	1786	1	24
F. di Costa	1786	1	3
W. Crafts and Co.	1786	1	3
D. O'Hara and William Trenholm	1786	1	80
D. Jennings	1786	1	5
G. Saltonstall	1786	1	4
Henry Todd and Frank Forbes	1786	1	5
Thomas Stewart	1787	1	14
Will Cooke	1787	1	2
Jennings and Co.	1787	1	2
Edward Penman, J. Neilson, and R. and W. Lindsey	1787	1	11
J. C. Todd	1787	1	1
Wilkinson, Cooke, and Peppin	1787	2	173
William Trenholm	1787	1	12
George Houstoun	1787	1	20
David Denoon	1787–88	2	58
T. Anderson	1787	1	50
Colcock and Grahm	1790	1	100
F. Fitzsimmons and William Stephens	1792	1	50

Merchant or Consignee	Years in Trade	Sales	Slaves Vended
Daniel O'Hara and John Connaly	1793	1	50
Henry O'Hara	1804	1	20
James Scott	1804–5	4	18
John Hanahan	1804	1	30
Verree and Blair	1804–7	6	588
Tunno and Cox	1804–7	10	1,446
Mortimer and Heron	1804	1	100
S. E. Turner	1804–5	2	113
W. T. Hudson	1804	1	215
Macbeth, Henry, and Co.	1804	2	225
Thomas Tunno and John Price; and Tunno and Cox	1804 and 1806	3	913
William Boyd	1804–7	26	7,218
J. and N. Bixby	1804	1	148
Andrew Smylie	1804	2	42
Napier, Smith, and Co.	1804–5	3	318
James Miller, Sr.	1804 and 1806	4	544
Cohen and Moses	1804 and 1807	3	71
Alex McGillivray	1804	1	50
Thomas Tunno and John Price	1804–7	7	1,726
William Holmes and Co.	1804–5	3	29
Alexander and John McClure	1804	1	243
James Broadfoot	1804 and 1806	5	942
James Broadfoot and James Lee	1804	1	165
John Potter	1804–5	2	198
Jacob De Leon	1804	1	20
James Miller, Jr.	1804	1	67
M. M. Campbell	1804–5 and 1807	7	179
Phillips and Gardner	1804–7	27	2,973
Gibson and Broadfoot	1804–7	12	3,097
William Payne	1804	1	30

Merchant or Consignee	Years in Trade	Sales	Slaves Vended
David M'Kelvey	1804 and 1806–7	3	418
John S. Adams	1804–7	13	2,375
Peter Ayrault	1805	1	116
Charles Bishop	1805	1	40
Cooper (master)	1805	1	224
George Parker	1805 and 1807	2	173
N. Bixby	1805	2	245
Clarke Cooke	1805 and 1807	3	375
Thomas Baker	1805	1	30
Ellison and Kennedy	1805	1	99
John Price	1805	3	722
William Porter	1805–7	4	88
C. Fitzimmons	1805 and 1807	2	259
John Duncan	1805 and 1807	2	215
T. W. Rawlinson	1806	2	530
J. Kennedy	1806	1	200
Everingham and Bineham	1806	2	340
James Quin	1806	1	67
J. Cooper	1806–7	2	386
Ebenezer P. Shearman (master)	1806	1	102
John Watson and Co.	1806	4	1,233
Spencer Mann	1806	1	230
Martin Benson (master)	1806	1	33
Adam Gilchrist	1806	1	198
John W. Footman	1806	1	5
William Aiken	1806	1	30
J. Callaghan and Thomas Vincent	1806	1	120
William McCormick	1806	1	54
Boothroyd (master)	1806–7	2	117
F. Tavel	1806	1	105
P. Mooney and John Everingham	1806	1	205

Merchant or Consignee	Years in Trade	Sales	Slaves Vended
Josh A. Brown	1806	1	10
M. Kelly	1806–7	3	488
Charles Christian	1806–7	3	248
Henry and John Kerr	1806–7	3	520
Nathaniel Ingram	1806–7	2	360
Robert Eason	1806–7	6	72
John Callaghan	1806–7	3	295
David Lopez	1806–7	3	60
Christian and D'Wolf	1806–7	18	2,262
Delaire and Canut	1807	3	312
P. Cassin	1807	1	78
Andrew Holmes	1807	1	55
J. Christie and G. Parker	1807	1	100
William Gray	1807	1	240
Hamilton and Gray	1807	1	302
R. Eason			
J. Cashman	1807	1	200
A. Isaacks, Jr.	1807	1	15
William Porter	1807	2	32
Thomas Ogier	1807	1	76
Benjamin Eddy (master)	1807	1	157
Frances Depau	1807	8	1,441
Nautre (master)	1807	1	39
Jacob DeLeon	1807	2	37
J. Christie	1807	1	200
James D'Wolf	1807	1	162
William Gray and William Timmons	1807	1	117
Thomas Vincent	1807	2	238
William Broadfoot	1807	1	460
A. Collins	1807	1	70
Peter Kennedy	1807	1	125
John MacNamara	1807	1	95

Merchant or Consignee	Years in Trade	Sales	Slaves Vended
Bailey and Waller	1807	1	40
J. B. Cotton	1807	1	218
Lyon (master)	1807	1	242
William Timmons	1807	1	156
William Timmons and John Timmons	1807	1	100
John Everingham	1807	1	162
Thomas Tunno	1807	1	80
John Stone	1807	1	136
C. and H. O'Hara	1807	1	214

The Florida Territory

Zephaniah Kingsley	1802 and 1806	3	269
Panton, Leslie, and Co.	1802	2	177
Juan Vermonet, William Cook, and Luis Gleuse	1804	1	200
Daniel Hurlburt (master)	1810	1	39
James Cashen	1810	1	28
Aerendondo and Son	1810	1	548
John Fraser	1810	2	266
Joseph Walden and Co.	1810	1	300

NORTH AMERICAN FOREIGN
SLAVE ARRIVALS, SLAVE VOYAGES,
AND FOREIGN SLAVE SALES, 1783–1810

This appendix is a compilation of post–Revolutionary War documentation of North American foreign slave arrivals, slave voyages, and foreign slave sales encountered during the research for this project. Each departure and North American disembarkation has been listed separately. If the only information available on a North American slave voyage or disembarkation is a sales advertisement or news of a slaving voyage or venture, it has also been listed. The information has been grouped into fourteen categories:

1. Date
2. Vessel type (rigging) and name
3. Master(s)
4. Activity (cleared, arrived, reported, disembarked, advertised, etc.) and location
5. Number of slaves
6. Origin of slaves
7. Consignee
8. Middle passage in days
9. Transshipment in days
10. Registry location
11. Owners (either vessel owners or voyage sponsors)
12. Vessel size in tons
13. Source(s)
14. Notes

The appendix layout was patterned after similar compilations in Elizabeth Donnan's *Documents Illustrative of the History of the Slave Trade to America,* Jay Coughtry's *The Notorious Triangle: Rhode Island and the African Slave Trade, 1700–1807,* and David Eltis, David Richardson, Stephen D. Behrendt, and Herbert S. Klein's *The Transatlantic Slave Trade: A Database on CD-Rom.*

These works greatly facilitated research for this project, but despite their richness they provide only limited information on the post–Revolutionary War North

American slave trade. Elizabeth Donnan, who performed her research long before microfilming and many southern archives had come into being, had access to only a handful of newspapers and merchants and customs records. In his study of the Rhode Island trade, Jay Coughtry included information on the post–Revolutionary War trade to North America only when the slavers from the region disembarked captives there. *The Transatlantic Slave Trade* database is more comprehensive, but for the North American trade David Eltis and his colleagues relied heavily on Donnan's and Coughtry's research and western European archival materials.

Drawing upon archival materials such as southern North American newspapers, other port and customhouse records, and merchant's and planter's papers this appendix provides a more comprehensive compilation of post–Revolutionary War North American foreign slave trade arrivals and voyages, the foreign slave trade between the West Indies and the North American mainland, clearances from the Carolinas and Georgia for Africa, foreign slave sales, slave vessel owners, and slaving venture investors. When available the primary source or sources were listed for a clearing, voyage, report, or sale. Therefore secondary sources such as *The Transatlantic Slave Trade* are cited only when primary sources were not located. It is hoped that slave trade scholars and nonacademics will find this approach and the information contained herein useful and accessible.

THE CD-ROM DATABASE

The database for this appendix is available on the accompanying CD-ROM as an Adobe Acrobat PDF file. Adobe Acrobat Reader, version 4 or higher, is required for viewing the database. A free copy can be downloaded from www.adobe.com. Please note that the database, because of the historical nature of the records surveyed, contains many variant spellings. Below is a list of people, vessels, and places that appear in the records.

SEARCH TERMS FOR THE CD-ROM DATABASE

People and Firms

Adams. *See also* J. S. Adams, John Adams, John S. Adams, Jonathon Adams, William Adams
Adams, J. S. *See also* John S. Adams
Adams, John. *See also* J. S. Adams, John S. Adams
Adams, John S. *See also* J. S. Adams, John Adams
Adams, Jonathon
Adams, William

Adamson
Addison, John
Ad[?]ain, George
Aiken, William
Ainsworth, John
Alexander
Allen, Caleb. *See also* Caleb, W. Allen
Allen, Caleb W. *See also* Caleb, Allen
Allen, Cyrus
Allen, Philip

Allen, Samuel
Allen, William S.
Allen, Zachariah
Almy, Job
Almy, John
Almy, Samuel
Ambrose
Ambrose, Robert
Anderson
Anderson, James
Anderson, John
Anderson, T.

Anderson, William
Armand, Sebastián
Arnold
Arnold, Joseph
Arnold, Perry, G.
Arredondo. *See also*
   Arredondo
Arrendondo. *See also*
   Arredondo
Ashston, John. *See also* John
   Ashton
Ashton, John. *See also* John
   Ashton
Aspinall
Atkins. *See also* Atkus
Atkus. *See also* Atkins
Auchmuty, Robert N. *See also*
   Robert Auchumty
Auchumty, Robert. *See also*
   Robert N. Auchmuty
Austin, Samuel
Ayala
Ayrault, Peter

Babbit, Jacob
Backhouse, Daniel
Bacon, John
Bailey
Bain, John
Baker, John
Baker, Thomas
Baker, William
Baldwin, Henry
Baldwin, P.
Ball
Ballenton, Thomas
Ballou, David
Bannatyne, A.
Barbados
Barber
Barber, Elijah
Barlow
Barnard
Barnet
Barracoa
Barrow, John
Barton, Thomas
Basden
Bass, Edward

Bates
Bates, Merit. *See also* Merrit
   Bates
Bates, Merrit. *See also* Merit
   Bates
Batty
Baxter, James
Beck
Begg
Begg, William
Bel
Belcher
Belhome
Bennet. *See also* Bennett
Bennet, Robert. *See also*
   Bennett, Finley
Bennett. *See also* Pardon
   Bennett, Bennet
Bennett, Pardon
Bennox
Benson, Martin
Berry
Bert
Biddicar
Bidlake, John
Bigley, John
Billings
Billings, Rufus
Bineham
Bixby
Bixby, J.
Bixby, N.
Blair
Blake, John
Blanck
Blight
Bloy, James
Boit, John
Bolton
Bonny
Bonsall, Thomas
Boothroyd
Boss
Boss, Chilcutt
Boss, Edward
Boss, John
Bosworth, Benjamin
Bosworth, Benjamin, II
Bosworth, Benjamin, Jr.

Bourdeaux, Daniel
Bourdeaux, David
Bourn. *See also* Bourne
Bourn, Shearjashub,
Bourn, Shearyashub
Bourne, John
Bourne, Shearjashub
Boutcher, James
Bowen, Hail
Bowen, Jabaez, Jr. *See also*
   Jabez Bowen, Jr.
Bowen, Jabez, Jr. *See also*
   Jabaez Bowen, Jr.
Bowen, Jonathon
Bowen, Mary
Bowen, Pardon
Bowers
Bowes
Bowes, Edward
Bowie, James
Bowman
Boyd
Boyd, Edward
Boyd, William
Bradford
Bradford, Henry
Bradford, Leonard. *See also*
   Leonard J. Bradford
Bradford, Leonard J.
Bradford, William. *See also*
   William Bradford, III
Bradford, William, III
Bradley
Brailsford
Brand
Branley
Branley, Pedro
Brattel, James. *See also* James
   Brattell, James Brattle
Brattell, James. *See also* James
   Brattel, James Brattle
Brattle, James. *See also* James
   Brattel, James Brattell
Brattle, John
Bray
Brayton, James
Brew. *See also* Brow
Briggs
Briggs, Benjamin

Briggs, Elijah
Briggs, Nathaniel
Briggs, Thomas
Briggs, Willard
Broadfoot
Broadfoot, J. *See also* James
  Broadfoot
Broadfoot, James. *See also*
  J. Broadfoot
Broadfoot, William
Brodie
Brookings
Brooks
Broomley, John
Brow. *See also* Brew
Brown. *See also* Browne
Brown, Benjamin
Brown, Daniel M.
Brown, Elisha
Brown, James
Brown, John
Brown, Josh A. *See also*
  Joshua Brown
Brown, Joshua. *See also* Josh
  A. Brown
Brown, Oliver
Brown, Sam. *See also* Samuel
  Brown
Brown, Samuel. *See also* Sam
  Brown
Brown, Shearjashub
Brown, Thomas
Brown, William, Jr.
Brownbill
Brownell, Paul
Browns
Brownton, Thomas
Bryan
Buchanan
Buell, Benjamin
Builbert, Augustus
Bulls
Bulls, Zenon
Buncombe, William
Burdett. *See also* Burditt
Burditt. *See also* Burdett
Burges
Burling
Burnet
Burr

Burr, Shubael
Burt
Burt, Alvan
Butler, Cyrus
Butler, William
Butman, John. *See also* John
  Buttman
Buttman, John. *See also* John
  Butman
Butts, John
Byrne, Michael

Cabot
Caig
Cain
Caldcleugh
Callaghan, J. *See also* John
  Callaghan
Callaghan, John. *See also*
  J. Callaghan
Calvert, Anthony
Camden, William
Campbell
Campbell, L. *See also*
  Lawrence Campbell
Campbell, Lawrence. *See also*
  L. Campbell
Campbell, M'M. *See also*
  Mc. M. Campbell
Campbell, Mc. M. *See also*
  M'M Campbell
Canut
Capauze, J.Castle
Carey, Archibald
Carey, Frederick
Carg, John
Carlile, Ludwick. *See also*
  Carlite
Carlite. *See also* Ludwick
  Carlile
Carlton
Carnes, John
Carr
Carr, George W.
Carr, Isaac
Carr, Samuel
Carroll, James P.
Carson. *See also* John Carson
Carson, John
Carter, Alfred

Caruth
Cashen, James
Cashman, J.
Cassin, P.
Castandet, Louis
Cathelin
Catlin
Caton, Joseph
Cayenne
Chace. *See also* Chase,
  Samuel
Chace, Jesse
Chace, Samuel
Champlin
Champlin, Christian
Champlin, George
Champlin, John
Champlin, Robert
Champlin, William
Channing, Walter
Chaple, Jose
Charters, Thomas
Chase, Samuel
Chew
Cheyney, Daniel
Child, Cromwell
Chilton, John
Chinic
Christian. *See also* Charles
  Christian
Christian, Charles
Christie, J.
Church
Church, Edward
Church, William
Churchill
Churchill, Ansell
Clare, Thomas
Clark. *See also* Clarke
Clark, Charles. *See also*
  Charles Clarke
Clark, Daniel
Clark, John. *See also* John
  Clarke
Clark, Jonathan
Clark, Peleg. *See also* Peleg
  Clarke
Clark, Samuel
Clark, Seth
Clarke. *See also* Clark

Willing, Richard
Willis, William
Willy
Wilson
Windsor
Winthrop
Wise, Diedereck
Wood
Wood, Godfrey

Wood, John
Wood, Joseph
Wood, Peleg. *See also* Peleg
   Wood, Jr.
Wood, Peleg, Jr. *See also*
   Peleg Wood
Wood, William
Woodberry, Isachar
Woodman, Richard

Woodward
Wordrop, John
Wright, Samuel
Wright, Thomas
Wyer

Yeates
Young
Young, John

Vessels

Abeona (schooner)
Abigail (schooner)
Active (schooner)
Active (ship)
Actor (schooner)
Adherbal (brig)
Adriana (brig)
Adventure (brig)
Adventure (schooner)
Africa (brig)
Africa (ship)
Agenora (brig)
Agenoria (ship)
Agent (ship)
Albert (brig)
Alcade (ship)
Alcaid (Alcade) (schooner)
Alert
Alert (brig)
Alert (ship)
Alerto (brig)
Alexander (brig)
Alexander (ship)
Alexandria (brig)
Alfred (brig)
Alice (Ellis) (ship)
Aligator (brig)
Alliance (sloop)
Almira (schooner)
Almy (brig)
Amanda (schooner)
Amastad (ship)
Amazon (ship)
Amelia (Amedie) (brig)
Amelia (brig)
Amelia (schooner)
America (brig)
America (ship)

America (snow)
Amistad
Amity
Amity (sloop)
Andromache
Andromache (ship)
Angenoria (ship)
Ann (Anna) (ship)
Ann (schooner)
Ann (ship)
Ann and Harriot (schooner)
Ann and Hope (brig)
Anna (schooner)
Anna (ship)
Anna Maria (brig)
Anne
Anne (Anna or Ann) (ship)
Anne (ship)
Antigallican (ship)
Aquila
Argus (Argo) (brig)
Argus (brig)
Ariel (schooner)
Armed Neutrality (brig)
Armed Neutrality (ship)
Ascension (ship)
Aspinall (ship)
Aurora
Aurora (brig)
Aurora (schooner)
Aurora (sloop)

Balandra La Favorecida
Baltimore (brig)
Baltimore (sloop)
Barbados Packet (brig)
Batcan Ranger
Batty

Bayard (brig)
Bayard (ship)
Beaver (schooner)
Becca (sloop)
Bellona (ship)
Belvidere (schooner)
Benjamin (ship)
Bennington (brig)
Betsey
Betsey (brig)
Betsey (schooner)
Betsey (ship)
Betsey (sloop)
Betsey and Polly (brig)
Betsey and Polly (ship)
Betsy (schooner)
Betsy (sloop)
Blackney (schooner)
Brandywine (brig)
Brilliant (brig)
Brother and Sister
   (schooner)
Brothers
Brothers (ship)
Bruges-Burgh

Cambridge (schooner)
Camden (brig)
Carolina (brig)
Carolina (sloop)
Caroline (sloop)
Castlesemple
Catalán (brig)
Catherine (brig)
Ceres (ship)
Chance (schooner)
Charles and Harriot (ship)
Charles-Town (ship)

Charleston (ship)
Charlotte (brig)
Charlotte (schooner)
Charlotte (ship)
Chatham (schooner)
Christiana (schooner)
Christopher (ship)
Cirjla (schooner)
Clara (ship)
Clarissa (snow)
Clementia (ship)
Clementine (ship)
Cleopatra (ship)
Clinton (brig)
Collector (schooner)
Columbia (brig)
Columbia (ship)
Columbia (sloop)
Commerce (brig)
Commerce (schooner)
Commerce (ship)
Commerce (sloop)
Comte du Norde (frigate)
Concord
Concord (schooner)
Constance (brig)
Coralline (sloop)
Cornwallace (brig)
Cotton Planter
Craydon (ship)

Daniel and Mary (brig)
Daphne (ship)
Davenport
Davis (schooner)
Deborah (sloop)
Delight (schooner)
Desire (brig)
Diana (frigate)
Diana (ship)
Diana (sloop)
Dispatch (brig)
Dispatch (schooner)
Doe (ship)
Dolphin (brig)
Dolphin (schooner)
Dolphin (ship)
Don Galvez
Don Galvez (brig)
Don Quijote (brig)

Donâ Juana (frigate)
Doria (schooner)
Dove (sloop)
Dove (snow)
Duddon (brig)
Duddon (ship)

Eagle
Eagle (brig)
Eagle (schooner)
Eagle (ship)
Eagle (sloop)
Edward and Edmund
   (schooner)
Edward and Mary (brig)
El Gobernador Miró
   (schooner)
El Guipuscoano
El Mississippian
El Postillón (brig)
Eleanor (ship)
Eliza
Eliza (brig)
Eliza (Elisa) (brig)
Eliza (schooner)
Eliza (ship)
Eliza (snow)
Eliza and Mary (brig)
Elizabeth (brig)
Elizabeth (ship)
Elizabeth (sloop)
Elizabeth and Sarah (brig)
Emily (ship)
Empresa
Empress (brig)
Enterprise
Enterprise (brig)
Enterprize (schooner)
Enterprize (ship)
Espasia
Ester (schooner)
Esther (Easter) (ship)
Esther (ship)
Ethiopian (brig)
Eunice (brig)
Eunice (schooner)
Euphemia (brig)
Exchange (sloop)
Experiment (brig)
Experiment (schooner)

Experiment (ship)
Experiment (sloop)

Fabian (ship)
Factor (brig)
Fair American (brig)
Fair American (ship)
Fair Eliza (brig)
Fair Eliza (ship)
Fair Eliza (snow)
Fair Trader (schooner)
Fairy (schooner)
Fame (brig)
Fanny (brig)
Fanny (schooner)
Fanny (ship)
Fanny (sloop)
Farmer (brig)
Farnham (ship)
Faulkner (brig)
Fausse Riviére (brig)
Favorite
Favorite (brig)
Fawn (brig)
Felicity (schooner)
Felix
Felix (schooner)
Ferret (cutter)
Ferrit (cutter)
Firebrand
Flora (schooner)
Flora (ship)
Flying Fish (schooner)
Fortuna (William and Mary)
Fortunas
Fortune (sloop)
Fourth of July (brig)
Fourth of July (ship)
Fox (sloop)
Frances (ship)
Franklin (frigate)
Franklin (schooner)
Franklin (ship)
Free Love (sloop)
Friends Adventure
Friends Adventure
   (schooner)
Friendship (brig)
Friendship (schooner)
Friendship (sloop)

Gambia (brig)
Gangonelli (schooner)
Gehermaads Gregers Jual
  (ship)
General Campbell (brig)
General Claiborne (ship)
General Eaton (ship)
General Greene (schooner)
General Greene (sloop)
General Huth (ship)
General Nichols (ship)
General Shirley (schooner)
George (brig)
George (ship)
George and Mary (ship)
George Clinton (brig)
Georgetown (schooner)
Gibralter (sloop)
Gibralter (sloop)
Gold Dust (schooner)
Good Intent (schooner)
Good Intent (sloop)
Good Intentions (sloop)
Governor Claiborne (ship)
Governor Dodeswell (ship)
Governor Dodsworth (ship)
Governor Miró (schooner)
Governor Wentworth (ship)
Gustavia (ship)

Haabet (brig)
Halifax Packet (brig)
Hamilton (ship)
Hampden (ship)
Hannah
Hannah (brig)
Hannah (schooner)
Hannah (snow)
Happy Return (brig)
Harmony (schooner)
Harriet (schooner)
Hawke (brig)
Hawthorne (cutter)
Hazard
Hazard (lugger)
Hazard (schooner)
Hazzard (lugger)
Heart of Oak (ship)
Hector (ship)
Hercules

Hercules (schooner)
Heroine (brig)
Heroine (ship)
Heron
Hibernia (schooner)
Hibernia (ship)
Hindostan (ship)
Hindustan
Hiram (brig)
Hiram (schooner)
Hiram (ship)
Hiram (sloop)
Hope
Hope (brig)
Hope (schooner)
Hope (ship)
Hope (sloop)
Hope (snow)
Hopewell (schooner)
Horizon (brig)
Horizon (ship)

Ida (brig)
Independence (ship)
Independence (sloop)
Industry (brig)
Industry (schooner)
Industry (ship)
Industry (sloop)
Isabella (brig)

Jack Park (ship)
James
James (brig)
James (schooner)
James (ship)
Jane (brig)
Jane (ship)
Jane and Eliza (brig)
Jason
Jason (brig)
Jennett (brig)
Jenny (ship)
Jesse (brig)
Jeune Felicité (brig)
Joana (frigate)
John
John (brig)
John (ship)
John Jones (ship)

Juliana
Juliet (sloop)
Juno
Juno (brig)
Juno (schooner)
Juno (ship)
Jupiter (brig)

Kate (Katy) (brig)
Kate (ship)
Katy
Katy (brig)
Katy (schooner)
Kerrie (snow)
Kingston (schooner)
Kitty (schooner)

L'Epine
La Confiance (brig)
La Diana
La Dichosa (frigate)
La Feliz (frigate)
La Joven Feliciana (brig)
La Louisiana (schooner)
La Margarita (frigate)
La Paloma (ship)
La Rosalía (brig)
La Thètes
La Victoria
La Victoria (sloop)
Lady Langford (brig)
Lady Nelson (brig)
Lady Shammelmann (ship)
Lady Walterstorff (ship)
Lafourche
Lark (brig)
Lark (ship)
Lark (sloop)
Laurel (brig)
Laurel (schooner)
Lavina (sloop)
Lavinia (brig)
Lavinia (sloop)
Le Guillamne
Le Leger (brig)
Le Vigilante (brig)
Leander (brig)
Lear (Lier) (brig)
Leon (brig)
Liberty

Liberty (schooner)
Liberty (ship)
Liberty (sloop)
Lindamen (brig)
Lindeman (brig)
Little Ann (brig)
Little Hornet (snow)
Little Jean (brig)
Little Mary
Little Mary (brig)
Little Mary (sloop)
Little Ned (sloop)
Little Peggy (sloop)
Little Sally (brig)
Little Watt (brig)
Littlewill (schooner)
Lively (ship)
Lonely Mary (sloop)
Lord Rodney (ship)
Loren (brig)
Los Siete Hermanos
   (schooner)
Louisa
Louisa (brig)
Louisa (cutter)
Louisa (ship)
Louisa (sloop)
Louisiana
Louisiana (brig)
Louisiana (ship)
Louisiana Packet (brig)
Love and Mary (sloop)
Love and Unity (sloop)
Lucky (brig)
Lucy (schooner)
Lupin
Lydia (ship)
Lydia (sloop)

Macclesfield (ship)
Mae (ship)
Magdeleine (ship)
Manning
Margaret (ship)
Maria (brig)
Maria (schooner)
Maria (ship)
Mariah (brig)
Mariam (brig)
Marian (brig)

Marie (ship)
Marion (brig)
Marquis of Huntley (ship)
Martha Crawley (schooner)
Mary
Mary (brig)
Mary (schooner)
Mary (ship)
Mary (sloop)
Mary (snow)
Mary Ann
Mary Ann (schooner)
Mary-Ann (brig)
Mary-Ann (schooner)
Mendon (ship)
Mentor (brig)
Mentor (ship)
Mercury (brig)
Mercury (schooner)
Mercury (ship)
Mercury (sloop)
Merry Quaker
Minerva
Minerva (brig)
Minerva (brig)
Minerva (ship)
Minerva (sloop)
Minerva (snow)
Miriam (schooner)
Molly (schooner)
Molly (sloop)
Molly (snow)
Montezuma (ship)
Monticello (ship)
Moreveto (brig)
Morning Star (sloop)

Nabby (schooner)
Nancies (schooner)
Nancy
Nancy (brig)
Nancy (Nanna or Nanny)
   (ship)
Nancy (schooner)
Nancy (ship)
Nancy (sloop)
Nancy (snow)
Nancy Wright (schooner)
Nantasket (schooner)
Navarro (brig)

Navarro (schooner)
Neptune (brig)
Neptune (schooner)
Neptune (snow)
New Hope (schooner)
New Hope (sloop)
New Orleans
New Orleans (schooner)
New York Packet (sloop)
Nicholson (ship)
Nile (ship)
Ninfa (frigate)
Norfolk (brig)
Notre Dame des Carmes
Nymph (ship)

Ocean
Old England (ship)
Olive Branch
   (schooner)
Onieda (ship)
Orange (brig)

Pacific (ship)
Patience (sloop)
Patty (brig)
Patty (ship)
Paul Hamilton (brig)
Peace of Plenty (sloop)
Peacock (schooner)
Pearl (brig)
Peatt (snow)
Peggy (brig)
Peggy (schooner)
Peggy (sloop)
Peje
Perserverance (ship)
Perseverance (brig)
Peter (sloop)
Phoebe
Phoebe (schooner)
Pigou
Polly (brig)
Polly (schooner)
Polly (ship)
Polly (sloop)
Polly and Harriot (brig)
Polly and Harriot (sloop)
Polly and Sally
Porgy (sloop)

Port Mary (ship)
Prince William (ship)
Providence (brig)
Providence (schooner)
Providence (ship)
Prudence (brig)
Prudent (brig)
Prudent (schooner)
Punch (brig)

Queen of Naples (brig)

Rachel (brig)
Rackoon (schooner)
Rambler (brig)
Ranger (sloop)
Rebecca (brig)
Rebecca (sloop)
Reliance
Reliance (schooner)
Reliance (sloop)
Republican (brig)
Republican (schooner)
Resolution (brig)
Resolution (schooner)
Resource (ship)
Richmond
Rio (brig)
Rising Sun (sloop)
Rising Sun (snow)
Robert (brig)
Robert (ship)
Robin (ship)
Roebuck (schooner)
Rolla (ship)
Rosalie
Roseau (brig)
Ruby (ship)
Ruth

St. John
St. Loren (brig)
Sally (brig)
Sally (schooner)
Sally (ship)
Sally (sloop)
Sally (snow)
Sampson (brig)
Samuel (ship)
San Francisco (schooner)

Sandwich (brig)
Santa Catalina (frigate)
Sarah (brig)
Sarah (ship)
Savana (sloop)
Schooner
Sea Flower
Sea Flower (ship)
Seaflower (schooner)
Seminarius (ship)
Semiramis (ship)
Sevilla (frigate)
Sidney (sloop)
Sir William Douglas (brig)
Sir William Douglas (ship)
Sisters (ship)
Sophie (brig)
Speculation (lugger)
Speedwell
Speedwell (brig)
Speedwell (sloop)
Sprightly (cutter)
Stork (brig)
Success (brig)
Success (schooner)
Success (ship)
Suckey and Sophia (schooner)
Sugary (schooner)
Sukey (schooner)
Sukey (snow)
Sukey and Polly (brig)
Sultan (ship)
Superior
Surprise (schooner)
Susan
Susan (schooner)
Susan (Susannah) (schooner)
Susannah (brig)
Susannah (schooner)
Swallow (schooner)
Swan (brig)
Swift (brig)
Swift (ship)
Sydney (sloop)
Syren (brig)
Syren of Kennebeck
   (schooner)

Tamez
Tartar (brig)

Tartar (ship)
Terrible (brig)
Thomas (brig)
Thomas (ship)
Thomas Jefferson (ship)
Three Brothers (ship)
Three Friends (schooner)
Three Friends (ship)
Three Sisters (brig)
Three Sisters (schooner)
Trenton (ship)
Trenton (Truxton) (ship)
Trial (brig)
Triton (sloop)
Triumph (schooner)
Trusty
Tryal (brig)
Tryal (schooner)
Two Brothers
Two Brothers (ship)
Two Friends (brig)
Two Friends (schooner)
Two Friends (sloop)

Union
Union (brig)
Union (schooner)
Union (ship)
United States (ship)

Venus (brig)
Venus (ship)
Venus (sloop)
Vulture (schooner)

Wanton (schooner)
Warren (brig)
Washington (brig)
Washington (schooner)
Washington (ship)
Wealthy Ann (brig)
Whim (snow)
Wilhelmina (brig)
William
William (brig)
William (schooner)
William (ship)
William (sloop)
William and Margaret
   (schooner)

William and Mary (ship)
Willing Quaker (ship)
Woodburn (schooner)

Yeopim (schooner)
Young Adam
Young Adam (schooner)

Places

Abaco
Africa
Anomabu, Gold Coast
Augusta, GA

Bahamas
Baltimore, MD
Bance Island, Sierra Leone
Bath, NC
Beaufort, NC
Beaufort, SC
Berry Islands, Bahamas
Bight of Benin
Bight of Biafra
Boston, MA
Bristol, RI
Britain. *See also* England
Brunswick, NC
Buenos Aires, Argentina

Cape Coast, Gold Coast
Cape Mount, Sierra Leone
Cape of Good Hope
Cape Verde
Cape Vine
Cartegena
Cartegena
Charleston, SC
Congo, West-Central Africa
Connecticut (CT)
Cuba

Denmark
Dominica
Dominica, West Indies

Edenton, NC
England

Florida (FL)
France

Gambia, Senegambia
Gambia River, Senegambia
Georgetown, SC
Georgia (GA)
Gold Coast

Gorée, Senegambia
Green Island, GA
Grenada

Havana, Cuba
Hispaniola

Iles de Loss, Sierra Leone
Isle de France

Kingston, Jamaica

Little Compton, RI
Liverpool, England
Loango, West-Central Africa
London, England
Louisiana (LA)

Martinique
Maryland (MD)
Massachusetts (MA)
Mississippi (MS)
Mississippi River
Mobile, West Florida
Montevideo, Uruguay
Montserrat

Nassau, Bahamas
Natchez, MS
New Bern, NC
New England
New Hampshire (NH)
New Haven, CT
New London, CT
New Orleans, LA
New York
Newburyport, MA
Newport, RI
Norfolk County, VA
Norfolk, VA
North Carolina (NC)
North Kingston, RI

Philadelphia
Portland, MA
Portsmouth, NH
Portugal

Prince's Island, Bight of Biafra
Providence, RI

Rhode Island (RI)
Rio de la Plata, South America
Rio Nunez, Sierra Leone
Rio Pongo, Sierra Leone
River Gambia, Senegambia
Roanoke, NC

St. Augustine, FL
St. Croix, Virgin Islands
St. Eustatia
St. Johns River, Florida
St. Thomas
Salem, MA
Salem, RI
Savannah, GA
Senegal
Senegambia
Sheba (Sherbro), Sierra Leone
Sherba (Sherbro), Sierra Leone
Sierra Leone
South Carolina (SC)
Spain
Stono Inlet, SC
Surinam

Tiverton, RI
Tortola

United States

Virginia (VA)

Warren, RI
Windward Coast

Zanzibar

NOTES

INTRODUCTION

1. "Sullivan's Island Honors Slaves," *(Columbia) State*, July 3, 1999, B5.

2. Peter H. Wood, *Black Majority: Negroes in South Carolina from 1670 through the Stono Rebellion* (New York: Alfred A. Knopf, 1974), xiv.

3. Elizabeth Donnan, "The New England Slave Trade after the Revolution," *New England Quarterly* 3 (January 1930): 804–28; B. M. Bigelow, "Aaron Lopes, Merchant of Newport," *New England Quarterly* 4 (October 1931): 757–76; Sarah Deutsch, "The Elusive Guineamen: Newport Slavers, 1735–1774," *New England Quarterly* 55, no. 2 (1982): 229–53; Jay Coughtry, *Liquid Gold: Rhode Island Rum and the International Slave Trade to West Africa in the Eighteenth Century* (Philadelphia: Temple University Press, 1970); Elaine F. Crane, "'The First Wheel of Commerce': Newport, Rhode Island and the Slave Trade, 1760–1776," *Slavery and Abolition* 1 (September 1980): 178–98; Jay Coughtry, *The Notorious Triangle: Rhode Island and the African Slave Trade, 1700–1807* (Philadelphia: Temple University Press, 1981); and James G. Lydon, "New York and the Slave Trade," *William and Mary Quarterly* 35, no.2 (1978): 375–94; Darold D. Wax, "Quaker Merchants and the Slave Trade in Colonial Pennsylvania," *Pennsylvania Magazine of History and Biography* 86 (April 1962): 44–59.

4. Herbert S. Klein, "Slaves and Shipping in Eighteenth-Century Virginia," *Journal of Interdisciplinary History* 5 (winter 1975): 383–412; Darold D. Wax, "Black Immigrants: The Slave Trade to Colonial Maryland," *Maryland Historical Magazine* 73 (March 1978): 30–45; Walter E. Minchinton, ed., *Virginia Slave-Trade Statistics, 1698–1775* (Richmond: Virginia State Library, 1984); Walter E. Minchinton, "The Seaborne Slave Trade of North Carolina," *North Carolina Historical Review* 71 (January 1994): 1–62; and Darold D. Wax, "'New Negroes Are Always in Demand': The Slave Trade in Eighteenth-Century Georgia," *Georgia Historical Quarterly* 68 (summer 1984): 193–220.

5. Patrick S. Brady, "The Slave Trade and Sectionalism in South Carolina, 1707–1808," *Journal of Southern History* 38 (November 1972): 601–20. Elizabeth Donnan, "The Slave Trade into South Carolina before the Revolution," *American Historical Review* 33 (July 1928): 804–28; W. Robert Higgins, "Charles Town Merchants and Factors Dealing in the External Negro Trade, 1735–1775," *South Carolina Historical Magazine* 65 (October 1964): 205–17; W. Robert Higgins, "The Geographic Origins of Negro Slaves in Colonial South Carolina," *South Atlantic Quarterly* 70 (winter 1971): 34–47; Peter H. Wood, *Black Majority*, 333–41; W. Robert Higgins, "Charleston: Terminus and Entrepôt of the Colonial Slave Trade," in Martin L. Kilson and Robert I. Rotberg, eds., *The African Diaspora: Interpretive Essays* (Cambridge: Harvard University Press, 1976), 114–31; Peter H. Wood, "'More like a Negro Country': Demographic Patterns in Colonial South Carolina, 1700–1740," in Stanley L. Engerman and Eugene D. Genovese, eds., *Race and Slavery in the Western Hemisphere: Quantitative Studies* (Princeton: Princeton University Press, 1975), 131–69; Daniel C. Littlefield, *Rice and Slaves: Ethnicity and the Slave Trade in Colonial South Carolina* (Baton Rouge: Louisiana State University Press, 1981),

74–114; and David Richardson, "The British Slave Trade to Colonial South Carolina," *Slavery and Abolition: A Journal of Comparative Studies* 12 (December 1991): 125–71.

6. Gwendolyn Midlo Hall, *Africans in Colonial Louisiana: The Development of Afro-Creole Cultures in the Eighteenth Century* (Baton Rouge: Louisiana State University Press, 1992); Paul F. LaChance, "The Politics of Fear: French Louisianians and the Slave Trade, 1769–1809," *Plantation Society* 1 (June 1979): 162–97; and Jane Landers, *African Society* (forthcoming).

7. Philip D. Curtin, *The Atlantic Slave Trade: A Census* (Madison: University of Wisconsin Press, 1969), 142–45; Roger Anstey, "The Volume of the North American Slave-Carrying Trade from Africa, 1761–1810," *Revue francaise d'histoire d'outre-mer* 62, no.2 (1975): 47–66; and Steven Dyle, "'By farr the most profitable trade'; Slave Trading in British Colonial North America," *Slavery and Abolition: A Journal of Comparative Studies* 10 (September 1989): 107–25.

8. Coughtry, *Notorious Triangle*.

9. Minchinton, "Seaborne Slave Trade," 1–62; Wax, "New Negroes," 193–220; LaChance, "Politics of Fear," 162–97; and Anstey, "Volume of the North American Slave-Carrying Trade," 47–66.

10. Elizabeth Donnan, "New England Slave Trade," 251–78.

11. Stephen D. Behrendt, "The British Slave Trade, 1785–1807: Volume, Profitability, and Mortality," Ph.D. diss., University of Wisconsin, 1993, 1–5.

12. Curtin, *Atlantic Slave Trade*, 73 and 140.

13. For representative treatments of this view, see George Bancroft, *History of the United States of America from the Discovery of the Continent*, 6 vols. (New York: D. Appleton, 1886), 4:440–46; John Fiske, *The Critical Period of American History, 1783–1789* (New York: Houghton Mifflin, 1888), 283–90; Norman K. Risjord, *Jefferson's America, 1760–1815* (Madison, Wisc.: Madison House, 1991), 178; and William W. Freehling, "The Founding Fathers and Slavery," *American Historical Society* 77 (February 1972): 81–93.

CHAPTER 1: DEMAND AND SUPPLY

1. Henry Laurens to Edward Bridgen, September 23, 1784, Henry Laurens Papers, South Caroliniana Library, University of South Carolina, Columbia.

2. Clay, Telfair and Co. to Nicholas and Jacob Van Staphorst, February 7, 1784, Clay, Telfair and Co. Letter Book, vol. 1, 1783–1784, Georgia Historical Society, Savannah. Although this letter is not signed by Joseph Clay, the subject matter and style strongly suggest he penned it.

3. Robert William Fogel and Stanley L. Engerman, *Time on the Cross: The Economics of American Negro Slavery* (Boston: Little, Brown, 1974), 86–94. For prices and demand, see figs. 23 and 24, p. 86.

4. J. D. B. De Bow, *Statistical View of the United States, Embracing Its Territory, Population— White, Free Colored, and Slave—Moral and Social Condition, Industry, Property, and Revenue; the Detailed Statistics of Cities, Towns and Counties: Being a Compendium of the Seventh Census, to which Are Added the Results of Every Previous Census, Beginning with 1790, in Comparative Tables, with explanatory and illustrative notes, Based upon the Schedules and other Official Sources of Information. By J. D. B. De Bow, Superintendent of the United States Census* (Washington: A. O. P. Nicholson, Public Printer, 1854), 63 and 82. Because the first federal census was not taken until 1789, no federal records exist of the southern black population before 1783.

5. Ibid.; Gwendolyn Midlo Hall, *Africans in Colonial Louisiana: The Development of Afro-Creole Cultures in the Eighteenth Century* (Baton Rouge: Louisiana State University Press, 1992), 280–81; Paul F. LaChance, "Politics of Fear: French Louisianians and the Slave Trade, 1786–1809," *Plantation Society* 1 (June 1979): 21; Patrick Riordan, "Finding Freedom in Florida:

Native Peoples, African Americans, and Colonists, 1670–1816," *Florida Historical Quarterly* 75 (summer 1996): 34–40; Edwin L. Williams, Jr., "Negro Slavery in Florida," *Florida Historical Quarterly* 28 (October 1949): 93–110; and Daniel H. Usner, Jr., *Indians, Settlers, and Slaves in a Frontier Exchange Economy* (Chapel Hill: University of North Carolina Press, 1990), 112–16.

6. Fogel and Engerman, *Time on the Cross*, 23–25. Fogel and Engerman do not agree with this assertion but do state that it is widely supported.

7. David Brion Davis, *The Problem of Slavery in the Age of Revolution, 1770–1823* (Ithaca: Cornell University Press, 1975), 7–14.

8. Henry Laurens to John Laurens, September 21, 1779, Henry Laurens Papers.

9. Darold D. Wax, "'New Negroes Are Always in Demand': The Slave Trade in Eighteenth-Century Georgia," *Georgia Historical Quarterly* 68 (summer 1984): 214–15. Another slave vessel arrived two months later with two hundred people from Senegambia, but the captain was not allowed to disembark any of the Africans, and it sailed a short time later.

10. Thomas Nicholson, "On Keeping Negroes," Pennsylvania Abolition Society Miscellaneous Collection, Historical Society of Pennsylvania, Philadelphia.

11. Davis, *Problem of Slavery*, 213–84.

12. Ibid.; and W. E. B. Du Bois, *The Suppression of the African Slave Trade to the United States of America, 1638–1870* (1896; reprint, Baton Rouge: Louisiana State University Press, 1969), 39–69.

13. Sylvia R. Frey, *Water from the Rock: Black Resistance in a Revolutionary Age* (Princeton: Princeton University Press, 1991), 81–142; and Walter Edgar, *South Carolina: A History* (Columbia: University of South Carolina Press, 1998), 226–44.

14. Henry Laurens to John Lewis Gervais, January 29, 1766, Henry Laurens Papers.

15. Robert Olwell, *Masters, Slaves, and Subjects: The Culture of Power in the South Carolina Low Country* (Ithaca: Cornell University Press, 1998), 223–25.

16. Peter Force, *American Archives*, 2 vols., 4th ser. (Washington, D.C.: United States Congress, 1837–54), 1:370; and McIntosh Papers, Georgia Historical Society, Savannah. After the War for American Independence, McIntosh changed his mind on slavery and the slave trade, and during the 1788 debates surrounding the ratification of the Constitution he defended both.

17. *South Carolina Gazette and General Advertiser*, October 18, 1783.

18. Quoted in Stanley K. Deaton, "Revolutionary Charleston, 1765–1800" (Ph.D. diss., University of Florida, 1997), 310.

19. For antislavery and antislave trade arguments between 1783 and 1791, see *South Carolina Gazette and General Advertiser*, *State Gazette of South Carolina*, *Charleston Morning Post*, *State Gazette of Georgia*, *Gazette of the State of Georgia*, *Georgia Gazette*, and Deaton, "Revolutionary Charleston," 298–343.

20. Du Bois, *Suppression of the African Slave Trade*, 49.

21. Quoted in Gary B. Nash, *Race and Revolution* (Madison, Wisc.: Madison House, 1990), 27.

22. Max Farrand, ed., *The Records of the Federal Convention of 1787*, 4 vols. (1913; rev. ed., New Haven: Yale University Press, 1937), 2:370.

23. Ibid., 364.

24. Ibid.

25. *Debates Which Arose in the House of Representatives of South Carolina, on the Constitution Framed for the United States, by a Convention of Delegates at Philadelphia* (Charleston: City Gazette, 1788), 16.

26. Alice Hanson Jones, *Wealth of a Nation to Be: The American Colonies on the Eve of the Revolution* (New York: Columbia University Press, 1980), 50–53; and Lewis Cecil Gray, *A History of*

Agriculture in the Southern United States to 1860, 2 vols. (Washington, D.C.: Carnegie Institution of Washington, 1933), 1:289.

27. Helen Tunnicliff Catterall, ed., *Judicial Cases Concerning American Slavery and the Negro*, 5 vols. (Washington, D.C.: Carnegie Institution of Washington, 1926–37), 2:290–91.

28. Joyce E. Chaplin, *An Anxious Pursuit: Agricultural Innovation and Modernity in the Lower South, 1712–1911* (Chapel Hill: University of North Carolina Press, 1993), 321–24; and Ira Berlin, *Many Thousands Gone: The First Two Centuries of Slavery in North America* (Cambridge: Belknap Press, 1998), 290–324.

29. Frey, *Water from the Rock*, 212.

30. Johann David Scheopf, *Travels in the Confederation*, 2 vols. (New York: Burt Franklin, 1968), 2.221.

31. John Drayton, *A View of South Carolina As Respects Her Natural and Civil Concerns* (Charleston: W. P. Young, 1802), 166–67; Joseph Clay to James Snelgrove, February 5, 1783, *Letters of Joseph Clay, Merchant of Savannah, 1776–1793* (Savannah: Morning News, 1913), 174–76; and Peter C. Mancall, Joshua L. Rosenbloom, and Thomas Weiss, "Slave Prices and the South Carolina Economy, 1722–1809," *Journal of Economic History* 61 (September 2001): 619–20.

32. Edgar, *South Carolina*, 245–87; and *Charleston Morning Post*, March 29, 1787.

33. *Charleston Evening Gazette*, September 27, 1785.

34. Winthrop D. Jordan, *White over Black: American Attitudes toward the Negro, 1550–1812* (New York: W. W. Norton, 1977), 318.

35. Allan Kulikoff, "Uprooted Peoples: Black Migrants in the Age of the American Revolution, 1790–1820," in *Slavery and Freedom in the Age of American Revolution*, ed. Ira Berlin and Ronald Hoffman (Urbana: University of Illinois Press, 1986), 143–67.

36. Edward Countryman, *Americans: A Collision of Histories* (New York: Hill and Wang, 1996), 88–108.

37. Clay, Telfair and Co. to Nicholas and Jacob Van Staphorst, February 7, 1784, Clay, Telfair and Co. Letter Book, vol. 1.

38. Rachel N. Klein, *Unification of a Slave State: The Rise of the Planter Class in the South Carolina Backcountry, 1760–1808* (Chapel Hill: University of North Carolina Press, 1990), 178–202; Usner, *Indians, Settlers, and Slaves*, 276–86.

39. John Hebron Moore, *The Emergence of the Cotton Kingdom in the Old Southwest: Mississippi, 1770–1860* (Baton Rouge: Louisiana University Press, 1988), 1–17.

40. Petitions to the South Carolina General Assembly, 1802, nos. 129 and 153, South Carolina Department of Archives and History, Columbia.

41. William C. C. Claiborne to James Madison, May 8, 1804, in *Official Letter Books of W. C. C. Claiborne, 1801–1816*, 3 vols., ed. Dunbar Rowland (Jackson: State Department of Archives and History, 1917), 2:135.

42. Chaplin, *Anxious Pursuit*, 279.

43. Gray, *History of Agriculture in the Southern United States*, 1:675–90.

44. Evarts B. Greene and Virginia D. Harrington, *American Population before the Federal Census of 1790* (New York: Columbia University Press, 1932), 123–86; De Bow, *Statistical View of the United States*, 63 and 82; Hall, *Africans in Colonial Louisiana*, 280–81; LaChance, "Politics of Fear," 21; and Usner, *Indians, Settlers, and Slaves*, 112–16.

45. Terry Alford, *Prince among Slaves* (New York: Harcourt Brace Jovanovich, 1977), 39–53.

46. Alford, *Prince among Slaves*, 39–84.

47. Moore, *Emergence of the Cotton Kingdom*, 1–17.

48. C. C. Robin, *Voyage to Louisiana, 1803–1805* (New Orleans: Pelican, 1966), 134–41.

49. William C. C. Claiborne to Thomas Jefferson, July 10, 1806, in *Official Letter Books*, ed. Rowland, 3:361–65.

50. *Louisiana Gazette*, April 11, 1811.

51. Adam Rothman, "The Expansion of Slavery in the Deep South, 1790–1820," Ph.D. diss., Columbia University, 2000, 71–76; and De Bow, *Statistical View of the United States*, 63 and 82.

52. Quoted in Fogel and Engerman, *Time on the Cross*, 68.

53. Chaplin, *Anxious Pursuit*, 8–10; Moore, *Emergence of the Cotton Kingdom*, 1–17; William Dusinberre, *Them Dark Days: Slavery in the American Rice Swamps* (New York: Oxford University Press, 1996), 28–47; and Robin, *Voyage to Louisiana*, 134–41.

54. For slave vessel arrivals, see appendix B; and, for estimate of the volume of the slave trade to South Carolina, see chapter 2.

55. For colonial slave prices, see Mancall, Rosenbloom, and Weiss, "Slave Prices and the South Carolina Economy," 616–39, and for postwar prices see Fogel and Engerman, *Time on the Cross*, 86–106; for slave prices in 1783–1785, see *Charleston Evening Gazette*, September 28, 1785; and, for slave prices in 1806 and 1807, see David Fleming to Mordecai Cohen, September 22 and October 2 and 22, 1806, and Myer Jacobs to Mordecai Cohen, November 5 and 16, 1807, Lewis Malone Ayer Papers, Rare Book, Manuscript, and Special Collections Library, Duke University, Durham, North Carolina. Although prices do not always mirror demand, in some cases declining or stable prices imply that supplies are meeting or increasing more rapidly than demand; in this case they were representative.

56. Phillip D. Curtin, *The Atlantic Slave Trade: A Census* (Madison: University of Wisconsin Press, 1969), 73 and 140.

57. Jack Ericson Eblen, "On the Natural Increase of Slave Populations: The Example of the Cuban Black Population, 1775–1900," in *Race and Slavery in the Western Hemisphere: Quantitative Studies*, ed. Stanley L. Engerman and Eugene D. Genovese (Princeton: Princeton University Press, 1975), 212–13. Eblen's definition of natural growth rate is used throughout this book. It takes into consideration births and deaths and represents the actual number a population increases, decreases, or remains the same. For instance, if births outnumbered deaths by twenty in a population of one thousand, then this would equate to an annual growth rate of twenty per thousand, which is the same thing as a 2 percent annual rate of increase. Because black populations were not closed during the period of study and not enough data is available to estimate the number of foreign-born women in the black population, the native-born progeny of foreign-born women are included in the natural growth rate. This is known as an observed, or crude, rate of natural increase.

58. H. C. Carey, *The Slave Trade, Domestic and Foreign: Why It Exists, and How It May Be Extinguished* (Philadelphia: John A. Norton, 1859), 16–21.

59. Ibid., 18. It is entirely possible that he meant the seventy thousand figure to include not only those slaves imported from 1791 to 1807, but also the slaves imported illegally between 1808 and 1861.

60. Ibid., 16–21.

61. Noel Deerr, *The History of Sugar*, 2 vols. (London: Chapman and Hall, 1950), 2:282–84; and Speech of S. L. Mitchell of New York, February 14, 1804, *Annals of Congress, First Session*, 1000.

62. Deerr, *History of Sugar*, 282–84.

63. For a discussion of modern data-oriented methods, see Stephen D. Behrendt, "The British Slave Trade, 1785–1807: Volume, Profitability, and Mortality," Ph.D. diss., University of Wisconsin, 1993, 1–10.

64. Basil Davidson, *Black Mother* (London, 1961), 89. Like most historians of his generation, Davidson relied mainly on the incomplete records of the London-based African and South Sea Companies and Elizabeth Donnan's four-volume compilation, *Documents Illustrative of the History of Slave Trade to America*, published from 1930 to 1935.

65. Marcus Lee Hansen, *The Atlantic Migration, 1607–1860* (Cambridge: Harvard University Press, 1940), 77; and Michael Kraus, *Immigration, the American Mosaic: From Pilgrims to Modern Refugees* (New York: Van Norstrand, 1966), 19.

66. Harry H. Laughlin, *Immigration and Conquest* (Washington, D.C.: Carnegie Institute of Washington, 1939), 52.

67. Conversation with David Eltis of the Du Bois Institute, Cambridge, Massachusetts, in March 1997.

68. Curtin, *Atlantic Slave Trade*, 3–16 and 265–73.

69. J. E. Inikori, introduction, in *Forced Migration: The Impact of the Export Slave Trade on African Societies* (London: Afrikana, 1981), 20. Inikori rejects the validity of Curtin's entire census and maintains that the old guess of 15 million — 15.4 million was his estimate — is much more accurate. James Rawley, *The Transatlantic Slave Trade: A History* (New York: W. W. Norton, 1981), 428. Rawley estimates 11,345,000 slaves were imported. Paul Lovejoy, "The Volume of the Atlantic Slave Trade: A Synthesis," *Journal of African History*, 23, no. 4 (1982): 494–501. Lovejoy suggests that 11,698,000 slaves were sent from Africa but only 9,778,500 may have survived. Jean-Michel Déveaux, in *France au temps des négrier* (Paris, 1994), gives his total as 11,500,000. Stephen D. Behrendt, "The Annual Volume and Regional Distribution of the British Slave Trade, 1780–1807," *Journal of African History*, 38, no. 2 (1997): 187–211. Behrendt suggests the number of British slave trade voyages have been overestimated by almost 15 percent. According to the scholar, a reduced number of British voyages suggests Curtin's estimate of 10 million should be adjusted down. Behrendt is the only scholar to date who has argued that Curtin overestimated the volume of the slave trade.

70. Curtin, *Atlantic Slave Trade*, 72.

71. Fogel and Engerman, *Time on the Cross*, 1:20–29; and *Time on the Cross* worksheets. Stanley Engerman kindly provided the worksheets and an explanation of how he and Fogel arrived at their estimate. They conjectured that 55,750 slaves were imported between 1780 and 1790, 79,041 slaves were imported between 1790 and 1800, and 156,335 were imported between 1800 and 1810, for a total of 291,126 from 1780 to 1810.

72. For discussions of Fogel and Engerman's estimate, see Roger Anstey, "The Volume of the North American Slave-Carrying Trade from Africa, 1761–1810," *Revue francaise d'histoire d'outre-mer* 62, no. 2 (1975): 63; and Philip D. Morgan, "African Migration," in *Encyclopedia of American Social History*, 3 vols., ed. Mary Kupiec Cayton, Elliott J. Gorn, Peter W. Williams (New York: Scribner, 1993), 2: 802.

73. Kulikoff, "Uprooted Peoples," 143–74. Kulikoff estimates that more than 20,000 foreign slaves were imported into South Carolina, Louisiana, and Mississippi from 1782 to 1790, 30,000 Africans were imported in the 1790s, and 63,000 more arrived in the 1800s. Of the 63,000, Kulikoff suggests 39,000 were imported legally into Charleston between 1804 and 1808, and 24,000 were smuggled into South Carolina and Georgia and along the Gulf coast in the 1800s.

74. Ibid., 169.

CHAPTER 2: THE VOLUME OF THE FOREIGN SLAVE
TRADE TO NORTH AMERICA, 1783–1810

1. Edward Hooker to Colonel Noadiah Hooker, Farmington, Connecticut, January 7, 1806, 169, Edward Hooker Papers, Rare Book, Manuscript, and Special Collections Library, Duke University, Durham, North Carolina.

2. J. D. B. De Bow, *Statistical View of the United States, Embracing Its Territory, Population — White, Free Colored, and Slave — Moral and Social Condition, Industry, Property, and Revenue; the Detailed Statistics of Cities, Towns and Counties: Being a Compendium of the Seventh Census, to which Are Added the Results of Every Previous Census, Beginning with 1790, in Comparative*

Tables, with explanatory and illustrative notes, Based upon the Schedules and other Official Sources of Information. By J. D. B. De Bow, Superintendent of the United States Census (Washington: A. O. P. Nicholson, Public Printer, 1854), 63 and 82.

3. In this book "foreign slave" is defined as any slave imported from outside North America.

4. Philip D. Curtin, *The Atlantic Slave Trade: A Census* (Madison: University of Wisconsin Press, 1969), 72–73, 140.

5. Ibid., 72–73; Jack Ericson Eblen, "On the Natural Increase of Slave Populations: The Example of the Cuban Black Population, 1775–1900," in *Race and Slavery in the Western Hemisphere: Quantitative Studies*, ed. Stanley L. Engerman and Eugene D. Genovese (Princeton: Princeton University Press, 1975), 212–13. See note 57, chapter 1, above.

6. Carey, Fogel, Engerman, Kulikoff, and Morgan made estimates of the volume of the foreign slave trade based on census data. See H. C. Carey, *The Slave Trade, Domestic and Foreign: Why It Exists, and How It May Be Extinguished* (Philadelphia: John A. Norton, 1859), 16–21; Robert William Fogel and Stanley L. Engerman, *Time on the Cross: The Economics of American Negro Slavery* (Boston: Little, Brown, 1974), 20–29; Allan Kulikoff, "Uprooted Peoples: Black Migrants in the Age of the American Revolution, 1790–1820," in *Slavery and Freedom in the Age of American Revolution,* ed. Ira Berlin and Ronald Hoffman (Urbana: University of Illinois Press, 1986), 148–50; and Philip D. Morgan, "Black Society in the Lowcountry, 1760–1810," in *Slavery and Freedom in the Age of the American Revolution*, ed. Ira Berlin and Ronald Hoffman (Urbana: University of Illinois Press, 1986), 84–89. For census data, see De Bow, *Statistical View of the United States*, 62 and 83; Evarts B. Greene and Virginia D. Harrington, *America Population before the Federal Census of 1790* (New York: Columbia University Press, 1932), 123–86; Gwendolyn Midlo Hall, *Africans in Colonial Louisiana: The Development of Afro-Creole Cultures in the Eighteenth Century* (Baton Rouge: Louisiana State University Press, 1992), 280–81; Paul F. LaChance, "The Politics of Fear: French Louisianians and the Slave Trade, 1786–1809," *Plantation Society* 1 (June 1979): 196–97; David C. Rankin, "The Tannenbaum Thesis Reconsidered: Slavery and Race Relations in Antebellum Louisiana," *Southern Studies* 18 (spring 1979): 21; Patrick Riordan, "Finding Freedom in Florida: Native Peoples, African Americans, and Colonists, 1670–1816," *Florida Historical Quarterly* 75 (summer 1996): 34–40; Edwin L. Williams, Jr., "Negro Slavery in Florida," in *Florida Historical Quarterly* 28 (October 1949): 93–110; and Daniel H. Usner, Jr., *Indians, Settlers, and Slaves in a Frontier Exchange Economy* (Chapel Hill: University of North Carolina Press, 1990): 112–16.

7. Kulikoff, "Uprooted Peoples," 168–69. Most scholars agree that the rate of under- or over-recording of the 1790, 1800, and 1810 censuses was insignificant.

8. Robert H. Steckel, "Birth Weights and Infant Mortality among American Slaves," *Explorations in Economic History* 3, no. 4 (1979): 86–113. According to Steckel, only one full set of plantation records of rice slaves' birth and death dates survives from before 1803.

9. Allan Kulikoff, "A 'Prolifick' People: Black Population Growth in the Chesapeake Colonies, 1700–1790," *Southern Studies* 16 (winter 1977): 409–14; John Hebron Moore, *The Emergence of the Cotton Kingdom in the Old Southwest: Mississippi, 1770–1860* (Baton Rouge: Louisiana State University Press, 1988), 1–17; and for the 1810 to 1820 estimate, see Kulikoff, "Uprooted Peoples," 168–69. North Carolina, Virginia, and Maryland experienced less destruction than the Deep South during the war, and their environments were more healthy than those of the lower South and Southwest.

10. Max Farrand, ed., *The Records of the Federal Convention of 1787*, 4 vols. (1913; rev. ed., New Haven, 1937), 2:371.

11. Julia Floyd Smith, *Slavery and Rice Culture in Low Country Georgia, 1750–1860* (Knoxville: University of Tennessee Press, 1985), 130–32; William Dusinberre, *Them Dark Days: Slavery in the American Rice Swamps* (New York: Oxford University Press, 1996), 48–83. Dusinberre shows

that lowcountry rice slaves' mortality rates were much higher than those for slaves on inland cotton plantations. He estimates that in the mid nineteenth century, the slave populations on tidal swamp rice plantations experienced a 4 percent decennial growth rate (p. 415). This was far below the slave norm of the whole South of 26.6 percent. He claims rice slave mortality rates were even worse in the eighteenth century and early nineteenth century before the reform movement of 1820. The 4 percent decennial rate equates to a less than .5 percent annual natural growth rate.

12. Morgan, "Black Society," 11; Darold D. Wax, "'New Negroes Are Always in Demand': The Slave Trade in Eighteenth-Century Georgia," *Georgia Historical Quarterly* 68 (summer 1984): 214–15; Sylvia R. Frey, *Water from the Rock: Black Resistance in a Revolutionary Age* (Princeton: Princeton University Press, 1991), 174; and Ira Berlin, *Many Thousands Gone: The First Two Centuries of Slavery in North America* (Cambridge: Belknap, 1998), 290–324. Morgan maintains that during the war the South Carolina slave population declined by 25,000. Wax argues several thousand Georgia slaves departed when the British evacuated. Frey estimates that as many as 10,000 Georgia slaves were relocated or lost during the war. Berlin concludes that South Carolina lost 25,000 slaves and Georgia 10,000.

13. Joseph Clay to John Wilcox, April 16, 1783, *Letters of Joseph Clay, Merchant of Savannah, 1776–1793* (Savannah: Morning News, 1913), 185–87; Frey, *Water from the Rock*, 206–42; and David Ramsay, *The History of South Carolina from Its First Settlement in 1670 to the Year 1808*, 2 vols. (Charleston: David Longworth for the author, 1809), 1:230–40.

14. George Baillie to John McIntosh, September 7, 1783, John McIntosh, Jr., Papers, Georgia Historical Society, Savannah.

15. Joyce E. Chaplin, "Tidal Rice Cultivation and the Problem of Slavery in South Carolina and Georgia, 1760–1815," *William and Mary Quarterly* 49 (January 1992): 36–50.

16. Dusinberre, *Them Dark Days*, 66–72, and 79; John Drayton, *A View of South Carolina As Respects Her Natural and Civil Concerns* (Charleston: W. P. Young, 1802), 116.

17. Charles William Janson, *Stranger in America: Containing Observations Made during a Long Residence in That Country, on the Genius, Manners, and Customs of People of the United States; with Biographical Particulars of Public Characters; Hints and Facts Relative to the Arts, Sciences, Commerce, Agriculture, Manufactures, Emigration, and the Slave Trade* (London: Printed for James Cundee by Albion Press, 1807), 358–59.

18. Frey, *Water from the Rock*, 210–14.

19. Joseph Lee Boyle, ed., "The Revolutionary War Diaries of Captain Walter Finney," *South Carolina Historical Magazine* 98 (April 1997): 140; and Frey, *Water from the Rock*, 213.

20. W. E. B. Du Bois, *The Suppression of the African Slave Trade to the United States of America, 1638–1870* (1896; reprint, Baton Rouge: Louisiana State University Press, 1969), 229.

21. *Columbian Herald*, May 23,1785; and *South Carolina Weekly Gazette*, October 27, 1785; quoted in Morgan, "Black Society," 131.

22. Kulikoff, "Black Migrants," 153–57.

23. Lawrence S. Rowland, Alexander Moore, and George C. Rogers, Jr., *The History of Beaufort County, South Carolina: Volume I, 1514–1861* (Columbia: University of South Carolina Press, 1996), 347–67; De Bow, *Statistical View of the United States*, 62 and 83; and Morgan, "Black Society," 84–89. Morgan calculated that the South Carolina black population natural growth rate was 2.2 percent in the 1780s and 1790s and 2 percent in the first decade of the 1800s. He attributed the low rate (in the Chesapeake it averaged 2.5) to the large number of Africans in the population, and the harmful living and working conditions in the lowcountry. The natural growth rates Morgan used in "Black Society" were slightly higher than the rates here, and thus his estimates of the number of foreign and domestic imports were slightly lower than the ones in this book. For instance, he estimated that, between 1801 and 1810, 30,195 slaves were imported into South Carolina; Morgan, "Black Society," 87. For the same period this book's data estimates

33,094 slaves were imported into the state (table 6). However, apparently Morgan later re-assessed his previous estimates of slave natural growth rates and slave migrants. In an article published in 1993, Morgan posited that many more Africans arrived after the Revolution than previously thought, about 140,000 in the first decade of the nineteenth century alone. The scholar based his new estimate on the work of Robert W. Fogel and Stanley L. Engerman; Philip D. Morgan, "African Migration," in *Encyclopedia of American Social History*, 3 vols., ed. Mary Kupiec Cayton, Elliott J. Gorn, Peter W. Williams (New York: Scribner, 1993), 802. As previously mentioned, this study indicates that Fogel and Engerman underestimated the natural growth rate.

24. The estimate of the number of lowcountry cotton slaves was arrived at by subtracting the number of lowcountry rice workers from the total slave population of the lowcountry counties. The estimate of the number of rice slaves was arrived at by dividing the lowcountry annual rice production by the average of clean rice produced per slave. For rice production, see Dusinberre, *Them Dark Days*, 460–62; Edward Ruffin, ed., *Report of the Agricultural History of South Carolina* (Columbia: A. H. Pemberton, 1843), 21–25; and George K. Holmes, *Rice Crop of the United States, 1712–1911* (Washington, D.C.: U.S. Department of Agriculture, Bureau of Statistics, Circular 34, 1912). For rice worker output, see Joyce E. Chaplin, *An Anxious Pursuit: Agricultural Innovation and Modernity in the Lower South, 1712–1911* (Chapel Hill: University of North Carolina Press, 1993), 246–50.

25. Rowland, Moore, and Rogers, *History of Beaufort County*, 348.

26. Smith, *Slavery and Rice Culture*, 131–32; Rowland, Moore, and Rogers, *History of Beaufort County*, 347–67; and "Inventory of slaves belonging to Colonel Stapleton on his Plantation at St. Helena Island" and "William Joyner Account Book," John Stapleton Papers, South Caroliniana Library, University of South Carolina, Columbia.

27. Morgan, "Black Society," 84–90; Kulikoff, "Black Migrants," 153–57; and Edward Countryman, unpublished paper on antebellum black migrants.

28. Curtin, *Atlantic Slave Trade*, 83; Paul LaChance, "Politics of Fear," 196–97; and Hall, *Africans in Colonial Louisiana*, 280–81.

29. For estimates of Florida, Louisiana, and Mississippi slave populations, natural growth rates, and foreign slave imports, see Hall, *Africans in Colonial Louisiana*, 280–81; LaChance, "Politics of Fear," 196–97; Rankin, "Tannenbaum Thesis," 21; Riordan, "Finding Freedom in Florida," 34–40; Usner, *Indians, Settlers, and Slaves*, 112–16; and Paul F. LaChance, "The Immigration of Saint-Dominique Refugees to New Orleans: Reception, Integration, and Impact," in *A Refuge for All Ages: Immigration in Louisiana History*, ed. Carl A. Brasseaux (Lafayette: University of Southwestern Louisiana Press, 1996), 25–26.

30. Jack D. L. Holmes, *Gayoso: The Life of a Spanish Governor in the Mississippi Valley, 1789–1799* (Baton Rouge: Louisiana State University Press, 1965), 114–17; Greene and Harrington, *American Population*, 7–9; De Bow, *Statistical View of the United States*, 62 and 83; and Riordan, "Finding Freedom in Florida," 37–39. For examples of sales in South Carolina and Georgia, see *Gazette of the State of Georgia*, February 27, 1784; and *South Carolina Gazette and General Advertiser*, February 21, 1784.

31. For advertisements and duties listings to which the phrase *a few* can be matched up, see September 8, 1785, and January 21, 1786, *State Gazette of South Carolina*, and Duties on Trade at Charleston, 1784–1787, South Carolina Department of Archives, Columbia, 232 and 274. By comparing the newspaper advertisements to the manifests, "a few" averages twenty appearances. Merchants used "a few" twenty-one times, "a parcel," twice, "several," four times, and "a gang" and "a group" only once each. No comparable listing in a duties or customs report for "a parcel," "a gang," or "a group" were located. Therefore, because the words *few*, *several*, and *parcel* are synonymous, "a parcel," "a gang," "a group," and "several" were assigned the same value as "a few."

32. No dual listings in advertisements and duties or customs reports were uncovered to define accurately "a number." However, for the most part, "a number" was probably greater than "a few" but less than "a small cargo." For an ad and a duties listing that define "a small cargo," see October 19, 1786, *State Gazette of South Carolina* and Duties on Trade at Charleston, 322. It should be noted that this particular ad was referring to a schooner's "small cargo." For advertisements and duties and customs officials' reports that define a brig's "cargo," see *Gazette of South Carolina*, June 13, 1785; Duties on Trade at Charleston, 215; *Gazette of the State of Georgia*, August 18 and 25, 1785; *State Gazette of South Carolina*, July 31, 1786, and Duties on Trade at Charleston, 311. For advertisements and duties and customs officials' reports that define a ship's "cargo," see *State Gazette of South Carolina*, July 4, 1785; Duties on Trade at Charleston, 218; and *Charleston Courier*, June 2 and 3, 1785. Merchants used the term *cargo* fourteen times and *small cargo* four times. For the vessels for which no comparisons were found, it was assumed 1.7 slaves were delivered per vessel ton in the 1780s, 1.3 in the 1790s, and 1.1 in the first decade of the 1800s. These estimates were arrived at by combining the research conducted for this study of North American slaving vessels and the work of Roger Anstey and Stephen D. Behrendt on the annual numbers of slaves landed per ton by British slavers; Roger Anstey, "The Volume and Profitability of the British Slave Trade, 1761–1807," in *Race and Slavery in the Western Hemisphere: Quantitative Studies*, ed. Stanley L. Engerman and Eugene D. Genovese (Princeton: Princeton University Press, 1975), 10–12; and Stephen D. Behrendt, "The Annual Volume and Regional Distribution of the British Slave Trade, 1780–1807," *Journal of African History* 38, no. 2 (1997): 192–94.

33. See appendix B for tonnages and the size of cargoes.

34. Duties on Trade at Charleston and *Annals of the Congress of the United States, Sixteenth Congress, Second Session; Comprising the Period from November 13, 1820 to March 3, 1821, Inclusive* (Washington: Gales and Seaton, 1855), 70–78.

35. For newspaper reports of arrivals not found in Duties on Trade at Charleston, see *State Gazette of South Carolina*, August 25 and October 13, 1785. The *Prudent* arrived on August 25 and the *Greyson* on October 13. For local observation, see Nathaniel Russel to Joseph and Joshua Grafton, July 2, 1785, quoted in Elizabeth Donnan, ed., *Documents Illustrative of the History of the Slave Trade to America*, 4 vols. (1930–35; reprint, New York: Octagon Books, 1969), 4:478–80.

36. Duties on Trade at Charleston, 360; and Lark Emerson Adams, ed., *Journals of the House of Representatives, 1785–1786* (Columbia: University of South Carolina Press, 1979), 567.

37. Edward Hooker, January 7, 1806, Edward Hooker Papers, Rare Book, Manuscript, and Special Collections Library, Duke University, Durham, North Carolina; *Annals of Congress, Sixteenth Congress, Second Session*, 74–75; and appendix B. Smith's list included only one arrival in November and December, the *Prince William*. The *Charleston Courier* reported five arrivals, *Rambler, Speedwell, Brandywine, Washington*, and the *Prince William*. Hooker probably saw two of these vessels, the *Washington* and the *Prince William*. The others, *Rambler, Speedwell*, and *Brandywine*, arrived in early November, and sales of their cargoes ended by early December. Advertisements for the sales stopped running before Hooker arrived.

38. For instance, the *Charleston Courier* reported on January 19, 1807, that the lugger *Speculation* arrived at Beaufort, South Carolina, in January with seventy-one slaves from Africa; and the arrival of another slave ship was reported in Rowland, Moore, and Rogers, *History of Beaufort County*, 347–50.

39. *Charleston Courier*, June 1, August 17, and September 27, 1805.

40. See Duties on Trade at Charleston. During 1785 the report listed thirty-three small cargoes of 40 slaves or less, totaling 520 persons. They made up 11 percent of the total volume of slaves delivered that year. In 1805, for instance, eight advertisements for small cargoes appeared in the *Charleston Courier*.

41. *Charleston Courier*, April 3, May 21, June 1, June 6, July 10, August 17, September 18, and October 29, 1805. In their defense, late-eighteenth- and early-nineteenth-century customs officials faced on impossible task. Thousands of vessels entered and cleared Charleston each year, and hundreds were anchored in Charleston harbor each day. For a list of vessels in Charleston harbor see the *Times*, January 11, 1808. For that day the harbormaster, William Conyers, reported that seventy-eight ships, forty-two brigs, and eighty-five schooners and sloops were in the port of Charleston.

42. *Annals*, 73–74; and appendix B.

43. Until the 1830s customs officials considered records made during their service as their personal property, and thus, when they left office, they took documents with them. Subsequently many of the records were lost. Fires, especially in Charleston, destroyed others. To make matters worse, the extant customs records have been shuffled back and forth between various federal agencies, which has resulted in many documents being lost since the 1930s. For instance, in *Documents*, Elizabeth Donnan lists the Savannah Customs Records as a source for a number of slave vessel arrivals, but current National Archive employees have been unable to locate the documents that Donnan lists. Interview with National Archives representative, October 3, 1997.

44. For information on extant newspapers for the period, 1783–1810, see Clarence S. Brigham, *History and Bibliography of American Newspapers, 1690–1820*, 2 vols. (Worcester, Mass.: American Antiquarian Society, 1947).

45. Roger Anstey, "The Volume of the North American Slave-Carrying Trade from Africa, 1761–1810," *Revue francaise d'histoire d'outre-mer* 62, no. 2 (1975): 52; and see the lists of Newport, Rhode Island, clearances for the years 1786–1790 and 1794–1800 in Donnan, ed., *Documents*, 3:337–40, 358, and 378–79.

46. For information on privileged slaves see "Journal of the Ship *Mary*, 1795–1796," Donnan, ed., *Documents*, 3:360–78; Duties on Trade at Charleston, 130; and Robert Mackay, *Letters of Robert Mackay to His Wife, Written from Ports in America and England, 1772–1816* (Athens: University of Georgia Press, 1949), 302–3.

47. *State Gazette of South Carolina*, August 10, 1785; Duties on Trade at Charleston, 226; and *Charleston Courier*, July 24, 1807.

48. Fogel and Engerman, *Time on the Cross*, 88–89.

49. David Brion Davis, *The Problem of Slavery in the Age of Revolution, 1770–1823* (Ithaca: Cornell University Press, 1975), 28–29; Du Bois, *Suppression of the African Slave Trade*, 70–93 and 230–46; and LaChance, "Repercussions of the Haitian Revolution," in *The Impact of the Haitian Revolution in the Atlantic World*, ed. David P. Geggus (Columbia: University of South Carolina Press, 2001), 209–14. Between 1793 and 1795 North Carolina, South Carolina, Georgia, and Louisiana passed legislation or issued edicts aimed at preventing the immigration of St. Dominique slaves.

50. *Maryland Journal*, July 26, 1793; and Lothrop Stoddard, *The French Revolution in San Domingo* (New York: Houghton Mifflin, 1914), 214–21. Another 8,500 refugees (black and white) put to sea at the same time, but it is not known how many landed on the North American mainland.

51. Quoted in Robert Alderson, "Charleston's Rumored Slave Revolt of 1793," in *Impact of the Haitian Revolution in the Atlantic World*, ed. Geggus, 94.

52. Please see Alderson, "Charleston's Rumored Slave Revolt," 104, for Charleston runaway study.

53. Mackay, *Letters of Robert Mackay to His Wife*, 264.

54. For 1809 Louisiana arrivals see Gwendolyn Midlo Hall, chapter 3, *African Diaspora in the Americas: Continuities of Regions, Ethnicities, and Cultures* (Chapel Hill: University of North Carolina Press, forthcoming); Thomas N. Ingersoll, "The Slave Trade and the Ethnic Diversity

of Louisiana's Slave Community," *Louisiana History* 37 (spring 1996): 133–36; Hall, *Africans in Colonial Louisiana*, 277–82; and LaChance, "Politics of Fear," 196–97.

55. LaChance, "Repercussions of the Haitian Revolution," 209–14. Based on his study of census records, LaChance estimated that several thousand more refugees arrived before 1809 than previously believed. The additional people would raise the number of St. Dominique immigrants to between 13,000 and 15,000 people for the period.

56. Foreign slave ships are defined as French, Spanish, or British vessels.

57. Gwendolyn Midlo Hall, chapter 3, *African Diaspora in the Americas*; Thomas N. Ingersoll, "Slave Trade," 133–36; Hall, *Africans in Colonial Louisiana*, 277–82; and LaChance, "Politics of Fear," 196–97.

58. Davis, *Problem of Slavery*, 28–29; Du Bois, *Suppression of the African Slave Trade*, 70–92 and 230–46; and LaChance, "Repercussions of the Haitian Revolution," 209–46. When the War for American Independence ended in 1783, only three states, North Carolina, South Carolina, and Georgia, permitted the importation of foreign slaves. Over the next fifteen years, the legislatures of the states either banned or suspended the trade: South Carolina in 1787, North Carolina in 1794, and Georgia in 1798. South Carolina lifted its prohibition in 1804. Captives poured into the state until the federal government finally imposed a permanent ban on imports in 1808. In Louisiana and Mississippi the slave trade was suspended in early 1795. Two years later, when Mississippi became part of the United States, Congress outlawed direct imports of foreign slaves to the territory. In Louisiana the trade reopened for bozals, or slaves imported directly from Africa, in 1800. When the United States took possession of Louisiana in 1804, it banned direct shipments from foreign ports, but it allowed the transshipment of newly arrived Africans from Charleston.

59. For description of fugitive slaves, see Lathan A. Windley, *Runaway Slave Advertisements: A Documentary History from the 1730s to 1790*, 4 vols. (Westport, Conn.: Greenwood, 1983).

60. *Columbia Museum and Savannah Advertiser*, March 19, 1799.

61. Helen Tunnicliff Catterall, ed., *Judicial Cases Concerning American Slavery and the Negro*, 5 vols. (Washington, D.C.: Carnegie Institution of Washington, 1926–37), 2:390.

62. Savannah City Council Minutes, September 1802, Georgia Historical Society, Savannah. Smugglers had probably landed the slaves by the time the council acted. News of the landing had traveled from the island of Guadalupe to a northern port and finally to Savannah.

63. *Charleston Courier*, October 28, 1803.

64. *Providence Gazette*, August 20, 1803.

65. *Savannah Republican and State Intelligencia*, December 9, 1803.

66. *Georgia Republican and State Intelligencer*, January 17, 1804.

67. Drayton,*View of South Carolina*, 146.

68. Sam Brown to William Vernon, April 20 and June 8, 1789, Slavery Papers, Box 1, New-York Historical Society, New York City.

69. Mungo Park, *Travels in the Interior of Africa: Performed in the Years 1795, 1796, and 1797, with an Account of a Subsequent Mission to the Country in 1805* (London: T. Allman, 1839), 249–51.

70. Charles Clark to James D'Wolf, January 7, 1802, quoted in George Locke Howe, *Mount Hope: A New England Chronicle* (New York: Viking, 1959), 122–23. Newspaper "Marine Lists" report several vessels entered Charleston and Savannah from Africa "in ballast." Evidently, as Clark infers, slave vessel masters smuggled slaves ashore and then entered Charleston or Savannah. This strategy would have allowed them to settle accounts with local merchants, take on much-needed provisions, and repair their vessels.

71. Thomas Hart Benton, *Abridgement of the Debates of Congress, from 1789 to 1856, From Gales and Seaton's Annals of Congress; from their Register of Debates; and from the Official*

Reported Debates, by John C. Rives. By the author of the Thirty year's view [Thomas Hart Benton], 16 vols. (New York: D. Appleton and Co., 1857), Eighth Congress, First Session, February 14, 1804, 3:129.

72. Benton, *Abridgement of the Debates of Congress, from 1789 to 1856*, Eighth Congress, First Session, February 14, 1804, 3:133.

73. Kensil Bell, *"Always Ready": The Story of the United States Coast Guard* (New York: Mead, 1944), 10–14.

74. Smith, *Slavery and Rice Culture*, 98–101; and Phillip S. May, "Zephaniah Kingsley, Non-conformist, 1765–1843," *Florida Historical Quarterly* 23 (January 1945): 145–50.

75. Moore, *Emergence of the Cotton Kingdom*, 1–18; James C. Bonner, *History of Georgia Agri-culture, 1732–1860* (Athens: University of Georgia Press, 1964), 41–56; Drayton,*View of South Carolina*, 128; and J. Carlyle Sitterson, *Sugar Country: The Cane Sugar Industry in the South, 1753–1950* (Lexington: University of Kentucky Press, 1953), 3–12.

76. Fogel and Engerman, *Time on the Cross*, 24–25 and 86–89; and Drayton, *View of South Carolina*, 146.

77. Gene A. Smith, "U.S. Navy Gunboats and the Slave Trade in Louisiana Waters, 1808–1811," *Military History of the West* 23 (fall 1993): 135–47.

78. For previous estimates of the North American carrying capacity, see Curtin, *Atlantic Slave Trade*, 212; Anstey, "Volume of the North American Slave-Carrying Trade," 61–65; and Tommy Todd Hamm, "The American Slave Trade with Africa, 1620–1807," Ph.D. diss., Indiana Univer-sity, 1975, 279–84. For methodologies and estimates using slave vessel–carrying capacities, see Anstey, "Volume and Profitability of the British Slave Trade," 10–12; David Richardson, "The Eighteenth-Century British Slave Trade: Estimates of the Volume and Coastal Distribution in Africa," *Research in Economic History* 12 (1989): 151–95; J. E. Inikori, "Measuring the Atlantic Slave Trade: An Assessment of Curtin and Anstey," *Journal of African History* 17, no. (1976): 197–223; and Stephen D. Behrendt, "Annual Volume and Regional Distribution," 187–211.

79. Stephen D. Behrendt, "The British Slave Trade, 1785–1807: Volume, Profitability, and Mortality," Ph.D. diss., University of Wisconsin–Madison, 1993, xvi; Anstey, "Volume of the North American Slave-Carrying Trade," 47–64; and appendix B. As Anstey and Behrendt have shown and appendix B indicates, between 1783 and 1810, transatlantic slave vessels increased in size while the number of slaves they carried per ton decreased. Appendix B suggests that in the 1780s North American vessels carried on average 1.7 slaves per ton; in the 1790s, 1.5 slaves per ton; and in the first decade of the 1800s, 1.2 slaves per ton. These averages are in line with British capacities in the 1780s and 1790s but slightly higher in the first decades of the 1800s; Behrendt, "British Slave Trade," 77–78. Unlike British traders, North American slavers were not restricted by federal laws that limited the number of slaves carried per ton. Thus it is not surprising that North American slavers carried more slaves per ton than British after the passage of the Dolben Act in 1788. It should be noted that snows and other brigs were both two-masted vessels with two decks, but their tonnages varied widely according to decade. Moreover, appendix B indicates that in the 1780s, snows were slightly larger than brigs, in the 1790s they were about the same size, and in the first decade of the 1800s, snows were much larger than brigs. Also the average size of vessels assumed to calculate the carrying capacity of the North American slaving fleet is slightly smaller than the average size of vessels assumed for estimating the arrivals of foreign slaves com-piled in table 7, because the table 7 vessels included foreign slavers that were on average larger than North American slave ships; Anstey, "Volume of the North American Slave-Carrying Trade," 47–64.

80. Anstey, "Volume of the North American Slave-Carrying Trade," 56–62; and appendix B.

81. Herbert S. Klein, "The Cuban Slave Trade in a Period of Transition, 1790–1843," *Revue fran-caise d'histoire d'outre-mer* 62, no. 2 (1975): 67–73; and Anstey, "Volume of the North American

Slave-Carrying Trade," 47–64. Klein's research shows that U.S. slave vessels were active in Cuba, especially from 1790 to 1810. However, they rarely averaged more than fifty African slaves delivered per vessel, which indicates that masters were stopping at other ports to sell slaves before disembarking the remainder of their cargoes in Cuba. Because South Carolina, Georgia, and Florida were accessible and slaves brought high prices there, it is safe to assume that masters often sold part of their cargoes there. Also many slave ships cleared from Charleston for Havana between 1804 and 1808. Based on Klein's research and others, Anstey estimated that North American slavers delivered 60 percent of their human cargoes to North America.

82. Gwendolyn Midlo Hall, chapter 3, *African Diaspora in the Americas*. Although transshipments are not included in table 7, they are listed in appendix B.

83. *South Carolina State Gazette and Daily Advertiser*, August 29, 1787. Eighteenth- and nineteenth-century newspapers often carried reports from other newspapers. In Charleston and Savannah newspapers, items from other newspapers, especially involving the slave trade, were a regular feature.

84. Petition of Bristol (England) merchants, May 12, 1789, quoted in Donnan, "The New England Slave Trade after the Revolution," *New England Quarterly* 3 (January 1930): 255.

85. This estimate was reached by increasing the carrying capacity of the vessels for which the disembarkation point is unknown (4,704) by 20 percent and then multiplying the product (5,645) by .6 to allow for shipments to foreign ports.

86. Anstey, "Volume of the North American Slave-Carrying Trade," 47–64.

87. Howe, *Mount Hope*, 107–9.

88. Benton, *Abridgement of the Debates of Congress, from 1789 to 1856*, Sixth Congress, First Session, April 26, 1800, 2:474–75.

89. Howe, *Mount Hope*, 107–9.

90. Hugh Thomas, *The Slave Trade: The Story of the Atlantic Slave Trade, 1440–1870* (New York: Simon and Schuster, 1997), 519–20; and Pennsylvania Abolition Society, Minutes of April 7, 1800, Historical Society of Pennsylvania, Philadelphia. For specific cases, see *Charleston Gazette*, October 30, 1799, and *Newport Mercury*, March 1, 1797.

91. Anstey, "Volume of the North American Slave-Carrying Trade," 47–64.

92. Zachary Macaulay to Samuel Hopkins, October 20, 1796, quoted in Samuel Hopkins, *Works* (Boston, 1852), 1:152.

93. Quoted in Thomas, *Slave Trade*, 546.

94. The African Institute, *Thirteenth Report of the Directors*, London, 1813, in Anstey, "Volume of the North American Slave-Carrying Trade," 64.

95. Anstey, "Volume of the North American Slave-Carrying Trade," 47–64.

96. Fogel and Engerman estimated that nearly three hundred thousand African captives were imported into North America between 1780 and 1810. To arrive at their estimate, they assumed an annual natural growth rate of 2 percent for the entire southern black population. Kulikoff has shown that in the Chesapeake, and other regions, the natural growth rate was much higher (2.5 percent). See Fogel and Engerman, *Time on the Cross*, 1:20–29; and Kulikoff, "Black Migrants," 168–69.

97. Klein, "Cuban Slave Trade," 67–73. These cargoes were small; they averaged 41.6 slaves per cargo from 1790 to 1810, which indicates that masters unloaded one-half or more of their cargo at another port before arriving in Cuba or else that the cargoes were transshipments. Many of the masters may well have stopped first at a West Indies port, but others, as 1800s "Marine Lists" indicate, also entered U.S. ports. Of course, before 1804 masters unloaded slaves at the first stop surreptitiously. However, it should be noted that American traders participated in a profitable 1790s slave trade innovation. For a time, traders such as J. and T. Handasyde Perkins of Boston sent cargoes of rice from Charleston and Savannah to the Windward Islands in exchange for

slaves to be sold in Cuba; Lloyd Vernon Briggs, *The History and Genealogy of the Cabot Family, 1475–1927*, 2 vols. (Boston: Charles E. Goodspeed, 1927), 2:478.

98. George E. Brooks, Jr., *Yankee Traders, Old Coasters and African Middlemen: A History of American Legitimate Trade with West Africa in the Nineteenth Century* (Brookline, Mass.: Boston University Press, 1970), 25.

99. Anstey, "Volume of the North American Slave-Carrying Trade," 60–65.

100. This estimate was reached by increasing the carrying capacity of the vessels for which the disembarkation point is unknown (16,560) by 30 percent and then multiplying the product (21,528) by .5 to allow for shipments to foreign ports.

101. Thomas, *Slave Trade*, 546.

102. It appears that between 1804 and 1807 newspapers and customs officials reported most of North American slave voyages. Therefore the carrying capacity was raised by only 10 percent to allow for illegal voyages between 1801 and 1803 and between 1808 and 1810.

103. This estimate was reached by increasing the carrying capacity of the vessels for which the disembarkation point is unknown (34,944) by 10 percent and then multiplying the product (38,438) by .7 to allow for shipments to foreign ports.

104. For Spanish census data, see LaChance, "Politics of Fear," 196. For Curtin's discussion of Louisiana black population, see Curtin, *Atlantic Slave Trade*, 83.

105. LaChance, "Politics of Fear," 162–97; and appendix A.

CHAPTER 3: FOREIGN SLAVE ORIGINS

1. William Dunbar to Tunno and Price, February 1, 1807, in Mrs. Dunbar Rowland, ed., *Life, Letters, and Papers of William Dunbar* (Jackson: Press of the Mississippi Historical Society, 1930), 351–52 .

2. Ibid.

3. Daniel C. Littlefield, *Rice and Slaves: Ethnicity and the Slave Trade in Colonial South Carolina* (Baton Rouge: Louisiana State University Press, 1981), 8.

4. Herbert S. Klein, "Slaves and Shipping in Eighteenth-Century Virginia," *Journal of Interdisciplinary History* 5 (winter 1975): 382; and Littlefield, *Rice and Slaves*, 110–14.

5. Littlefield, *Rice and Slaves*, 8–23 and 118–22; and Philip D. Curtin, *The Atlantic Slave Trade: A Census* (Madison: University of Wisconsin Press, 1969), 127–32.

6. Curtin, *Atlantic Slave Trade*, 158.

7. Walter E. Minchinton, "The Seaborne Slave Trade of North Carolina," *North Carolina Historical Review* 71 (January 1994): 1–62.

8. For estimates, see Peter H. Wood, "'More like a Negro Country': Demographic Patterns in Colonial South Carolina, 1700–1744," in *Race and Slavery in the Western Hemisphere: Quantitative Studies*, ed. Stanley L. Engerman and Eugene D. Genovese (Princeton, N.J.: Princeton University Press, 1975), 150, table 4; Elizabeth Donnan, ed., *Documents Illustrative of the History of the Slave Trade to America*, 4 vols. (1930–35; reprint, New York: Octagon Books, 1969), 4:310–633; W. Robert Higgins, "The Geographical Origins of Negro Slaves in Colonial South Carolina," *South Atlantic Quarterly* 70 (winter 1971): 34–47; and Philip D. Morgan, "Black Society in the Lowcountry, 1760–1810," in *Slavery and Freedom in the Age of the American Revolution*, ed. Ira Berlin and Ronald Hoffman (Urbana: University of Illinois Press, 1986), 131–32.

9. Henry Laurens to Richard Oswald, May 17, 1756, quoted in Littlefield, *Rice and the Slaves*, 8.

10. Henry Laurens to Smith and Clifton, July 17, 1755, quoted in Littlefield, *Rice and the Slaves*, 8.

11. Henry Laurens to John Knight, February 12, 1756; Laurens to Richard Nicholas and Co., September 11, 2756; Laurens to Jonathan Blundell and Co., May 16, 1756; Laurens to John

Knight, July 11, 1755; Laurens to Devonshire, Reeve, and Lloyd, May 22, 1755; Laurens to Gidney Clarke, June 26, 1756; and Laurens to Samuel Linnecar, May 8, 1756; all quoted in Littlefield, *Rice and Slaves*, 8–10.

12. Morgan, "Black Society," 131–32. For his study Morgan used South Carolina Treasury General Duty Books; South Carolina Naval Office Shipping Lists; South Carolina newspapers; and Donnan, ed., *Documents*, 4, 235–471; and South Carolina Archives, Duties on Trade at Charleston, 1784–89, South Carolina Department of Archives and History, Columbia, South Carolina.

13. Wood, "'More like a Negro Country,'" 148–52; Margaret Washington Creel, "*A Peculiar People*": *Slave Religion and Community-Culture among the Gullahs* (New York: New York University Press, 1988), 29–44 and 329–34.

14. Donnan, ed., *Documents*, 372–73. A June 30, 1759, advertisement in the *South Carolina Gazette* describes the origin of the snow *Betsey* as "from the Factory at Sierra Leon on the Windward Coast of Guiney."

15. Morgan, "Black Society," 131–32.

16. Quoted in Darold D. Wax, "'New Negroes Are Always in Demand:' The Slave Trade in Eighteenth-Century Georgia," *Georgia Historical Quarterly* 68 (summer 1984): 207.

17. Curtin, *Atlantic Slave Trade*, 216.

18. Gwendolyn Midlo Hall, *Africans in Colonial Louisiana: The Development of Afro-Creole Culture in the Eighteenth Century* (Baton Rouge: Louisiana University Press, 1992), 56–65.

19. Ibid., 402–6.

20. Curtin, *Atlantic Slave Trade*, 171.

21. For these percentages the data presented in the discussions of each colony were used to extrapolate the African origins of a majority of imports between 1730 and 1774. These figures are highly speculative, but they are in line with other scholars' estimates. During this period, of 167,453 people imported whose origin can be conjectured, it is estimated that 50,256 were natives of Senegambia, 8,373 were natives of Sierra Leone, 18,820 were natives of the Windward Coast, 16,834 were natives of the Gold Coast, 8,242 were natives of the Bight of Benin, 13,521 were natives of the Bight of Biafra, 50,977 were natives of west-central Africa, and 430 were natives of Mozambique. For other estimates, see Curtin, *Atlantic Slave Trade*, 156–58; and Philip D. Morgan, "African Migration," in *Encyclopedia of American Social History*, 3 vols., ed. Mary Kupiec Cayton, Elliott J. Gorn, Peter W. Williams (New York: Scribner, 1993), 2:803.

22. Morgan, "African Migration," 2:803; Klein, "Slaves and Shipping," 382–412; Littlefield, *Rice and Slaves*, 109–114; and Curtin, *Atlantic Slave Trade*, 150, 156–58, 200, and 220–22.

23. *State Gazette of Georgia*, May 27, 1784; and *Charleston Courier*, September 20, 1783, and April 17, May 5 and 7, and July 6, 1784.

24. *State Gazette of Georgia*, May 6, 1784.

25. *South Carolina Gazette and General Advertiser*, November 11, 1783.

26. *Charleston Courier*, December 28, 1807.

27. *Gazette of the State of Georgia*, February 19, 1784, and April 29, 1784; and *Georgia Gazette*, April 30, 1795.

28. William Vernon to William Brown, August 27, 1786, Parish Transcripts, Miscellaneous Slave Papers, New-York Historical Society, New York City.

29. Charles Clark to James D'Wolf, January 7, 1802, quoted in George Locke Howe, *Mount Hope: A New England Chronicle* (New York: Viking, 1959), 122–23.

30. Curtin, *Atlantic Slave Trade*, 156–57; Donnan, ed., *Documents*, 4:230–36.

31. *Charleston Courier*, March 20 and 24, 1804.

32. Donnan, ed., *Documents*, 4:633.

33. W. E. B. Du Bois. *The Suppression of the African Slave Trade to the United States of America, 1638–1870* (1896; reprint, Baton Rouge: Louisiana State University Press, 1969), 7–38.

34. The Africans aboard the *Camden* were taken to Edenton, North Carolina, and sent into the cypress swamps to dig canals and clear fields for rice cultivation on what would become Somerset Plantation near Creswell, North Carolina; Dorothy S. Redford with Michael D'Orso, *Somerset Homecoming: Recovering a Lost Heritage* (New York: Doubleday, 1988), 90 and 128–30

35. Minchinton, "Seaborne Slave Trade," 1–61.

36. Du Bois, *Suppression of the African Slave Trade*, 240.

37. Curtin, *Atlantic Slave Trade*, 157.

38. *South Carolina Gazette*, May 30, 1785.

39. Ibid., July 11, 1785.

40. Ibid., May 6, 1784.

41. Ibid., August 25, 1785.

42. Ibid., December 16, 1784, through March 10, 1785; and Nathaniel Russell to Joseph and Joshua Grafton, July 2, 1785; Donnan, ed., *Documents*, 4:479–80.

43. Hugh Thomas, *The Slave Trade: The Story of the Atlantic Slave Trade, 1440–1870* (New York: Simon and Schuster, 1997), 281–84.

44. Jerome J. Nadelhaft, *The Disorders of War: The Revolution in South Carolina* (Orono: University of Maine Press, 1981), 144–46.

45. Donnan, ed., *Documents*, 3:468–73; and W. Robert Higgins, "Charles Town Merchants and Factors Dealing in the External Negro Trade, 1735–1775," *South Carolina Historical Magazine* 65 (October 1964): 205–17.

46. Nadelhaft, *Disorders of War*, 141–54.

47. *Georgia Gazette*, January 17 and 20, 1793; Helen Tunnicliff Catterall, ed., *Judicial Cases Concerning American Slavery and the Negro*, 5 vols. (Washington, D.C.: Carnegie Institution of Washington, 1926–37), 2:276; and Michael E. Stevens, ed., *Journals of the House of Representatives, 1787–1788* (Columbia: University of South Carolina Press, 1983), 159–60.

48. *Charleston Courier*, April 24, April 30, June 10, June 11, June 22, June 30, December 28, and December 29, 1807.

49. *Charleston Courier*, May 7 and 8, 1805. The brig *Thomas* reported arriving from Isles de Loss, but an advertisement lists the origin as the Windward Coast.

50. Curtin, *Atlantic Slave Trade*, 155–67.

51. Thomas, *Slave Trade*, 337–40; Curtin, *Atlantic Slave Trade*, 156–62.

52. John Adams, *Remarks on the Country Extending from Cape Palmas to the River Congo* (London, 1966), 217–18; quoted in Stephen D. Behrendt, "The Annual Volume and Regional Distribution of the British Slave Trade, 1780–1807," *Journal of African History* 38, no. 2 (1997): 203.

53. Curtin, *Atlantic Slave Trade*, 228–30. Quote on page 229.

54. Ibid., 278–79. For middle-passage lengths from Sierra Leone, see *Charleston Courier*, May 30, 1807, and June 25, 1807, forty days and fifty days, respectively.

55. For examples of middle-passage lengths from under the bulge of Africa, see *Charleston Courier*, April 2, 1807, and April 13, 1807, ninety-eight days from the Bight of Biafra and eighty-five days from the Gold Coast, respectively.

56. For examples of middle-passage lengths from West-Central Africa, see *Charleston Courier*, January 12, 1807, and January 28, 1807, fifty-six days from the Congo and fifty-four days from Angola, respectively.

57. Daniel Pratt Mannix, *Black Cargoes: A History of the Atlantic Slave Trade, 1518–1865* (New York: Viking, 1962), 112.

58. Thomas, *Slave Trade*, 360.

59. F. H. and E. to John Anderson, May 8, 1784, Slavery Mss., box 2, New-York Historical Society, New York City.

60. Nadelhaft, *Disorders of War*, 147–49.

61. Charles Ball, *Slavery in the United States: A Narrative of the Life and Adventures of Charles Ball, a Black Man* (Lewiston, Pa.: John W. Shugert, 1836), 58.

62. Ibid., 126–27.

63. Wax, "New Negroes," 216–18; Joseph Clay to James Jackson, February 16, 1784, Donnan, ed., *Documents*, 4, 630; and Clay, Telfair and Co. to James Jackson, March 29, 1784, Clay, Telfair and Co. Letter Book, vol. 1, 1783–1784, Georgia Historical Society, Savannah.

64. Du Bois, *Suppression of the African Slave Trade*, 250–60.

65. Ibid.

66. Clay and Telfair to Nathaniel Hall, March 11, 1784. Clay, Telfair and Co. Letter Book, vol. 1, 1782–1784.

67. For arrivals from Gambia touted as Windward Coast slaves, see *Georgia Gazette*, August 27, 1795; and for arrivals from Sierra Leone, see *Georgia Gazette*, August 12, 1795.

68. Wax, "'New Negroes,'" 193–220; and appendices A and B.

69. Lawrence S. Rowland, Alexander Moore, and George C. Rogers, Jr., *The History of Beaufort County, South Carolina: Volume I, 1514–1861* (Columbia: University of South Carolina Press, 1996), 346–49.

70. Joseph Clay to [?], December 13, 1786, Edward Telfair Papers, Duke Special Collections, Perkins Library, Duke University, Durham, North Carolina.

71. Ibid.

72. Ibid.

73. Wax, "New Negroes," 217.

74. Edwin L. Williams, Jr., "Negro Slavery in Florida," *Florida Historical Quarterly* 28 (October 1949): 93–110.

75. For arrivals of Florida slaves in Georgia, South Carolina, and North Carolina see *Gazette of the State of Florida*; *South Carolina Gazette and General Advertiser*; Duties on Trade at Charleston, 1784–1787, South Carolina Department of Archives, Columbia, South Carolina; *South Carolina Gazette and Daily Advertiser*; *State Gazette of South Carolina*; Walter E. Minchinton, "Seaborne Slave Trade of North Carolina," 1–62; *Gazette of the State of Georgia*; *Charleston Morning Post*; and *Republican and Savannah Ledger*.

76. Williams, "Negro Slavery in Florida," 93–110.

77. Ibid.

78. Terry Alford, *Prince among Slaves* (New York: Harcourt Brace Jovanovich, 1977), 40–42; and Thomas Ashe, *Travels in America Performed in 1806*, 2 vols. (London: Wm. Sawyer, 1808), 2:340–44.

79. Alford, *Prince among Slaves*, 42.

80. Paul F. LaChance, "The Politics of Fear: French Louisianians and the Slave Trade, 1786–1809," *Plantation Society* 1 (June 1979): 195; Alford, *Prince among Slaves*, 40–42; and Caroline Maude Burson, *The Stewardship of Don Esteban Miró, 1782–1792: A Study of Louisiana Based Largely on the Documents in New Orleans* (New Orleans: American Printing, 1940), 98–99.

81. Du Bois, *African Slave Trade*, 88.

82. LaChance, "Politics of Fear," 162–97.

83. Ashe, *Travels in America*, 2:216.

84. Curtin, *Atlantic Slave Trade*, 160.

85. Littlefield, *Rice and Slaves*, 25.

86. Curtin, *Atlantic Slave Trade*, 156–58.

87. Morgan, "Black Society," 130–33. Morgan estimated that in the 1780s the Gold Coast was the source for 46 percent of the African slaves of identifiable origin, Senegambia for 15 percent, Sierra Leone for 3 percent, the Windward Coast for 13 percent, and Angola for 19 percent. This study, for the same decade, indicates that the Gold Coast was the source for 41 percent, Senegambia for 20 percent, Sierra Leone for 8 percent, the Windward Coast for 7 percent, and Angola, 22 percent. For the first decade of the 1800s, Morgan estimated Angola, 49 percent; Senegambia, 6 percent; Sierra Leone, 2 percent; the Windward Coast, 23 percent; and the Gold Coast, 13 percent. This study indicates for Angola exports, 46 percent; Senegambia, 2 percent; Sierra Leone, 20 percent; the Windward Coast, 7 percent; and the Gold Coast, 10 percent. See table 10.

CHAPTER 4: NORTH AMERICAN SLAVE MERCHANTS

1. Philip D. Curtin, *The Atlantic Slave Trade: A Census* (Madison: University of Wisconsin Press, 1969), 71–73; and Herbert S. Klein, "Slaves and Shipping in Eighteenth-Century Virginia," *Journal of Interdisciplinary History* 5 (winter 1975): 392.

2. Jay Coughtry, *The Notorious Triangle: Rhode Island and the African Slave Trade* (Philadelphia: Temple University Press, 1981), 5–21.

3. David Richardson, "The British Slave Trade to Colonial South Carolina," *Slavery and Abolition: A Journal of Comparative Studies*, 12 (December 1991): 162–64.

4. Francis Jerdone to William Buchanan, May 26, 1750, Elizabeth Donnan, ed., *Documents Illustrative of the History of the Slave Trade to America*, 4 vols. (1930–35; reprint, New York: Octagon Books, 1969), 4:140.

5. William Allason to Crosbies and Traffords, August 4, 1761, quoted in Darold D. Wax, "Negro Import Duties in Colonial Virginia: A Study of British Commercial Policy and Local Public Policy," *Virginia Magazine of History and Biography* 79 (January 1975): 43.

6. Henry Laurens to Ross and Mills, September 2, 1768, quoted in Richardson, "British Slave Trade," 155.

7. Clay and Co. to Messrs. William Fox, Jr., and Co., September 1, 1774, quoted in Darold D. Wax, "'New Negroes Are Always in Demand': The Slave Trade in Eighteenth-Century Georgia," *Georgia Historical Quarterly* 68 (summer 1984): 206.

8. Edward Telfair to William Thompson, August 11, 1773, quoted in Wax, "'New Negroes,'" 207.

9. Edward McCrady, *South Carolina under the Royal Government, 1719–1776* (New York, 1899), 649.

10. Richardson, "British Slave Trade," 144–46.

11. Julia Floyd Smith, *Slavery and Rice Culture in Low Country Georgia, 1750–1860* (Knoxville: University of Tennessee Press, 1985), 99.

12. Edward Ball, *Slaves in the Family* (New York: Farrar, Straus and Giroux, 1998), 191.

13. Ibid., 177–256 and 329–54.

14. W. Robert Higgins, "Charles Town Merchants and Factors Dealing in the External Negro Trade, 1735–1775," *South Carolina Historical Magazine* 65 (October 1964): 205–17.

15. Higgins, "Charles Town Merchants," 206–17; and Wax, "'New Negroes,'" 206.

16. Henry Laurens to Wells, Wharton, and Doran, May 27, 1755, quoted from Elizabeth Donnan, "The Slave Trade into South Carolina before the Revolution," *American Historical Review* 33 (July 1928): 815.

17. David Duncan Wallace, *The Life of Henry Laurens* (New York: G. P. Putman, 1915), 72–94.

18. Wax, "'New Negroes,'" 214–17; and Wallace, *Life of Henry Laurens*, 420–31.

19. Joseph Clay to James Jackson, February 16, 1784, quoted in Donnan, ed., *Documents*, 4:630.

20. Joseph Clay to James Jackson, March 29, 1784, Clay, Telfair and Co., Letter Book, vol. 1, 1783–1784, Georgia Historical Society, Savannah.

21. Appendices A and B; and Donnan, ed., *Documents*, 4:475. For the sloop *Porgy*, see *State Gazette of South Carolina*, April 21, 1785; and Duties on Trade at Charleston, 1784–1787, South Carolina Department of Archives, Columbia, 124, 195, 208, and 222.

22. Joseph Clay to James Snelgrove, February 5, 1783, Joseph Clay, *Letters of Joseph Clay, Merchant of Savannah, 1776–1793* (Savannah: Morning News, 1913), 174–76.

23. *South Carolina Gazette and General Advertiser*, November 16, 1785.

24. See Duties on Trade at Charleston for imports from England.

25. *State Gazette of South Carolina*, March 5, 1785.

26. *Boston Gazette and Country Journal*, October 25, 1784.

27. *State Gazette of South Carolina*, August 29, 1785.

28. Nathaniel Russell to Stephen Deblois, April 7, 1786, Slavery Mss., box 2, New-York Historical Society, New York City.

29. Trustees of the Charleston Library Society, *The Charlestown Directory for 1782 and the Charleston Directory for 1785* (Richmond, Va.: Whittet and Shepperson, 1951), 13–19. In 1782 the *Charlestown Directory* listed 106 merchants and factors. Unfortunately, the 1785 directory does not list occupations.

30. Anonymous, *A Few Salutary Hints, Pointing out the Policy and Consequences of Admitting British Subjects to Engross Our Trade and Become Our Citizens*, Shipton, No. 19645 (Charleston and New York, 1786).

31. *State Gazette of South Carolina*, March 5, 1787.

32. George Abbott Hall to Thomas Jefferson, December 31, 1784, Julian P. Boyd, ed., *The Papers of Thomas Jefferson*, 26 vols. to date (Princeton, N.J.: Princeton University Press, 1950–), 8:201.

33. Malcolm Bell, Jr., *Major Butler's Legacy: Five Generations of a Slaveholding Family* (Athens: University of Georgia Press, 1987), 45–46.

34. George Abbott Hall to Thomas Jefferson, December 31, 1784, Boyd, ed., *Papers of Thomas Jefferson*, 8:201.

35. For slave-sale credit terms, see *Gazette of the State of Georgia*, February 5 and April 15, 1784, and January 1, 1787; and *Baillee vs. Hartley*, In the Court of Exchequer, 1784, Parish Transcripts, Miscellaneous Papers on Slavery, box 1, file 2, New-York Historical Society, New York City.

36. Richardson, "British Slave Trade," 151–55; Joseph and Joshua Grafton to Captain Robert Champlin, April 15, 1785, and Nathaniel Russell to Joseph and Joshua Grafton, July 2, 1785, in Donnan, ed., *Documents*, 4:479–80.

37. Patrick S. Brady, "The Slave Trade and Sectionalism in South Carolina, 1787–1808," *Journal of Southern History* 38 (November 1972): 601–20.

38. *South Carolina Gazette and General Advertiser*, July 19, 1783.

39. Joseph W. Barnwell, "Diary of Timothy Ford, 1785–1786," *South Carolina Historical and Genealogical Magazine* 13 (October 1912): 193.

40. *South Carolina State Gazette and Daily Advertiser*, August 21, 1786.

41. *State Gazette of South Carolina*, October 12, 1786.

42. John Lloyd to T. B. Smith, April 15, 1786, John Lloyd Papers, South Carolina Historical Society, Charleston, South Carolina.

43. Barnwell, "Diary of Timothy Ford," 201.

44. Joseph Clay to Nathaniel Hall, April 23, 1783, in Clay, *Letters of Joseph Clay*, 185–86.

45. James Baillee to James Rodgers, April 16, 1785, James Rodgers Papers, box 17, III-A, Rare Book, Manuscript, and Special Collections Library, Duke University, Durham, North Carolina.

46. Warren C. Ogden, "Langdon Cheves, 1776–1857," M.A. thesis, Duke University, 1930, 14–15.

47. Robert Molloy, *Charleston, a Gracious Heritage* (New York: D. Appleton–Century, 1947), 86.

48. Antonio Pace, trans. and ed., *Luigi Castiglioni's Viaggio: Travels in the United States of North America, 1785–1787* (Syracuse: Syracuse University Press, 1983), 165–66; and Ebenezer S. Thomas, *Reminiscences of the Last Sixty-Five Years*, 2 vols. (Hartford, Conn., 1840), 1:33–34 and 40.

49. *South Carolina State Gazette and Daily Advertiser*, September 6, 1784.

50. Brailsford and Morris to Thomas Jefferson, October 31, 1787, in "Letters of Morris and Brailsford to Thomas Jefferson," ed. Richard Walsh, *South Carolina Historical Magazine* 58 (1957): 135–36.

51. Appendix B.

52. Trustees of the Charleston Library Society, *Charlestown Directory for 1782 and the Charleston Directory for 1785*; John Dixon Nelson, *Nelson's Charleston Directory, and Strangers Guide, for the Year of Our Lord 1801. Being the Twenty-Fifth Year of the Independence of the United States of America, until July Fourth* (Charleston: John Dixon Nelson, 1801); J. J. Negrin, *Charleston Library Society New Charleston Directory, and Strangers's Guide, for the Year 1802. Being the Twenty-Sixth and Twenty-Seventh Year of the Independence of the United States of America* (Charleston: John A. Dacqueny, 1802).

53. Orlando Ridout V and Willie Graham, Draft Report of "An Architectural and Historical Analysis of the Nathaniel Russell House, Charleston, South Carolina," May 1996, 5–26, Historic Charleston Foundation.

54. Ibid.; and Nathaniel Russell to Joseph and Joshua Grafton, July 2, 1785, in Donnan, ed., *Documents*, 4:479–80.

55. Ridout and Graham, "Architectural and Historical Analysis," 5–26.

56. Ibid.; Duties on Trade at Charleston, 68, 215, 220, 227, 311, and 322; *State Gazette of South Carolina*, June 13 and July 31, 1784, and August 1, 1786; and Gibbs and Channing to Nathaniel Russell, February 28, 1805, Slavery Mss., box 2, New-York Historical Society, New York City.

57. George C. Rogers, Jr., *Evolution of a Federalist: William Loughton Smith of Charleston, 1758–1812* (Columbia: University of South Carolina Press, 1962), 384.

58. Ibid.; and Ridout and Graham, "Architectural and Historical Analysis," 5–26.

59. Ira Berlin, *Many Thousands Gone: The First Two Centuries of Slavery in North America* (Cambridge: Belknap, 1998), 290–324; Joyce E. Chaplin, *An Anxious Pursuit: Agricultural Innovation and Modernity in the Lower South, 1712–1911* (Chapel Hill: University of North Carolina Press, 1993), 321–24; and Wax, "New Negroes," 214–16.

60. Clay, Telfair, and Co. to Messrs. Coppells, March 11, 1784, Clay, Telfair and Co. Letter Book, Georgia Historical Society, Savannah.

61. Appendix B.

62. See appendices A and B for Savannah imports, merchants, and factors; and Wax, "New Negroes," 215–19.

63. Helen Tunnicliff Catterall, ed., *Judicial Cases Concerning American Slavery and the Negro*, 5 vols. (Washington: Carnegie Institution of North America, 1926–37), 2:294; *State Gazette of South Carolina*, March 1, 1790; and William Mein to Pierce Butler, May 24, 1803, Butler Family Papers, Historical Society of Pennsylvania, Philadelphia.

64. *Columbia Museum and Savannah Advertiser*, March 15, 1799.

65. Samuel Vernon to [?], January 20, 1800, quoted in Coughtry, *Notorious Triangle*, 196.

66. *Charleston Courier,* July 27 and December 2, 1807.

67. Appendices A and B.

68. "Account of Sales of 106 Africans brought into Charleston, S.C., on Brig *Three Sisters,* Captain Champlin, of Bristol, October 12, 1807," *Collections* (Rhode Island Historical Society) 12 (January 1919): 9–10; Walter Edgar, *South Carolina: A History* (Columbia: University of South Carolina Press, 1998), 265–87; Ronald Edward Bridwell, "The South's Wealthiest Planter: Wade Hampton I of South Carolina," Ph.D. diss., 2 vols., University of South Carolina, 1980, 2:749–86; and J. Carlyle Sitterson, *Sugar Country: The Cane Sugar Industry in the South, 1753–1950* (Lexington: University of Kentucky Press, 1953), 13–44.

69. Thomas, *Reminiscences,* 35–36.

70. "Diary of Edward Hooker," *American Historical Association Annual Report* 1 (1897): 867–70.

71. David Fleming to Mordecai Cohen, September 22, 1806, Lewis Malone Ayer Papers, 1772–1865, Rare Book, Manuscript, and Special Collections Library, Duke University, Durham, North Carolina.

72. David Fleming to Mordecai Cohen, September 22 and October 2, 1806, Ayer Papers.

73. David Fleming to Mordecai Cohen, October 6, 1806; and Myer Jacobs to Mordecai Cohen, November 5 and 16, 1807, Ayer Papers. For cotton prices, see John Hebron Moore, *The Emergence of the Cotton Kingdom in the Old Southwest: Mississippi, 1770–1860* (Baton Rouge: Louisiana State University Press, 1988), 6–10.

74. Darling Peoples to Lewis Malone Ayer, December 8, 1804, Ayer Papers.

75. Donnan, ed., *Documents,* 4:547–77.

76. For old and "refuse" slaves, see Frances Depau advertisement for "old slaves" in *Charleston Courier,* November 23, 1807, and *Murden v. Insurance Co.,* Catterall, ed., *Judicial Cases,* 2:302–3; for Bight of Benin and Bight of Biafra shipments, see *Charleston Courier,* January 26, May 27, 1806, and April 8, 1807.

77. *Charleston Courier,* November 28, 1807.

78. Ibid., February 11, 1808, and December 18, 1807.

79. Ibid., December 2, 1807; and March 4 and September 12, 1808.

80. *Annals of the Congress of the United States. Sixteenth Congress, Second Session: Comprising the Period from November 13, 1820 to March 3, 1821, Inclusive* (Washington: Gales and Seaton, 1855), 72–78; and appendix B.

81. *Annals of the Congress,* 72–78.

82. George Locke Howe, *Mount Hope; A New England Chronicle* (New York: Viking, 1959). 124; and appendix A.

83. Donnan, ed., *Documents,* 3:397; and appendix A.

84. Donnan, ed., *Documents,* 3:383–404; Trustees of the Charleston Library Society, *Charlestown Directory for 1782 and the Charleston Directory for 1785;* Milligan, *Charleston Directory* (1790); and Negrin, *Charleston Directory* (1802).

85. Donnan, ed., *Documents,* 4:552–58.

86. For Verree and Blair sales, see *Charleston Courier,* February 8 and 10, July 31, and August 2, 1804, and May 21, 1805; for M. M. Campbell sales, see *Charleston Courier,* September 25 and December 22, 1804, and January 31, June 6, and July 10, 1805; for David Lopez sales, see *Charleston Courier,* October 9 and November 11, 1806, and July 29 and September 29, 1807; for R. Eason sales, see *Charleston Courier,* June 12 and September 18, 1806, and February 24, 1807.

87. Fleming to Cohen, September 22 and October 2, 1806, Ayer Papers.

88. Appendix A.

89. David J. Weber, *The Spanish Frontier in North America* (New Haven, Conn.: Yale University Press, 1992), 283.

90. Phillip S. May, "Zephaniah Kingsley, Nonconformist (1765–1843)," *Florida Historical Quarterly* 23 (January 1945): 148–59; Daniel L. Schafer, *Anna Madgigine Jai Kingsley: African Princess, Florida Slave, Plantation Owner* (Gainesville: University Press of Florida, 2003), 20–26; June Landers, *Black Society in Spanish Florida* (Urbana: University of Illinois Press, 1999), 174–82; Edwin L. Williams, Jr., "Negro Slavery in Florida," *Florida Historical Quarterly* 28 (October 1949): 93–99; and Daniel L. Schafer, "Ties That Bind: Anglo-American Slave Traders in Africa and Florida, John Fraser and His Descendents," *Slavery and Abolition* 20 (December 1999): 1–21.

91. Thomas Ashe, *Travels in America Performed in 1806* (London: Wm. Sawyer, 1808), 341–42.

92. Introduction, 1–3, John McDonogh Papers, 1779–1850, Howard-Tilton Library, Tulane University, New Orleans, Louisiana.

93. Ibid., appendix B, and B. Lafon, *Calendrier de Commerce de la Nouvell-Orleans pour l'année 1807* (New Orleans: Chez Jean Renard, Imprimeur de la ville, 1806), 76–84.

94. Hamm, "American Slave Trade," 56–58.

95. Coughtry, *Notorious Triangle*, 106.

96. Appendix B.

97. *South Carolina State Gazette and Daily Advertiser*, August 29, 1785.

98. Walter E. Minchinton, "The Seaborne Slave Trade of North Carolina," *North Carolina Historical Review* 71 (January 1994): 17; and Dorothy S. Redford with Michael D'Orso, *Somerset Homecoming: Recovering a Lost Heritage* (New York: Doubleday, 1988), 90, 128–30. The holding company that Collins headed received another seventy slaves in 1787.

99. Hugh Thomas, *The Slave Trade: The Story of the Atlantic Slave Trade, 1440–1870* (New York: Simon and Schuster, 1997), 487.

100. *Charleston Morning Post*, January 18, 1787.

101. Thomas H. Perkins to M. Jean Laroque, December 16, 1791, in Lloyd Vernon Briggs, *The History and Genealogy of the Cabot Family, 1475–1927*, 2 vols. (Boston: Charles E. Goodspeed, 1927), 2:505.

102. Terry Alford, *Prince among Slaves* (New York: Harcourt Brace Jovanovich, 1977), 30–38 and 224–31.

103. Quoted in Roger Anstey, "The Volume of the North American Slave-Carrying Trade from Africa, 1761–1810," *Revue francaise d'histoire outre-mer* 62, no. 2 (1975): 47–66.

104. Appendix B.

105. Anstey, "Volume of the North American Slave-Carrying Trade," 52–58; and Curtin, *Atlantic Slave Trade*, 266–67.

106. Appendix B.

107. Anstey, "Volume of the North American Slave-Carrying Trade," 63–65.

108. Donnan, ed., *Documents*, 4:494–98 and 500.

109. Ibid., 4:515.

110. E. E. Charleston, July 24, 1799, "Sund's shipp'd by H. J. Jones on board the Schooner 'Charlotte.' Wm. Langster Master, for Africa on Acct. and risk of the Shipper and cons'd to the Master on Board," Slavery Papers, box 2, New-York Historical Society, New York City.

111. Hamm, "American Slave Trade," 180.

112. Appendix B.

113. Daniel Pratt Mannix, *Black Cargoes: A History of the Atlantic Slave Trade, 1518–1865* (New York: Viking, 1962), 188–89.

114. Thomas, *Reminiscences*, 2:35–36.

115. Coughtry, *Notorious Triangle*, 27–28. Between 1803 and 1808 African clearances from Bristol, Newport, Providence, and Warren totaled 142.

116. Stephen D. Behrendt, "The British Slave Trade, 1785–1807: Volume, Profitability, and Mortality," Ph.D. diss., the University of Wisconsin, 1993, 40.

117. Appendices A and B.

118. Vice Admiralty Briefs, Marine Research Society, in Donnan, ed., *Documents*, 4:551–70.

119. Chapter 2 includes estimates that, in the first decade of the 1800s, 79,490 foreign slaves were disembarked in South Carolina. However, not all of these were landed in Charleston. Therefore, to allow for arrivals in other locations in South Carolina, the number of Charleston arrivals was lowered to 75,000.

120. The slave-sales amount was reached by multiplying the estimated number of slaves arrived in Charleston, 75,000, by the average sales price, $240 per person, which totaled $18,000,000. The African trade-goods amount was reached by multiplying the number of slave voyages that originated in Charleston, 140, by the value of the African trade goods carried by an average slaver, $23,100, which totaled $3,234,000.

121. For evidence of transshipments, see appendix B.

122. For African trade goods, see *Charleston Courier*, October 28, 1803, and December 6, 1805; for collars, chains, and shackles, see *Charleston Courier*, July 12, 1804; for India goods, see *Charleston Courier*, October 21, 1805; for gunpowder and muskets, see *Charleston Courier*, June 3, 1805, February 25, August 21, September 4, October 18, and December 8, 1806; for officers and crew, see *Charleston Courier*, October 8 and 18, 1806; and for sales of slave ships, see *Charleston Courier*, January 20, April 5, and April 22, 1806.

CHAPTER 5: THE NATURE OF THE NORTH AMERICAN SLAVE TRADE BETWEEN 1787 AND 1808

1. W. E. B. Du Bois, *The Suppression of the African Slave Trade to the United States of America, 1638–1870* (1896; reprint, Baton Rouge: Louisiana State University Press, 1969), 53–62.

2. John P. Kaminski, ed., *A Necessary Evil? Slavery and the Debate over the Constitution* (Madison, Wisc.: Madison House, 1995), 62–63.

3. Ralph Ketcham, *James Madison: A Biography* (Charlottesville: University of Virginia Press, 1990), 315.

4. Michael E. Stevens, "To Get As Many Slaves As You Can: An 1807 Slaving Voyage," *South Carolina Historical Magazine* 87 (July 1986): 190.

5. Paul F. LaChance, "The Politics of Fear: French Louisianians and the Slave Trade, 1786–1809," *Plantation Society* 1 (June 1979): 195–97.

6. Quoted in LaChance, "Politics of Fear," 165.

7. Ibid., 164–70; and Gabriel Debien and René Le Gardeur, "The Saint-Domingue Refugees in Louisiana, 1792–1804," in *The Road to Louisiana: The Saint-Domingue Refugees, 1792–1809*, ed. Carl A. Brasseaux and Glenn R. Conrad (Lafayette: Center for Louisiana Studies, University of Southwestern Louisiana, 1992), 175–188.

8. LaChance, "Politics of Fear," 164–70; and Debien and Le Gardeur, "Saint-Domingue Refugees in Louisiana," 2:137.

9. Du Bois, *Suppression of the African Slave Trade*, 86–88.

10. Terry Alford, *Prince among Slaves* (New York: Harcourt Brace Jovanovich, 1977), 32–37.

11. Sir William Young, *West India Common-Place Book: Compiled from Parliamentary and Official Documents* (London, 1807), 170.

12. John Robinson, "Answers to Queries Respecting Slavery," quoted in Alford, *Prince among Slaves*, 34.

13. Alford, *Prince among Slaves*, 1–38.

14. Ibid.

15. *Charleston Courier*, April 14, 1807. According to the "Ship News," the schooner *Mercury* arrived in New Orleans twenty-one days after clearing Charleston.

16. *Charleston Courier*, July 1, 1806; and Helen Tunnicliff Catterall, ed., *Judicial Cases Concerning American Slavery and the Negro*, 5 vols. (Washington D.C.: Carnegie Institution of Washington, 1926–37), 2:298.

17. *Charleston Courier*, March 23 and May 8, 1807.

18. Ibid., September 28 and November 11, 1807.

19. Ibid., August 11, 1806.

20. Alford, *Prince among Slaves*, 36–37. Alford suggests that Ibrahima and his fellow captives may have pulled their barge upriver. According to Alford, the work was so strenuous that a number of slaves had died while performing the task. In April of 1808, an English traveler, Christian Schultz, Jr., witnessed part of a cargo of slaves pulling a brig upriver between New Orleans and Natchez. For his description, see Christian Schultz, Jr., *Travels on an Inland Voyage*, 2 vols. (New York: Isaac Riley, 1810), 2:137.

21. *Louisiana Gazette*, February 4, 1806; and *Charleston Courier*, December 15, 1806.

22. *Charleston Courier*, July 1, 1806; and Catterall, ed., *Judicial Cases*, 2:298.

23. George E. Brooks, Jr., *Yankee Traders, Old Coasters and African Middlemen: A History of American Legitimate Trade with West Africa in the Nineteenth Century* (Brookline, Mass.: Boston University Press, 1970), 25; and Roger Anstey, "The Volume of the North American Slave-Carrying Trade from Africa, 1761–1810," *Revue francaise d'histoire d'outre-mer* 62, no. 2 (1975): 56–64.

24. Brooks, *Yankee Traders*, 25.

25. *Charleston Courier*, February 18, July 12, and August 6, 1804; and *Louisiana Gazette*, September 28, 1804.

26. For the *Samuel*, see *Charleston Courier*, January 24, 1805; for *Seaflower*, see Gibbs and Channing to Nathaniel Russell, February 28, 1805, Slavery Mss., box 4, New-York Historical Society, New York City; for *Almira*, see *Charleston Courier*, May 3, 1805; for *Two Friends*, see *Charleston Courier*, June 7, 1805; for *Montezuma*, see Robert Mackay, *Letters of Robert Mackay to His Wife, Written from Ports in America and England, 1772–1816* (Athens: University of Georgia Press, 1949), 302–3, and *Charleston Courier*, September 11 and October 15, 1805; for the brig *Jane*, see *Charleston Courier*, January 20, 1806; and for the *Yeopum*, see *Charleston Courier*, January 20 and May 10, 1806.

27. *Charleston Courier*, June 16, 18, 19, 21, 1806.

28. For the *Fanny*, see *Charleston Courier*, April 20; for the *Truxton*, see *Charleston Courier*, May 16; for the *Port Mary*, see *Charleston Courier*, June 9 and 18, 1806.

29. For the *Lucy*, see *Charleston Courier*, September 11; and for the *Washington*, see *Charleston Courier*, November 10, 1806.

30. Thomas White to Gardner and Dean, January 1, 1806, Slavery Mss., box 2, New-York Historical Society, New York City.

31. For the *Ann*, see Elizabeth Donnan, ed., *Documents Illustrative of the History of the Slave Trade to America*, 4 vols. (1930–35; reprint, New York: Octagon Books, 1969), 3:388 and 394–404; for the *Juno*, see *Charleston Courier*, May 1, 1807; for the *Lavinia*, see *Charleston Courier*, May 9, 1807; for the *Eliza*, see *Charleston Courier*, October 20, 1807; for the *Nancy*, see *Charleston Courier*, December 28, 1807; and for the *Amedie*, see Donnan, ed., *Documents*, 3:531–50.

32. Donnan, ed., *Documents*, 3:531–50.

33. *Charleston Courier*, May 8, 1807.

34. Ibid., November 23, 1807.

35. Ibid., October 20, 1807.

36. Donnan, ed., *Documents*, 3:531–50.

37. Ibid., 551–70.

38. *Charleston Courier,* July 8, 11, and 12, 1805.

39. Eleazer Elizer, *A Directory For 1803; Containing The Names of all the Housekeepers and Traders in the City of Charleston, alphabetically arranged; their particular profession and their residence* (Charleston: W. P. Young, 1803), 38; and *Charleston Courier,* July 8, 11, and 12, 1805.

40. *Charleston Courier,* April 22, 1806, and December 14, 1807.

41. Samuel Brown to William Vernon, July 3, 1792, Slavery Mss., box 2, New-York Historical Society, New York City .

42. Captain Gray to (Samuel Brown?) November 26, 1793 (enclosed in Samuel Brown to William Vernon, March 1794), Slavery Mss., box 2, New-York Historical Society, New York City.

43. Quoted in Hugh Thomas, *The Slave Trade: The Story of the Atlantic Slave Trade: 1440–1870* (New York: Simon and Schuster, 1997), 414.

44. *Charleston Courier,* July 12 and 13, 1804.

45. Ibid., July 13, 1804.

46. *Charleston Courier,* July 16, 1804.

47. Ibid., July 12, 13, and 16, 1804. Evidently the *Horizon* did not sell or was sold to someone who hired Alexander M'Clure to undertake another slaving voyage. The *Charleston Courier* reported on December 4, 1804, that the *Horizon* had cleared Charleston for Africa with M'Clure as its master.

48. Du Bois, *Suppression of the African Slave Trade,* 94–96.

49. *Charleston Courier,* July 12 and 13, 1804.

50. Thomas, *Slave Trade,* 550–57.

51. Captain Wood to Gardner and Dean, January 25, 1807, Slavery Mss., box 2, New-York Historical Society, New York City .

52. *Murden v. Insurance Co.,* Catterall, ed., *Judicial Cases,* 2:302–3.

53. Quoted in Stevens, "To Get As Many Slaves As You Can," 189.

54. Ibid., 187–92.

55. *U.S. v. Schooner Kitty,* Catterall, ed., *Judicial Cases,* 2:291–92.

56. *Murden v. Insurance Co.,* Catterall, *Judicial Cases,* 2:302–3.

57. Letter of Instruction to the Master, William Boyd, July 24, 1807, in Donnan, ed., *Documents,* 4:568.

58. *Teasdale v. Insurance Co.,* Catterall, ed., *Judicial Cases,* 2:289–90.

59. Phillips and Gardner to Silas Dean, October 25, 1807, Slavery Mss., box 2, New-York Historical Society, New York City.

60. Wilfred Harold Munroe, *Tales of an Old Sea Port: A General Sketch of the History of Bristol, Rhode Island, Including, Incidentally, An Account of the Voyages of the Norsemen, So Far As They May Have Been Connected With Narragansett Bay: And Personal Narratives of Some Notable Voyages Accomplished By Sailors From the Mount Hope Lands* (London: Princeton University Press, 1917), 210–11.

61. *Murden v. Insurance Co.,* Catterall, ed., *Judicial Cases,* 2:302–3.

62. *U.S. v. Schooner Kitty,* Catterall, ed., *Judicial Cases,* 2:291–92.

63. "Report of Captain Street," *Charleston Courier,* December 10, 1807.

64. Philip D. Curtin, "Epidemiology and the Slave Trade," *Political Science Quarterly* 83 (June 1968): 203–5.

65. *U.S. v. Schooner Kitty,* Catterall, ed., *Judicial Cases,* 2:291–92.

66. *Murden v. Insurance Co.,* Catterall, ed., *Judicial Cases,* 2:302–3.

67. Mungo Park, *Travels in the Interior of Africa: Performed in the Years 1795, 1796, and 1797, with an Account of a Mission to the Country in 1805* (London: T. Allman, 1839), 249–51.

68. George E. Brooks, Jr., *Yankee Traders, Old Coasters and African Middlemen: A History of American Legitimate Trade with West Africa in the Nineteenth Century* (Brookline, Mass.: Boston

University Press, 1970), 30; Daniel Pratt Mannix, *Black Cargoes: A History of the Atlantic Slave Trade, 1518–1865* (New York: Viking, 1962), 112; Phillip D. Curtin, *The Atlantic Slave Trade: A Census* (Madison: University of Wisconsin Press), 278–79; and George Francis Dow, *Slave Ships and Slaving* (New York: Dover, 1790), 151.

69. Donnan, ed., *Documents,* 3:551–70; and *Charleston Courier,* July 24, 1807. Merchants avoided any references to trading with foreign powers in written instructions that might result in detainment and confiscation. In the case of the *Africa,* Boyd instructed Connolly in writing to enter a U.S. port even if he arrived after the deadline. However, a crewman testified that they were bound for Havana, where the *Africa* had previously delivered two cargoes of Africans. Cuba being a colony of England's enemy at the time, a British court awarded the *Africa* and its cargo to the captors.

70. For the ship *Lydia,* see *Charleston Courier,* May 30, 1807; for the brig *Eliza,* see *Charleston Courier,* November 23, 1807; for the ship *General Eaton,* see *Charleston Courier,* June 11, 1807; for the ship *Independence,* see Catterall, ed., *Judicial Cases,* 2:300; and for the brig *Nancy,* see *Charleston Courier,* December 14, 1807.

71. Joseph Ioor Waring, *A History of Medicine in South Carolina, 1670–1825* (Charleston: South Carolina Medical Society, 1964), 113. The "Pest House" on James Island replaced the Sullivans Island "pest house" in 1798.

72. For location of slave sales, see *Charleston Courier,* 1804, 1805, 1806, 1807, 1808; for locations of commercial houses, see J. J. Negrin, *Negrin's Charleston Directory, for 1807* (Charleston: J. J. Negrin, 1807).

73. For length of slave sales, see *Charleston Courier,* 1804, 1805, 1806, 1807, and 1808. Merchants usually advertised sales until all slaves were sold.

74. See appendix B for volume and origin of arrivals. For quote, see John Lambert, *Travels through Canada and the United States of North America in the Years 1806 and 1807,* 2 vols., 2d. ed. (London: Dorg and Storling, 1814), 165.

75. *Charleston Courier,* November 24, 1807 and January 15, 1808.

76. Ibid., December 14 and 16, 1807.

77. Stevens, "To Get As Many Slaves As You Can," 187–92.

78. In his research on California Indians, Sherburne F. Cook found that similar conditions dramatically increased mortality among the aborigine population. In the late 1700s and early 1800s, missionaries succeeded in converting Native Americans in large numbers, but the converts refused to remain near the missions. To prevent them from leaving, missionaries locked them up at night in cramped, unsanitary, and poorly ventilated buildings. Ironically Charleston merchants were confining Africans on the eastern coast of North America at the same time that Franciscan missionaries were confining Native Americans on the western coast. Sherburne F. Cook, *Population of the California Indians, 1769–1970* (Berkeley: University of California, 1976), 1–43.

79. In Africa populations were not as isolated as Native Americans in North America, but many Africans residing in the interior had not been exposed to various diseases. Adult Africans, the largest age group of captives, were especially vulnerable in many instances. When children were exposed to diseases, they usually survived and developed immunity to the diseases, but adults became much more ill, and many succumbed. Raymond L. Cohn and Richard A. Jensen, "The Determinants of Slave Mortality Rates on the Middle Passage," *Explorations in Economic History* 19 (July 1982): 269–82; Herbert S. Klein and Stanley I. Engerman, "Slave Mortality on British Ships, 1791–1797," in *Liverpool, the African Slave Trade, and Abolition,* Occasional Series, no. 2, ed. Roger Anstey and P. E. H. Hair (London: Historic Society of Lancashire and Cheshire, 1976), 113–22; and Curtin, "Epidemiology," 200–204.

80. Lambert, *Travels,* 167.

81. Ibid., 166.

82. Ibid.

83. Ibid., 167. The previous epidemic probably occurred in October and November of 1805. According to the *Charleston Courier*, November 22, 1805, "Whereas since the importation of slaves from Africa, several incidents have occurred of dead human bodies having been thrown into the waters of the harbour of Charleston."

84. *Charleston Courier*, November 28, 1807.

85. Ibid., December 18, 1807, and February 11, 1808.

86. Ibid., December 2, 1807; and March 4 and September 12, 1808.

87. Stevens, "To Get As Many Slaves As You Can," 187–92.

88. David Ramsay, "Remarks on the Yellow Fever and Epidemic Catarrh, as they appeared in South-Carolina, during the Summer and Autumn of 1807," *Medical Repository Comprehending Original Essays and Intelligence Relative to Medicine, Chemistry, Natural History, Agriculture, Geography, and the Arts; More Especially as They Are Cultivated in America; and A Review of American Publications on Medicine, and the Auxiliary Branches of Science* 5, second hexade (1808): 233–35.

89. Quoted in Stevens, "To Get As Many Slaves As You Can," 191.

90. See appendix B.

91. Curtin, *Atlantic Slave Trade*, 275–86; David Richardson, "The Eighteenth-Century British Slave Trade: Estimates of the Volume and Coastal Distribution in Africa," *Research in Economic History* 12 (1989): 156–57; and Stephen D. Behrendt, "The Annual Volume and Regional Distribution of the British Slave Trade, 1780–1807," *Journal of African History* 38, no. 2 (1997): 187–88.

92. Stevens, "To Get As Many Slaves As You Can," 187–92.

93. Curtin, *Atlantic Slave Trade*, 286.

CONCLUSION

1. Philip D. Curtin, *The Atlantic Slave Trade: A Census* (Madison: University of Wisconsin Press, 1969), 72–74.

2. Roger Anstey, "The Volume of the North American Slave-Carrying Trade from Africa, 1761–1810," *Revue francaise d'histoire d'outre-mer*, 62, no. 2 (1975): 65; and Curtin, *Atlantic Slave Trade*, 212. The figure 120,000 was taken from data extrapolated from data taken from table 64. Allowance was made for no traffic between 1775 and 1782, and 20,000 between 1804 and 1807.

3. Curtin, *Atlantic Slave Trade*, 268. Curtin estimated that about 288,000 Africans were imported during the colonial era, 92,000 from 1783 to 1810, and 50,000 from 1811 to 1861.

4. Ibid., 265–73.

5. Marcus Lee Hansen, *The Atlantic Migration, 1607–1860* (Cambridge: Harvard University Press, 1940), 77; Michael Kraus, *Immigration, the American Mosaic: From Pilgrims to Modern Refugees* (Princeton: Van Norstrand, 1966), 19; and David M. Reimers, "Immigration," in *Encyclopedia of American Social History*, 3 vols., ed. Mary Kupiec Cayton, Elliott J. Gorn, and Peter W. Williams (New York: Scribner, 1993), 1:579–81. The scholars estimate that from 1783 to 1815 about 250,000 English, French, and Irish immigrants landed in North America. Hansen and Kraus ignore Africans in their estimates and discussions of immigration during the period. Reimers discusses African immigrants, but he argues that immigration during the period was limited.

6. For discussion of slave prices and the foreign slave trade, see Robert William Fogel and Stanley L. Engerman, *Time on the Cross: The Economics of American Negro Slavery* (Boston: Little, Brown, 1974), 86–94.

7. Allan Kulikoff, "Uprooted Peoples: Black Migrants in the Age of the American Revolution, 1790–1820," in *Slavery and Freedom in the Age of the American Revolution*, ed. Ira Berlin and Ronald Hoffman (Urbana: University of Illinois Press, 1986), 161–63.

8. Philip D. Morgan, "Black Society in the Lowcountry, 1760–1810," in *Slavery and Freedom in the Age of the American Revolution*, ed. Ira Berlin and Ronald Hoffman (Urbana: University of Illinois Press, 1986), 91–93.

9. See table 5.

10. Donald R. Wright, *African Americans in the Colonial Era: From African Origins through the American Revolution* (Arlington Heights: Harlan Davidson, 1990), 3–5.

11. Quoted in David Brion Davis, *The Problem of Slavery in the Age of Revolution, 1770–1823* (Ithaca: Cornell University Press, 1975), 324–25.

12. Ibid.

13. For a discussion of American slave-carrying capacities, see part 3 in chapter 2. Research found no evidence of surgeons serving on American slavers.

14. Stephen D. Behrendt, "The British Slave Trade, 1785–1807: Volume, Profitability, and Mortality," Ph.D. diss., University of Wisconsin, 1993, 31; and appendix A. According to Behrendt, Liverpool merchants sponsored 111 slavers in 1806 and 71 in 1807. This study indicates that from 1803 to 1808 nearly 100 slavers were outfitted in Charleston.

15. Thomas M. Doerflinger, *A Vigorous Spirit of Enterprise: Merchants and Economic Development in Revolutionary Philadelphia* (Chapel Hill: University of North Carolina Press, 1986), 1–7 and 356–64.

16. William H. Pease and Jane H. Pease, *The Web of Progress: Private Values and Public Styles in Boston and Charleston, 1828–1843* (Athens: University of Georgia Press, 1991), 11.

BIBLIOGRAPHY

PRIMARY SOURCES

Manuscripts

Baker Library, Harvard University, Cambridge, Massachusetts
    James D'Wolf Mss.
Caroliniana Library, University of South Carolina, Columbia
    Henry Laurens Papers
    John Stapleton Papers
    John Walden Papers
Georgia Department of Archives and History, Atlanta
    Black Studies Papers
Georgia Historical Society, Savannah
    Clay, Telfair and Co. Letter Book
    John McIntosh, Jr., Papers
    Savannah City Council Minutes
Hargrett Rare Book and Manuscript Library, University of Georgia, Athens
    Keith Read Collection
Historic Charleston Foundation
Historical Society of Pennsylvania, Philadelphia
    Butler Family Papers
    Pennsylvania Abolition Society
    Anthony Wayne Papers
Howard-Tilton Library, Tulane University, New Orleans, Louisiana
    John McDonogh Papers
Library of Congress, Washington, D.C.
    "Extracts from Letters of the Government and Council at Sierra Leone to the Chairman
        and Court of Directors of the Sierra Leone Company"
Massachusetts Historical Society, Boston
    Boston Marine Insurance Papers
National Archives, Washington, D.C.
    John McDonogh Papers, Collector's Office of the Port of New Orleans, Shipping
        Records
    Records of the Customs Houses in the South-Atlantic States, Savannah, Georgia, Foreign
        Inward Cargo Manifests
    United States Customs Service, New Orleans, Louisiana, Foreign Inward Cargo Manifests,
        1804–08
New-York Historical Society, New York City
    Grand Jury Inquest, Newport, Rhode Island
    Slavery Papers
    Slavery Mss.

North Carolina State Archives, Raleigh
    Anne S. Graham Collection
    Ports, Treasurer's and Comptroller's Papers
Rare Book, Manuscript, and Special Collections Library, Duke University, Durham, North
    Carolina
    Lewis Malone Ayer Papers
    Edward Hooker Papers
    James Rodgers Papers
    Edward Telfair Papers
Rhode Island Historical Society
    Moses Brown Papers
    Charles D'Wolf Papers
South Carolina Department of Archives and History, Columbia
    Duties on Trade at Charleston, 1784–1787
South Carolina Historical Society, Charleston
    John Lloyd Papers

Government Documents

Adams, Lark Emerson, ed. *Journals of the House of Representatives, 1785–1786*. Columbia:
    University of South Carolina Press, 1979.
*Annals of the Congress of the United States. Sixteenth Congress, Second Session: Comprising
    the Period from November 13, 1820 to March 3, 1821, Inclusive*. Washington: Gales and
    Seaton, 1855.
Benton, Thomas Hart. *Abridgement of the Debates of Congress, from 1789 to 1856, From Gales
    and Seaton's Annals of Congress, from their Register of Debates; and from the Official
    Reported Debates, by John C. Rives. By the author of the Thirty year's view* [Thomas Hart
    Benton]. 16 vols. New York: D. Appleton and Co., 1857.
De Bow, J. D. B. *Statistical View of the United States, Embracing Its Territory, Population—
    White, Free Colored, and Slave—Moral and Social Condition, Industry, Property, and Rev-
    enue; the Detailed Statistics of Cities, Towns and Counties: Being a Compendium of the
    Seventh Census, to which Are Added the Results of Every Previous Census, Beginning with
    1790, in Comparative Tables, with explanatory and illustrative notes, Based upon the Sched-
    ules and other Official Sources of Information. By J. D. B. De Bow, Superintendent of the
    United States Census*. Washington: A. O. P. Nicholson, Public Printer, 1854.
Force, Peter. *American Archives*. 2 vols., 4th ser. Washington, D.C.: United States Congress,
    1837–54.
Holmes, George K. *Rice Crop of the United States, 1712–1911*. Washington, D.C.: United
    States Department of Agriculture, Bureau of Statistics, Circular 34, 1912.
Stevens, Michael E., ed. *Journals of the House of Representatives, 1787–1788*. Columbia: Uni-
    versity of South Carolina Press, 1983.
———, ed. *Journals of the House of Representatives, 1791*. Columbia: University of South
    Carolina Press, 1985.
———, ed. *Journals of the House of Representatives, 1792–1794*. Columbia: University of
    South Carolina Press, 1988.

Printed Primary Sources

"Account of Sales of 106 Africans Brought into Charleston, S.C., on Brig. *Three Sisters*, Cap-
    tain Champlin, of Bristol, October 12, 1807." *Collections* (Rhode Island Historical Soci-
    ety) 12 (January 1919): 9–11.
Adams, John. *Remarks on the Country Extending from Cape Palmas to the River Congo*. Lon-
    don, 1966.

African Institute. *Thirteenth Report of the Directors.* London, 1813.

Anonymous. *A Few Salutary Hints, Pointing out the Policy and Consequences of Admitting British Subjects to Engross Our Trade and Become Our Citizens.* Shipton No. 19645. Charleston and New York, 1786.

Ashe, Thomas. *Travels in America Performed in 1806.* 2 vols. London: Wm. Sawyer, 1808.

Ball, Charles. *Slavery in the United States: A Narrative of the Life and Adventures of Charles Ball, a Black Man.* Lewiston, Pa.: John W. Shugert, 1836.

Barnwell, Joseph W. "Diary of Timothy Ford, 1785–1786." *South Carolina Historical and Genealogical Magazine* 13 (October 1912): 181–204.

Boyd, Julian P., ed. *The Papers of Thomas Jefferson.* 26 vols. to date. Princeton, N.J.: Princeton University Press, 1950– .

Boyle, Joseph Lee, ed. "The Revolutionary War Diaries of Captain Walter Finney," *South Carolina Historical Magazine* 98 (April 1997): 126–41.

Bryce, Mrs. Campbell. *The Personal Experiences of Mrs. Campbell Bryce during the Burning of Columbia, South Carolina, by General W. T. Sherman's Army, February 17, 1865.* Philadelphia: J. B. Lippincott, 1899.

Catterall, Helen Tunnicliff, ed. *Judicial Cases Concerning American Slavery and the Negro.* 5 vols. Washington, D.C.: Carnegie Institution of Washington, 1926–37.

Clay, Joseph. *Letters of Joseph Clay, Merchant of Savannah, 1776–1793.* Savannah: Morning News, 1913.

Debates Which Arose in the House of Representatives of South Carolina, on the Constitution Framed for the United States, by a Convention of Delegates at Philadelphia. Charleston: City Gazette, 1788.

Derenne, W. J., Otis Ashmore, W. W. Gordon, and Thomas J. Charlton, M.D., eds. *Letters of Joseph Clay, Merchant of Savannah, 1776–1798.* Savannah: Morning News, 1913.

"Diary of Edward Hooker." *Annual Report of the American Historical Association* 1 (1897): 842–929.

Diary of William Bentley, D.D. 4 vols. Salem: Essex Institute, 1907.

Donnan, Elizabeth, ed. *Documents Illustrative of the History of the Slave Trade to America.* 4 vols. 1930–35. Reprint, New York: Octagon Books, 1969.

Drayton, John. *A View of South Carolina As Respects Her Natural and Civil Concerns.* Charleston: W. P. Young, 1802.

Duffy, John, ed. *The Rudolf Matus History of Medicine.* 2 vols. Baton Rouge: Louisiana State University Press, 1958.

Dunbar, Rowland, ed. *Official Letter Books of W. C. C. Claiborne, 1801–1816.* 3 vols. Jackson: State Department of Archives and History, 1917.

Elizer, Eleazer, A. *Directory For 1803; Containing The Names of all the Housekeepers and Traders in the City of Charleston, alphabetically arranged; their particular profession and their residence* Charleston: W. P. Young, 1803.

Elliott, John, ed. *The Debates in the Several States Conventions on the Adoption of the Federal Constitution.* 4 vols. Philadelphia: J. B. Lippincott, 1836–59.

Eltis, David, Stephen D. Behrendt, David Richardson, and Herbert S. Klein, eds. *The Transatlantic Slave Trade: A Database on CD-Rom.* Cambridge: Cambridge University Press, 1999.

Farrand, Max, ed. *The Records of the Federal Convention of 1787.* 4 vols. 1913. Rev. ed. New Haven: Yale University Press, 1937.

Gilpin, H. E., ed. *The Papers of James Madison.* 3 vols. Mobile: A. Mygatt, 1842.

Hall, Gwendolyn Midlo, ed. *Databases for the Study of Afro-Louisiana History and Genealogy, 1699–1860: Information from Original Manuscript Sources* (CD-ROM). Baton Rouge: Louisiana State University Press, 2000.

Hawkins, Joseph. *Voyage to the Coast of Africa and Travels into the Interior of That Country.* 1797. Reprint, London: Frank Cass, 1970.

Janson, Charles William. *Stranger in America: Containing Observations Made during a Long Residence in That Country, on the Genius, Manners, and Customs of People of the United States; with Biographical Particulars of Public Characters; Hints and Facts Relative to the Arts, Sciences, Commerce, Agriculture, Manufactures, Emigration, and the Slave Trade.* London: Printed for James Cundee by Albion Press, 1807.

Journal of an African Slaver, 1789–1792. Worcester, Mass.: American Antiquarian Society, 1930.

Knutsford, Viscountess. *The Life and Letters of Zachary Macauly.* London: Edward Arnold, 1900.

Lafon, B. *Calendrier de Commerce de la Nouvell-Orleans pour l'année 1807.* New Orleans: Chez Jean Renarcd, Imprimcur de la ville, 1806.

Lambert, John. *Travels through Canada and the United States of North America in the Years 1806 and 1807.* 2 vols. 2d ed. London: Dorg and Storling, 1814.

Mackay, Robert. *Letters of Robert Mackay to His Wife, Written from Ports in America and England, 1772–1816.* Athens: University of Georgia Press, 1949.

Moore, Frank, ed. *Materials for History Printed from Original Manuscripts: Correspondence of Henry Laurens.* New York: Zenger Club, 1861.

Mouser, Bruce L. *A Slaving Voyage to Africa and Jamaica: The Log of the* Sandown, *1793–1794* (Bloomington: Indiana University Press, 2002).

Negrin, *Charleston Library Society New Charleston Directory, and Strangers's Guide, for the Year 1802. Being the Twenty-Sixth and Twenty-Seventh Year of the Independence of the United States of America* (Charleston: J. J. Negrin, 1802).

———. *J. J. Negrin's Charleston Directory for the Year 1806* (Charleston: J. J. Negrin, 1806).

———. *Negrin's Charleston Directory, for 1807* (Charleston: J. J. Negrin, 1807).

Nelson, John Dixon. *Nelson's Charleston Directory, and Strangers Guide, for the Year of Our Lord 1801. Being the Twenty Fifth Year of the Independence of the United States of America, until July Fourth* (Charleston: John Dixon Nelson, 1801).

Pace, Antonia, trans. and ed. *Luigi Castiglioni's Viaggio: Travels in the United States of North America, 1785–1787.* Syracuse: Syracuse University Press, 1983.

Park, Mungo. *Travels in the Interior of Africa: Performed in the Years 1795, 1796, and 1797, with an Account of a Mission to the Country in 1805.* London: T. Allman, 1839.

Robin, C. C. *Voyage to Louisiana, 1803–1805.* New Orleans: Pelican, 1966.

Rowland, Mrs. Dunbar, ed. *Life, Letters, and Papers of William Dunbar.* Jackson: Press of the Mississippi Historical Society, 1930.

Scheopf, Johann David. *Travels in the Confederation.* 2 vols. New York: Burt Franklin, 1968.

Schultz, Christian, Jr. *Travels on an Inland Voyage.* 2 vols. New York: Isaac Riley, 1810.

Thomas, Ebenezer S. *Reminiscences of the Last Sixty-Five Years.* 2 vols. Hartford, Conn., 1840.

Trustees of the Charleston Library Society. *The Charlestown Directory for 1782 and the Charleston Directory for 1785.* Richmond, Va.: Whittet and Shepperson, 1951.

Walsh, Richard, ed. "Letters of Morris and Brailsford to Thomas Jefferson." *South Carolina Historical Magazine* 58 (1957): 129–44.

Windley, Lathan A. *Runaway Slave Advertisements: A Documentary History from the 1730s to 1790.* 4 vols. Westport, Conn.: Greenwood, 1983.

Young, Sir William. *West India Common-Place Book: Compiled from Parliamentary and Official Documents.* London, 1807.

Reference Sources

Brigham, Clarence S. *History and Bibliography of American Newspapers, 1690–1820.* 2 vols. Worcester, Mass.: American Antiquarian Society, 1947.

Greene, Evarts B., and Virginia D. Harrington. *American Population before the Federal Census of 1790.* New York, 1932.

Ruffin, Edmund. *Report on the Commencement and Progress of the Agricultural Survey of South-Carolina, for 1843.* Columbia, A. H. Pemberton, 1843.

Newspapers

Augusta Chronicle and Gazette of the State
Boston Gazette and Country Journal
Charleston Courier
Charleston Evening Gazette
Charleston Gazette
Charleston Morning Post
Columbia Museum and Savannah Advertiser
Columbian Herald, Savannah
Gazette of the State of Georgia, Savannah
Georgia Courier, Savannah
Georgia Gazette, Savannah
Georgia Republican, Savannah
Georgia Republican and State Intelligencer, Savannah
Louisiana Gazette, New Orleans
Maryland Journal, Baltimore
New Haven Gazette and the Connecticut Magazine
Newport Mercury, Newport, R.I.
New York Journal
Providence Gazette, Providence, R.I.
Republican and Savannah Evening Ledger
Republican and Savannah Ledger
Royal Gazette and Bahama Advertiser
Salem Gazette, Salem, Mass.
Savannah Republican and State Intelligencia
South Carolina Advertiser, Charleston
South Carolina Gazette and General Advertiser, Charleston
South Carolina State Gazette and Daily Advertiser, Charleston
South Carolina Weekly Gazette, Charleston
State, Columbia, South Carolina
State Gazette of Georgia, Savannah
State Gazette of South Carolina, Charleston
Times, Charleston

SECONDARY SOURCES

Books and Articles

Alford, Terry. *Prince among Slaves.* New York: Harcourt Brace Jovanovich, 1977.

Alderson, Robert. "Charleston's Rumored Slave Revolt of 1793," in *The Impact of the Haitian Revolution in the Atlantic World*, ed. David P. Geggus, 93–111. Columbia: University of South Carolina Press, 2001.

Anstey, Roger. "The Volume and Profitability of the British Slave Trade, 1761–1807." In *Race and Slavery in the Western Hemisphere: Quantitative Studies*, edited by Stanley L. Engerman and Eugene D. Genovese, 3–31. Princeton: Princeton University Press, 1975.

———. "The Volume of the North American Slave-Carrying Trade from Africa, 1761–1810." *Revue francaise d'histoire d'outre-mer* 62, no. 2 (1975): 47–66.

Bailyn, Bernard. *The Ideological Origins of the American Revolution.* Cambridge: Belknap, 1967.

Ball, Edward. *Slaves in the Family*. New York: Farrar, Straus and Giroux, 1998.

Bancroft, Frederic. *Slave Trading in the Old South*. 1931. Reprint, New York: Frederick Ungar, 1959.

Bancroft, George. *The History of the Formation of the Constitution of the United States of America*. New York: D. Appleton, 1885.

———. *History of the United States of America from the Discovery of the Continent*. 6 vols. New York: D. Appleton, 1886.

Barry, Richard. *Mr. Rutledge of South Carolina*. New York: J. J. Little and Ives, 1949.

Beard, Charles A. *An Economic Interpretation of the Constitution of the United States*. New York: Macmillan, 1913.

Becker, Carl L. *The Declaration of Independence: A Study in the History of Political Ideas*. New York: Alfred A. Knopf, 1960.

Behrendt, Stephen D. "The Annual Volume and Regional Distribution of the British Slave Trade, 1780–1807." *Journal of African History* 38, no. 2 (1997): 187–211.

Bell, Kensil. "*Always Ready*": *The Story of the United States Coast Guard*. New York: Mead, 1944.

Bell, Malcolm, Jr. *Major Butler's Legacy: Five Generations of a Slaveholding Family*. Athens: University of Georgia Press, 1987.

Berlin, Ira. *Many Thousands Gone: The First Two Centuries of Slavery in North America*. Cambridge: Belknap, 1998.

Bigelow, B. M. "Aaron Lopes, Merchant of Newport." *New England Quarterly* 4 (October 1931): 757–76.

Boles, John B. *The South through Time: A History of an American Region*. 2 vols. Englewood Cliffs, N.J.: Prentice Hall, 1995.

Bonner, James C. *History of Georgia Agriculture, 1732–1860*. Athens: University of Georgia Press, 1964.

Brady, Patrick S. "The Slave Trade and Sectionalism in South Carolina, 1787–1808." *Journal of Southern History* 38 (November 1972): 601–20.

Briggs, Lloyd Vernon. *The History and Genealogy of the Cabot Family, 1475–1927*. 2 vols. Boston: Charles E. Goodspeed, 1927.

Brooks, George E., Jr. *Yankee Traders, Old Coasters and African Middlemen: A History of American Legitimate Trade with West Africa in the Nineteenth Century*. Brookline, Mass.: Boston University Press, 1970.

Burson, Caroline Maude. *The Stewardship of Don Esteban Miró, 1782–1792: A Study of Louisiana Based Largely on the Documents in New Orleans*. New Orleans: American Printing, 1940.

Carey, H. C. *The Slave Trade, Domestic and Foreign: Why It Exists, and How It May Be Extinguished*. Philadelphia: John A. Norton, 1859.

Chaplin, Joyce E. "Tidal Rice Cultivation and the Problem of Slavery in South Carolina and Georgia, 1760–1815." *William and Mary Quarterly* 49 (January 1992): 29–61.

———. *An Anxious Pursuit: Agricultural Innovation and Modernity in the Lower South, 1712–1911*. Chapel Hill: University of North Carolina Press, 1993.

Cohn, Raymond L., and Richard A. Jensen. "The Determinants of Slave Mortality Rates on the Middle Passage." *Explorations in Economic History* 19 (July 1982): 269–82.

Collier, Christopher, and James Lincoln Collier. *Decision in Philadelphia: The Constitutional Convention of 1787*. New York: Random House, 1986.

Cook, Sherburne F. *Population of the California Indians, 1769–1970*. Berkeley: University of California, 1976.

Corbitt, D. C. "Shipments of Slaves from the United States to Cuba, 1789–1807." *Journal of Southern History* 7 (November 1941): 540–49.

Coughtry, Jay. *Liquid Gold: Rhode Island Rum and the International Slave Trade to West Africa in the Eighteenth Century.* Philadelphia: Temple University Press, 1970.

——. *The Notorious Triangle: Rhode Island and the African Slave Trade, 1700–1807.* Philadelphia: Temple University Press, 1981.

Countryman, Edward. *Americans: A Collision of Histories.* New York: Hill and Wang, 1996.

Crane, Elaine F. "'The First Wheel of Commerce': Newport, Rhode Island and the Slave Trade, 1760–1776." *Slavery and Abolition* 1 (September 1980): 178–98.

Creel, Margaret Washington. *A Peculiar People: Slave Religion and Community-Culture among the Gullahs.* New York: New York University Press, 1988.

Curtin, Philip D. "Epidemiology and the Slave Trade." *Political Science Quarterly* 83 (June 1968): 190–216.

——. *The Atlantic Slave Trade: A Census.* Madison: University of Wisconsin Press, 1969.

Davidson, Basil. *Black Mother.* London, 1961.

Davis, David Brion. *The Problem of Slavery in the Age of Revolution, 1770–1823.* Ithaca: Cornell University Press, 1975.

Debien, Gabriel, and René Le Gardeur. "The Saint-Domingue Refugees in Louisiana, 1792–1804," in *The Road to Louisiana: The Saint-Domingue Refugees, 1792–1809,* edited by Carl A. Brasseaux and Glenn R. Conrad. Lafayette: Center for Louisiana Studies, University of Southwestern Louisiana, 1992.

Deerr, Noel. *The History of Sugar.* 2 vols. London: Chapman and Hall, 1950.

Deutsch, Sarah. "The Elusive Guineamen: Newport Slavers, 1735–1774." *New England Quarterly* 55, no. 2 (1982): 229–53.

Déveaux, Jean-Michel. *France au temps des négrier.* Paris, 1994.

Din, Gilbert C. *Spaniards, Planters, and Slaves: The Spanish Regulation of Slavery in Louisiana, 1763–1803.* College Station: Texas A&M Press, 1999.

Doerflinger, Thomas M. *A Vigorous Spirit of Enterprise: Merchants and Economic Development in Revolutionary Philadelphia.* Chapel Hill: University of North Carolina Press, 1986.

Donnan, Elizabeth. "The Slave Trade into South Carolina before the Revolution." *American Historical Review* 33 (July 1928): 804–28.

——. "The New England Slave Trade after the Revolution." *New England Quarterly* 3 (January 1930): 251–78.

Dow, George Francis. *Slave Ships and Slaving.* New York: Dover, 1790.

Du Bois, W. E. B. *The Suppression of the African Slave Trade to the United States of America, 1638–1870.* 1896. Reprint, Baton Rouge: Louisiana State University Press, 1969.

Dusinberre, William. *Them Dark Days: Slavery in the American Rice Swamps.* New York: Oxford University Press, 1996.

Dyle, Steven. "'By farr the most profitable trade': Slave Trading in British Colonial North America." *Slavery and Abolition: A Journal of Comparative Studies* 10 (September 1989): 107–25.

Eblen, Jack Ericson. "On the Natural Increase of Slave Populations: The Example of the Cuban Black Population, 1775–1900." In *Race and Slavery in the Western Hemisphere: Quantitative Studies,* edited by Stanley L. Engerman and Eugene D. Genovese, 211–47. Princeton: Princeton University Press, 1975.

Edgar, Walter. *South Carolina: A History.* Columbia: University of South Carolina Press, 1998.

Felt, Joseph B. *Annals of Salem.* 2 vols. Boston: W. and S. B. Ives, 1845–49.

Fiske, John. *The Critical Period of American History, 1783–1789.* New York: Houghton Mifflin, 1888.

Fogel, Robert William, and Stanley L. Engerman. *Time on the Cross: The Economics of American Negro Slavery.* Boston: Little, Brown, 1974.

————. *Time on the Cross: Evidence and Methods—A Supplement.* Boston: Little, Brown, 1974.

Freehling, William W. "The Founding Fathers and Slavery." *American Historical Society* 77 (February 1972): 81–93.

Frey, Sylvia R. *Water from the Rock: Black Resistance in a Revolutionary Age.* Princeton: Princeton University Press, 1991.

Gray, Lewis Cecil. *A History of Agriculture in the Southern United States to 1860.* 2 vols. Washington, D.C.: Carnegie Institution of Washington, 1933.

Greene, Evarts B., and Virginia D. Harrington. *American Population before the Federal Census of 1790.* New York: Columbia University Press, 1932.

Hall, Gwendolyn Midlo. *Africans in Colonial Louisiana: The Development of Afro-Creole Cultures in the Eighteenth Century.* Baton Rouge: Louisiana State University Press, 1992.

————. *African Diaspora in the Americas: Continuities of Regions, Ethnicities, and Cultures.* Chapel Hill: University of North Carolina Press, forthcoming.

Hansen, Marcus Lee. *The Atlantic Migration, 1607–1860.* Cambridge: Harvard University Press, 1940.

Haw, James. *John and Edward Rutledge of South Carolina.* Athens: University of Georgia Press, 1997.

Hedges, James B. *The Browns of Providence Plantations: Colonial Years.* Cambridge: Harvard University Press, 1952.

Higgins, W. Robert. "Charles Town Merchants and Factors Dealing in the External Negro Trade, 1735–1775." *South Carolina Historical Magazine* 65 (October 1964): 205–17.

————. "The Geographical Origins of Negro Slaves in Colonial South Carolina." *South Atlantic Quarterly* 70 (winter 1971): 34 47.

————. "Charleston: Terminus and Entrepôt of the Colonial Slave Trade." In *The African Diaspora: Interpretive Essays*, edited by Martin L. Kilson and Robert I. Rotberg, 114–31. Cambridge: Harvard University Press, 1976.

Holmes, Jack D. L. *Gayaso: The Life of a Spanish Governor in the Mississippi Valley, 1789–1799.* Baton Rouge: Louisiana State University Press, 1965.

Hopkins, Samuel. *Works.* Boston, 1852.

Howe, George Locke. *Mount Hope: A New England Chronicle.* New York: Viking, 1959.

Ingersoll, Thomas N. "The Slave Trade and Ethnic Diversity of Louisiana's Slave Community." *Louisiana History* 37 (spring 1996): 133–61.

Inikori, J. E. "Measuring the Atlantic Slave Trade: An Assessment of Curtin and Anstey." *Journal of African History* 17, no. 2 (1976): 197–223.

————. Introduction. In *Forced Migration: The Impact of the Export Slave Trade on African Societies*, edited by J. E. Inikori, 1–20. London: Africana, 1981.

Jensen, Merrell. *The Founding of a Nation.* New York, 1968.

Jones, Alice Hanson. *Wealth of a Nation to Be: The American Colonies on the Eve the Revolution.* New York: Columbia University Press, 1980.

Jordan, Winthrop D. *White over Black: American Attitudes toward the Negro, 1550–1812.* New York: W. W. Norton, 1977.

Kaminski, John P., ed. *A Necessary Evil? Slavery and the Debate over the Constitution.* Madison, Wisc.: Madison House, 1995.

Ketcham, Ralph. *James Madison: A Biography.* Charlottesville: University of Virginia Press, 1990.

Klein, Herbert S. "North American Competition and the Characteristics of the American Slave Trade to Cuba, 1790–1794," *William and Mary Quarterly* 28 (January 1971): 86–102.

————. "Slaves and Shipping in Eighteenth-Century Virginia." *Journal of Interdisciplinary History* 5 (winter 1975): 383–412.

————. "The Cuban Slave Trade in a Period of Transition, 1790–1843," *Revue francaise d'histoire d'outre-mer* 62, no. 2 (1975): 67–73.

————, and Stanley I. Engerman. "Slave Mortality on British Ships, 1791–1797." In *Liverpool, the African Slave Trade, and Abolition*, Occasional Series, no. 2, edited by Roger Anstey and P. E. H. Hair, 113–25. London: Historic Society of Lancashire and Cheshire, 1976.

Klein, Rachel N. *Unification of a Slave State: The Rise of the Planter Class in the South Carolina Backcountry, 1760–1808*. Chapel Hill: University of North Carolina Press, 1990.

Kolchin, Peter. *American Slavery, 1619–1877*. New York: Hill and Wang, 1993.

Kraus, Michael. *Immigration, the American Mosaic: From Pilgrims to Modern Refugees*. Princeton, N.J.: Van Norstrand, 1966.

Kulikoff, Allan. "A 'Prolifick' People: Black Population Growth in the Chesapeake Colonies, 1700–1790." *Southern Studies* 16 (winter 1977): 391–428.

————. "Uprooted Peoples: Black Migrants in the Age of the American Revolution, 1790–1820." In *Slavery and Freedom in the Age of the American Revolution*, edited by Ira Berlin and Ronald Hoffman, 143–71. Urbana: University of Illinois Press, 1986.

LaChance, Paul F. "The Politics of Fear: French Louisianians and the Slave Trade, 1786–1809." *Plantation Society* 1 (June 1979): 162–97.

————. "The Immigration of Saint-Dominigue Refugees to New Orleans: Reception, Integration and Impact." In *A Refuge for All Ages: Immigration in Louisiana History*, ed. Carl A. Brasseaux. Lafayette: Center for Louisiana Studies, Univ. of Southwestern Louisiana, 1996.

————. "Repercussions of the Haitian Revolution." In *The Impact of the Haitian Revolution in the Atlantic World*. ed. David P. Geggus, 209–30. Columbia: University of South Carolina Press, 2001.

Landers, Jane. *Black Society in Spanish Florida*. Urbana: University of Illinois Press, 1999.

Laughlin, Harry H. *Immigration and Conquest*. Washington, D.C.: Carnegie Institute of Washington, 1939.

Liscomb, Terry W. "The Legacy of Ainsley Hall." *South Carolina Historical Magazine* 99 (April 1998): 154–79.

Littlefield, Daniel C. *Rice and Slaves: Ethnicity and the Slave Trade in Colonial South Carolina*. Baton Rouge: Louisiana State University Press, 1981).

Lovejoy, Paul. "The Volume of the Atlantic Slave Trade: A Synthesis." *Journal of African History* 23, no. 4 (1982): 473–501.

Lydon, James G. "New York and the Slave Trade." *William and Mary Quarterly* 35, no. 2 (1978): 375–94.

Mancall, Peter C., Joshua L. Rosenbloom, and Thomas Weiss. "Slave Prices and the South Carolina Economy, 1722–1809." *Journal of Economic History* 61 (September 2001): 616–40.

Mannix, Daniel Pratt. *Black Cargoes: A History of the Atlantic Slave Trade, 1518–1865*. New York: Viking, 1962.

May, Phillip S. "Zephaniah Kingsley, Nonconformist (1765–1843)." *Florida Historical Quarterly* 23 (January 1945): 145–59.

McCrady, Edward. *South Carolina under the Royal Government, 1719–1776*. New York, 1899.

McDonald, Forrest, *E Pluribus Unum: The Formation of the American Republic, 1776–1790*. Boston: Houghton Mifflin, 1962).

Minchinton, Walter E. "The Seaborne Slave Trade of North Carolina." *North Carolina Historical Review* 71 (January 1994): 1–62.

————, ed. *Virginia Slave-Trade Statistics, 1698–1775*. Richmond: Virginia State Library, 1984.

Molloy, Robert. *Charleston, a Gracious Heritage*. New York: D. Appleton–Century, 1947.

Moore, John Hebron. *The Emergence of the Cotton Kingdom in the Old Southwest: Missis-sippi, 1770–1860.* Baton Rouge: Louisiana State University Press, 1988.

Morgan, Philip D. "Black Society in the Lowcountry, 1760–1810." In *Slavery and Freedom in the Age of the American Revolution,* edited by Ira Berlin and Ronald Hoffman, 83–141. Urbana: University of Illinois Press, 1986.

———. "African Migration." In *Encyclopedia of American Social History,* 3 vols., edited by Mary Kupiec Cayton, Elliott J. Gorn, and Peter W. Williams, 2:795–809. New York: Scrib-ner, 1993.

Munroe, Wilfred Harold. *Tales of an Old Sea Port: A General Sketch of the History of Bristol, Rhode Island, Including, Incidentally, An Account of the Voyages of the Norsemen, So Far As They May Have Been Connected With Narragansett Bay: And Personal Narratives of Some Notable Voyages Accomplished By Sailors From the Mount Hope Lands.* London: Princeton University Press, 1917.

Nadelhaft, Jerome J. *The Disorders of War: The Revolution in South Carolina.* Orono: Univer-sity of Maine Press, 1981.

Nash, Gary B. *Race and Revolution.* Madison, Wisc.: Madison House, 1990.

Olwell, Robert. *Masters, Slaves, and Subjects: The Culture of Power in the South Carolina Low Country.* Ithaca: Cornell University Press, 1998.

Pease, William H., and Jane H. Pease. *The Web of Progress: Private Values and Public Styles in Boston and Charleston, 1828–1843.* Athens: University of Georgia Press, 1991.

Pope-Hennessy, James. *Sins of the Fathers: A Study of Atlantic Slave Traders, 1441–1807.* Lon-don: Weidenfeld and Nicolson, 1967.

Ramsay, David. "Remarks on the Yellow Fever and Epidemic Catarrh, as they appeared in South-Carolina, during the Summer and Autumn of 1807." *Medical Repository Compre-hending Original Essays and Intelligence Relative to Medicine, Chemistry, Natural History, Agriculture, Geography, and the Arts; More Especially as They Are Cultivated in America; and A Review of American Publications on Medicine, and the Auxiliary Branches of Science.* 5, second hexade (1808): 233–35.

———. *The History of South Carolina from Its First Settlement in 1670 to the Year 1808.* 2 vols. Charleston: David Longworth for the author, 1809.

Rankin, David C. "The Tannenbaum Thesis Reconsidered: Slavery and Race Relations in Antebellum Louisiana." *Southern Studies* 18 (spring 1979): 5–32.

Rawley, James. *The Transatlantic Slave Trade: A History.* New York: W. W. Norton, 1981.

Redford, Dorothy S., with Michael D'Orso. *Somerset Homecoming: Recovering a Lost Heri-tage.* New York: Doubleday, 1988.

Reimers, David M. "Immigration." In *Encyclopedia of American Social History,* 3 vols., edited by Mary Kupiec Cayton, Elliot J. Gorn, and Peter W. Williams, 1:577–91. New York: Scribner, 1993.

Richardson, David. "The Eighteenth-Century British Slave Trade: Estimates of the Volume and Coastal Distribution in Africa." *Research in Economic History* 12 (1989): 151–95.

———. "The British Slave Trade to Colonial South Carolina." *Slavery and Abolition: A Jour-nal of Comparative Studies* 12 (December 1991): 125–71.

Ridout, Orlando, V, and Willie Graham. Draft Report of "An Architectural and Historical Analysis of the Nathaniel Russell House, Charleston, South Carolina." Historic Charleston Foundation.

Riordan, Patrick. "Finding Freedom in Florida: Native Peoples, African Americans, and Colonists, 1670–1816." *Florida Historical Quarterly* 75 (summer 1996): 24–43.

Risjord, Norman K. *Jefferson's America, 1760–1815.* Madison, Wisc.: Madison House, 1991.

Robinson, Donald L. *Slavery in the Structure of American Politics, 1765–1820.* New York: Harcourt Brace Jovanovich, 1971.

Rogers, George C., Jr. *Evolution of a Federalist: William Loughton Smith of Charleston, 1758–1812,* Columbia: University of South Carolina Press, 1962.

———. *The History of Georgetown County.* Columbia: University of South Carolina Press, 1970.

Rowland, Lawrence S., Alexander Moore, and George C. Rogers, Jr. *The History of Beaufort County, South Carolina: Volume I, 1514–1861.* Columbia: University of South Carolina Press, 1996.

Ruffin, Edward, ed. *Report of the Agricultural History of South Carolina.* Columbia: A. H. Pemberton, 1843.

Schafer, Daniel L. "Ties That Bind: Anglo-American Slave Trades in Africa and Florida, John Fraser and His Descendents." *Slavery and Abolition* 20 (December 1999): 1–21.

———. *Anna Madgigine Jai Kingsley: African Princess, Florida Slavery Plantation Owner.* Gainsville: University Press of Florida, 2003.

Siebert, Wilbur Henry. *Loyalists in East Florida, 1774–1785.* 2 vols. Deland: Florida, State Historical Society, 1929.

Sitterson, J. Carlyle. *Sugar Country: The Cane Sugar Industry in the South, 1753–1950.* Lexington: University of Kentucky Press, 1953.

Smith, Gene A. "U.S. Navy Gunboats and the Slave Trade in Louisiana Waters, 1808–1811." *Military History of the West* 23 (fall 1993): 135–47.

Smith, Julia Floyd. *Slavery and Rice Culture in Low Country Georgia, 1750–1860.* Knoxville: University of Tennessee Press, 1985.

Steckel, Robert H. "Birth Weights and Infant Mortality among American Slaves." *Explorations in Economic History* 3, no. 4 (1979): 86–113.

Stevens, Michael E. "To Get As Many Slaves As You Can: An 1807 Slaving Voyage." *South Carolina Historical Magazine* 87 (July 1986): 187–92.

Stoddard, Lothrop. *The French Revolution in San Domingo* (New York: Houghton Mifflin, 1914).

Thomas, Hugh. *The Slave Trade: The Story of the Atlantic Slave Trade, 1440–1870.* New York: Simon and Schuster, 1997.

Usner, Daniel H., Jr. *Indians, Settlers, and Slaves in a Frontier Exchange Economy.* Chapel Hill: University of North Carolina Press, 1990.

Wallace, David Duncan. *The Life of Henry Laurens.* New York: G. P. Putnam, 1915.

Waring, Joseph Ioor. *A History of Medicine in South Carolina, 1670–1825.* Charleston: South Carolina Medical Society, 1964.

Wax, Darold D. "Quaker Merchants and the Slave Trade in Colonial Pennsylvania." *Pennsylvania Magazine of History and Biography* 86 (April 1962): 44–59.

———. "Negro Import Duties in Colonial Virginia: A Study of British Commercial Policy and Local Public Policy." *Virginia Magazine of History and Biography* 79 (January 1971): 29–44.

———. "Preferences for Slaves to Colonial America." *Journal of Negro History* 58 (October 1973): 371–401.

———. "Black Immigrants: The Slave Trade to Colonial Maryland." *Maryland Historical Magazine* 73 (March 1978): 30–45.

———. "'New Negroes Are Always in Demand': The Slave Trade in Eighteenth-Century Georgia." *Georgia Historical Quarterly* 68 (summer 1984): 193–220.

Weber, David J. *The Spanish Frontier in North America.* New Haven, Conn.: Yale University Press, 1992.

Williams, Edwin L., Jr. "Negro Slavery in Florida." *Florida Historical Quarterly* 28 (October 1949): 93–110.

Wood, Gordon S. *Creation of the American Republic, 1776–1787.* Chapel Hill: Published for the Institute of Early American History and Culture at Williamsburg, Va., by the University of North Carolina Press, 1969.

Wood, Peter H. *Black Majority: Negroes in Colonial South Carolina from 1670 through the Stono Rebellion.* New York: Alfred A. Knopf, 1974.

———. "'More like a Negro Country': Demographic Patterns in Colonial South Carolina, 1700–1740." In *Race and Slavery in the Western Hemisphere: Quantitative Studies,* edited by Stanley L. Engerman and Eugene D. Genovese, 131–69. Princeton, N.J.: Princeton University Press, 1975.

Wright, Benjamin F. *Consensus and Continuity, 1776–1787.* Boston: Boston University Press, 1958.

Wright, Donald R., *African Americans in the Colonial Era: From African Origins through the American Revolution.* Arlington Heights: Harland Davidson, 1990.

Theses and Dissertations

Behrendt, Stephen D. "The British Slave Trade, 1785–1807: Volume, Profitability, and Mortality." Ph.D. diss., University of Wisconsin, 1993.

Bridwell, Ronald Edward. "The South's Wealthiest Planter: Wade Hampton I of South Carolina." Ph.D. diss., 2 vols., University of South Carolina, 1980.

Deaton, Stanley K. "Revolutionary Charleston, 1765–1800." Ph.D. diss., University of Florida, 1997.

Hamm, Tommy Todd. "The American Slave Trade with Africa, 1620–1807." Ph.D. diss., Indiana University, 1975.

Ogden, Warren C. "Langdon Cheves, 1776–1857." M.A. thesis, Duke University, 1930.

Rothman, Adam. "The Expansion of Slavery in the Deep South, 1790–1820." Ph.D. diss., Columbia University, 2000.

INDEX

Abaco, 100

Adams, John (British slave captain), 60

advertisements, 32, 36, 64, 105; newspaper, 20, 30, 35, 116; for slave sales, 33, 47, 55, 75, 96; as source of slave trade estimates, 34, 117

Africa, 8, 18, 30, 33, 43–44, 61, 73, 88, 98, 103–4, 106–7, 109–10, 112, 114; captives purchased on the coast of, 49–50; clearances from Charleston for, 92–94; *Kitty* (schooner) sailed for, 108; migrants imported from, 15, 23; "New Negroes from Africa," 4; origin of slaves imported from, 71; reports of clearances to, 34–38; 1783 to 1810 slave arrivals from, 119; ships detained sailing from, 100–102; slave shipments from, 52–60, 62–69, 76, 85–86; slaving voyages to the coast of, 42, 45

Africa (ship), 95, 99, 103

African Americans, 13, 17, 19, 49

African coast, 37, 45, 72, 90, 101, 106, 109; American slavers flooded the, 43–44; price of slaves on the, 43; products traded on the, 73, 91; ships left Charleston for the, 93–94; ships sailed to New Orleans from the, 100; slave voyages to the, 95; slavers cleared Charleston port for the, 102; slaves smuggled on the, 56

African Institute in London, 44

Africans, 6–9, 21, 37–38, 49, 55–56, 58, 64, 66, 68, 75, 80, 86, 90, 100, 106, 110–11, 118; from Angola, 69; arrived in large numbers until 1810, 119; average price of, 13; Carey's calculations of imported, 14; Charleston-owned slavers transported, 120; from the Congo, 69; Curtin's estimate of imported, 15, 18, 71, 116; died during middle passage, 103; died on brig *Three Sisters*, 100; disembarked in Charleston, 20, 95; disembarked in Louisiana, 47; disembarked in Mississippi, 47; disembarked in North America, 45; disembarked in South Carolina, 46; Fogel and Engerman's estimate of imported, 16; forced migration of, 50; held off market to increase prices, 88, 113; imported from the West Indies, 57, 65; imports into South Carolina discouraged, 52; mortality rates of transported, 112, 115, 117; newspaper advertisements for missing, 36; number of imported, 114; planter bias toward, 59, 67; purchase of, 10, 92; purchased for cotton cultivation, 87; purchased for rice cultivation, 53; 1790s demand for, 62; smuggled into Georgia, 43; smuggled into Louisiana, 43; smuggled into South Carolina, 43; South Carolina population of, 54; transported by American slavers, 77; transshipped from Charleston, 96; transshipped from the West Indies, 33, 42, 76; transshipped to New Orleans, Louisiana, 31, 93, 98; transshipped to Spanish North America, 94; vended by Boyd, 89; vended by Caig, Macleod & Co., 85; vended by Penmans, 82; vended by Russell, 84

Alabama, 5, 66

Alford, Terry, 99

Almira (schooner), 102

Amedie (ship), 103

Amelia (schooner), 37

America, 6, 10, 74, 120

Americans, 5, 10, 17, 19, 91, 101, 105–6, 120; began restoration after war, 4; crew on slave ship *Africa*, 95; delivered captives to West Indies, 102; Mississippi population of white, 98

American Revolution, 4–6, 7, 10, 12–17, 20, 42, 46, 50, 65, 69, 75, 81, 88, 90–91, 117, 119–20; created financial catastrophe, 19; Georgia severely damaged by, 85; slave

Timbalier Islands, 39

Tories, 8, 84

Tortola, 103, 109

trade, 6–7, 19, 38, 53–54, 61–62, 75, 81, 85–86, 94–95, 98, 101–2, 107, 113; Atlantic slave, 34, 58, 115; Britain banned direct, 79; Carey's calculations of, 15; Caribbean slave, 90; Charleston slave, 33, 77, 88–89, 105; conditions of middle passage slave, 114; Congress closed, 13; Curtin's estimate of foreign slave, 16, 18; effects of American Revolution on slave, 119; estimates of foreign slave, 5, 14; European wars curtailed, 40; Florida slave, 67; foreign slave, 39, 87, 97; French slave, 106; between Georgia and West Indies, 65; Georgia slave, 74; illegal foreign slave, 37, 47; increase in Georgia slave, 64; interruption of African, 8; Kulikoff's estimates of domestic slave, 17; Louisiana slave, 67; middle passage of slave, 109; New Orleans slave, 91; North American slave, 43, 71; North Carolina prohibited slave, 46; post–Revolutionary War foreign slave, 30, 32, 50, 63, 68–69, 76, 96, 116; Rhode Island participation in slave, 73; slave rebellion halted, 52; South Carolina foreign slave, 57, 78; transatlantic slave, 41–42, 55, 72, 93, 117, 120; U.S. vessels involved in slave, 44–45; volume of foreign slave, 36, 118; West Indies slave, 92

traffic, 5, 7, 13, 40, 43–44, 57, 86, 89, 97, 98; foreign slave, 18, 119; North American slave, 16; Savannah slave, 85

transshipments, 69, 73; of Africans, 56, 64–65, 76; from Charleston, 66–67, 98; West Indies, 33

Truxton (ship), 102

Tunno, Adam (British vendor), 81–82

Tunno, William (British vendor), 82

Tunno and Price (Charleston firm), 49

Two Friends (ship), 82

United States, 9, 22–23, 42, 44–45, 47–48, 57, 65, 93, 95, 97, 102, 106, 118, 120; banned foreign slave imports, 90; Britain banned trade with, 79; closed direct trade, 67; conflicts with France, 100–101; estimate of captives landed in, 46; foreign slave imports prohibited in, 66; foreign slave trade, 15; slave trade prohibited from, 43; slave trade with Britain, 8; took control of Louisiana territory, 98

U.S. census records, 4, 17

U.S. Constitution, 7, 94, 119

U.S. government, 68

U.S. House of Representatives, 118

U.S. Navy, 39

U.S. Bureau of the Census, first, second, third, and fourth censuses, 24

U.S. House of Representatives, 38, 43

University of South Carolina, 111

upper South, 6, 50

Uruguay, 103

Usner, Daniel H., Jr., 24–27, 29–30

van Wyck, William (Baltimore merchant), 92

vendors, 76, 89; British, 82; slave, 73, 75, 78

Vengeance (French privateer), 102

Venus (brig), 106, 112–14

Verree and Blair (firm), 89–90

Vermont, 6

Vernon, Samuel, 86

Vernon, William, 55

Veterans of the Revolutionary War, 6

Viaggio, Luigi Castiglioni (French traveler), 81

Villepontoux and Co., 82

Vincent, Thomas (Charleston merchant), 106, 112–14

Virginia, 10, 19, 22–23, 56, 91; banned foreign slave trade, 6; delegates argued for abolition, 97; Gabriel's rebellion in, 57

Volta River, 50

Wando River, 84

War of the First Coalition, 100

War of the Second Coalition, 101–2

War of the Third Coalition, 101

Washington (ship), 102

Watson, John (vendor), 89

Watts, Robert (trader), 85–86

Wayne, Richard (trader), 85–86

Wenton (ship), 33

West Africa, 98

West Florida, 39, 47, 90, 93, 96; permitted foreign slave imports, 97; Spain gained control of, 65

Minimum requirements for use of this CD database:

Adobe Acrobat Reader 4.0 or higher

Adobe Acrobat Reader is required to use this CD database.
Adobe Acrobat Reader is available as a free internet download from
www.adobe.com/reader

PC Operating Systems
Windows XP Home, Windows XP Professional, Windows 2000 Professional,
Windows ME, Windows 98

Macintosh Operating Systems
Mac OS X, Mac OS 9

PC users:
• Insert CD into CD drive

If CD fails to self-launch:
• Open My Computer: *double click on the desktop icon My Computer or select the My Computer icon from the Start menu*
• Double click on the CD icon
• Double click on the file appendixB.pdf

Mac users:
• Insert CD into CD drive
• Double click on the CD icon on the desktop
• Double click on the folder Mac
• Double click on the file appendixB.pdf